IRON MAN

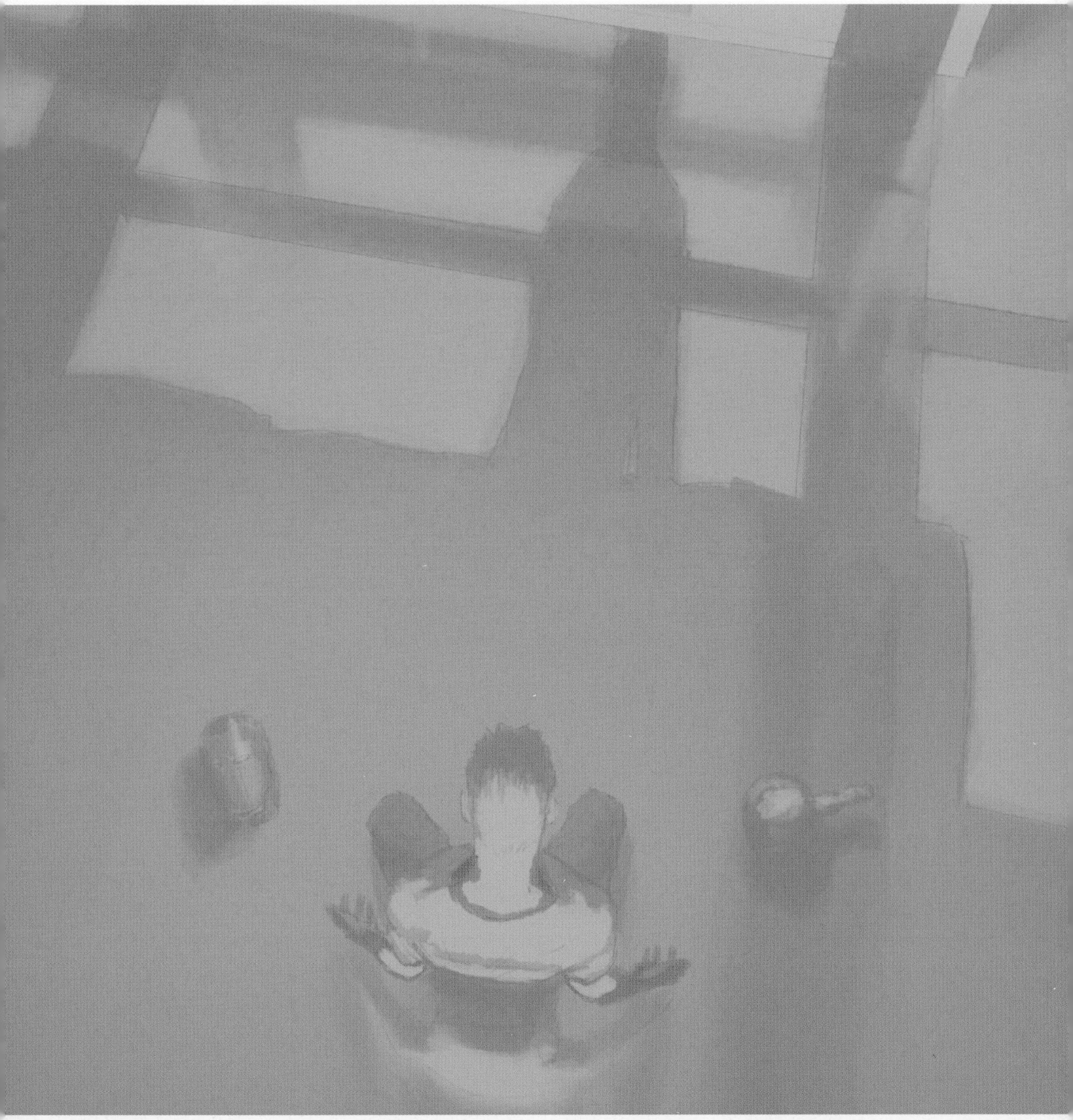

COLLECTION EDITOR: **JENNIFER GRÜNWALD**
ASSISTANT EDITORS: **ALEX STARBUCK & NELSON RIBEIRO**
EDITOR, SPECIAL PROJECTS: **MARK D. BEAZLEY**
SENIOR EDITOR, SPECIAL PROJECTS: **JEFF YOUNGQUIST**
SVP OF PRINT AND DIGITAL PUBLISHING SALES: **DAVID GABRIEL**
COVER & BOOK DESIGN: **JEFF POWELL**

EDITOR IN CHIEF: **AXEL ALONSO**
CHIEF CREATIVE OFFICER: **JOE QUESADA**
PUBLISHER: **DAN BUCKLEY**
EXECUTIVE PRODUCER: **ALAN FINE**

IRON MAN: SEASON ONE. First printing 2013. ISBN# 978-0-7851-6670-2. Published by MARVEL WORLDWIDE, INC., a subsidiary of MARVEL ENTERTAINMENT, LLC. OFFICE OF PUBLICATION: 135 West 50th S York, NY 10020. Copyright © 2012 and 2013 Marvel Characters, Inc. All rights reserved. All characters featured in this issue and the distinctive names and likenesses thereof, and all related indicia are trad Marvel Characters, Inc. No similarity between any of the names, characters, persons, and/or institutions in this magazine with those of any living or dead person or institution is intended, and any such simil may exist is purely coincidental. **Printed in the U.S.A.** ALAN FINE, EVP - Office of the President, Marvel Worldwide, Inc. and EVP & CMO Marvel Characters B.V.; DAN BUCKLEY, Publisher & President - Print & Digital Divisions; JOE QUESADA, Chief Creative Officer; TOM BREVOORT, SVP of Publishing; DAVID BOGART, SVP of Operations & Procurement, Publishing; RUWAN JAYATILLEKE, SVP & Associate Publisher, C.B. CEBULSKI, SVP of Creator & Content Development; DAVID GABRIEL, SVP of Print & Digital Publishing Sales; JIM O'KEEFE, VP of Operations & Logistics; DAN CARR, Executive Director of Publishing Technolo CRESPI, Editorial Operations Manager; ALEX MORALES, Publishing Operations Manager; STAN LEE, Chairman Emeritus. For information regarding advertising in Marvel Comics or on Marvel.com, please c Disla, Director of Marvel Partnerships, at ndisla@marvel.com. For Marvel subscription inquiries, please call 800-217-9158. **Manufactured between 2/4/2013 and 3/8/2013 by R.R. DONNELLEY, INC., SALEM**

10 9 8 7 6 5 4 3 2 1

IRON MAN

WRITER
HOWARD CHAYKIN

ARTIST
GERALD PAREL

LETTERER
VC'S CLAYTON COWLES

COVER ARTIST
JULIAN TOTINO TEDESCO

EDITORS
ANDY SCHMIDT
AUBREY SITTERSON
MICHAEL HORWITZ
JAKE THOMAS

EXECUTIVE EDITOR
TOM BREVOORT

SEASON ONE

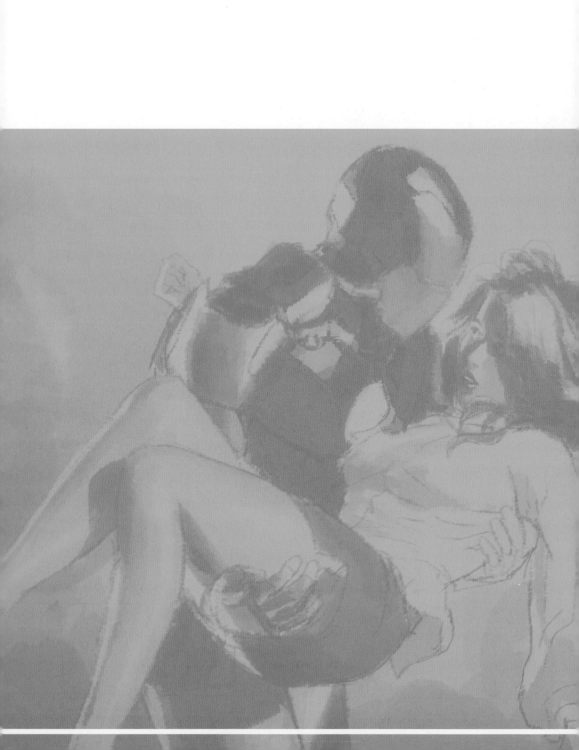

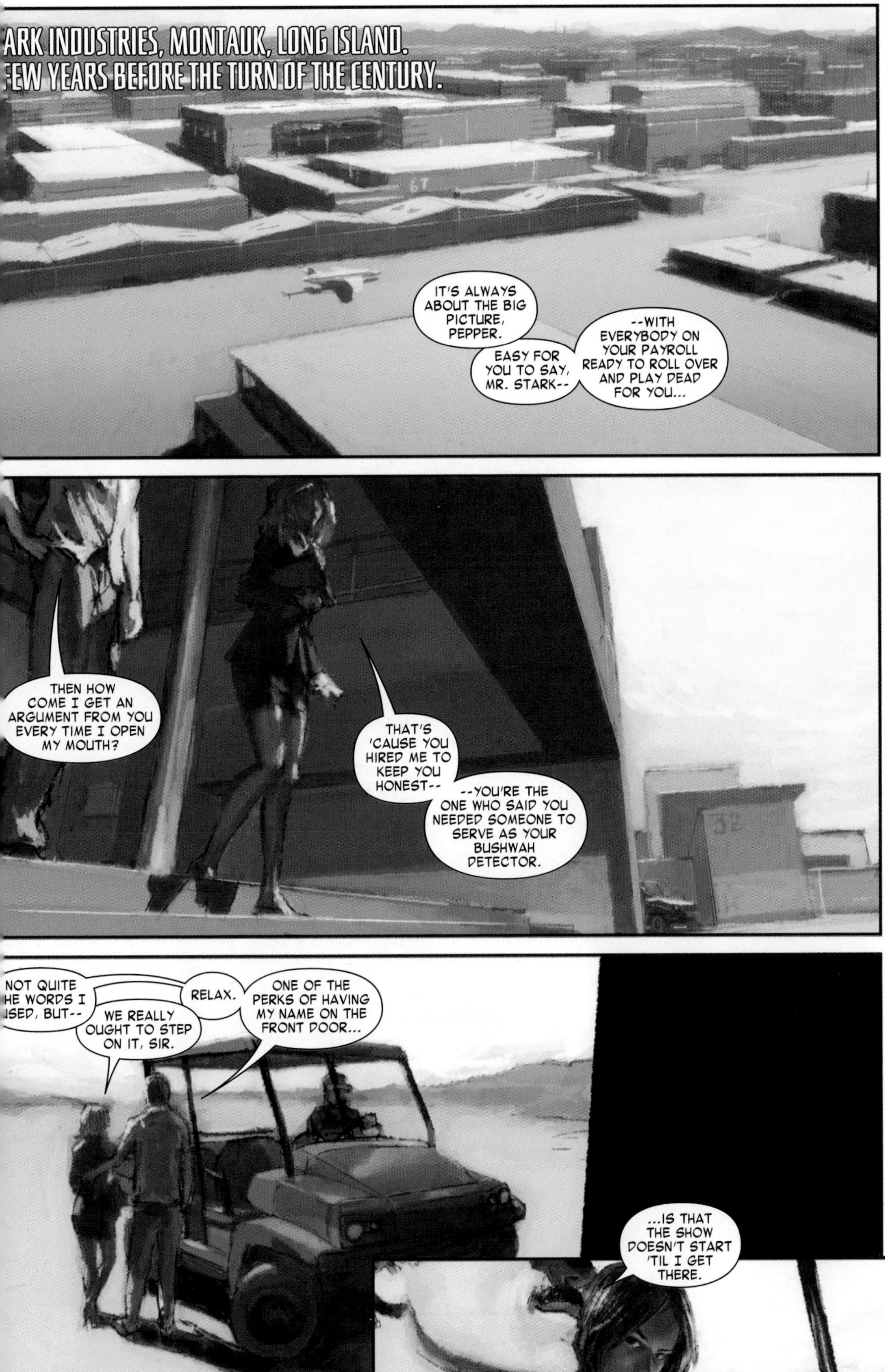
ARK INDUSTRIES, MONTAUK, LONG ISLAND.
EW YEARS BEFORE THE TURN OF THE CENTURY.
IT'S ALWAYS ABOUT THE BIG PICTURE, PEPPER.
EASY FOR YOU TO SAY, MR. STARK--
--WITH EVERYBODY ON YOUR PAYROLL READY TO ROLL OVER AND PLAY DEAD FOR YOU...
THEN HOW COME I GET AN ARGUMENT FROM YOU EVERY TIME I OPEN MY MOUTH?
THAT'S 'CAUSE YOU HIRED ME TO KEEP YOU HONEST--
--YOU'RE THE ONE WHO SAID YOU NEEDED SOMEONE TO SERVE AS YOUR BUSHWAH DETECTOR.
NOT QUITE HE WORDS I SED, BUT--
RELAX.
WE REALLY OUGHT TO STEP ON IT, SIR.
ONE OF THE PERKS OF HAVING MY NAME ON THE FRONT DOOR...
...IS THAT THE SHOW DOESN'T START 'TIL I GET THERE.

DAMN IT, VAN ZANDT--WHO DOES THIS BUTTWIPE THINK HE IS?

HE THINKS HE'S THE ONLY GAME IN TOWN.

AND RIGHT NOW, DIRECTOR BIRCH, CONSIDERING WHAT YOU'RE LOOKING FOR...

...STARK INDUSTRIES IS YOUR ONLY HOPE.

AND ANTHONY STARK IS STARK INDUSTRIES.

YOU ASS ME YOU'D HIS, SHALL MISBEHA UNDER CO MS. SIM

IF HIS FATHER WERE STILL ALIVE--

BUT HE'S NOT, NEAL--SO LET'S FORGET ABOUT FANTASY AND DEAL WITH REALITY. WE'RE PAID BY ANTHONY STARK...

RUNNING A LITTLE LATE, TONY?

ONLY BY YOUR CLOCK, MR. DIRECTOR...

...AND YOU SHOULD KNOW BY NOW...

...CRISES CAUSED BY YOUR S.H.I.E.L.D. AGENTS'LL STILL BE CRISES...

...WHEN I SHOW UP TO STRAIGHTEN OUT THE CRAPSTORM YOUR PEOPLE'VE STIRRED UP.

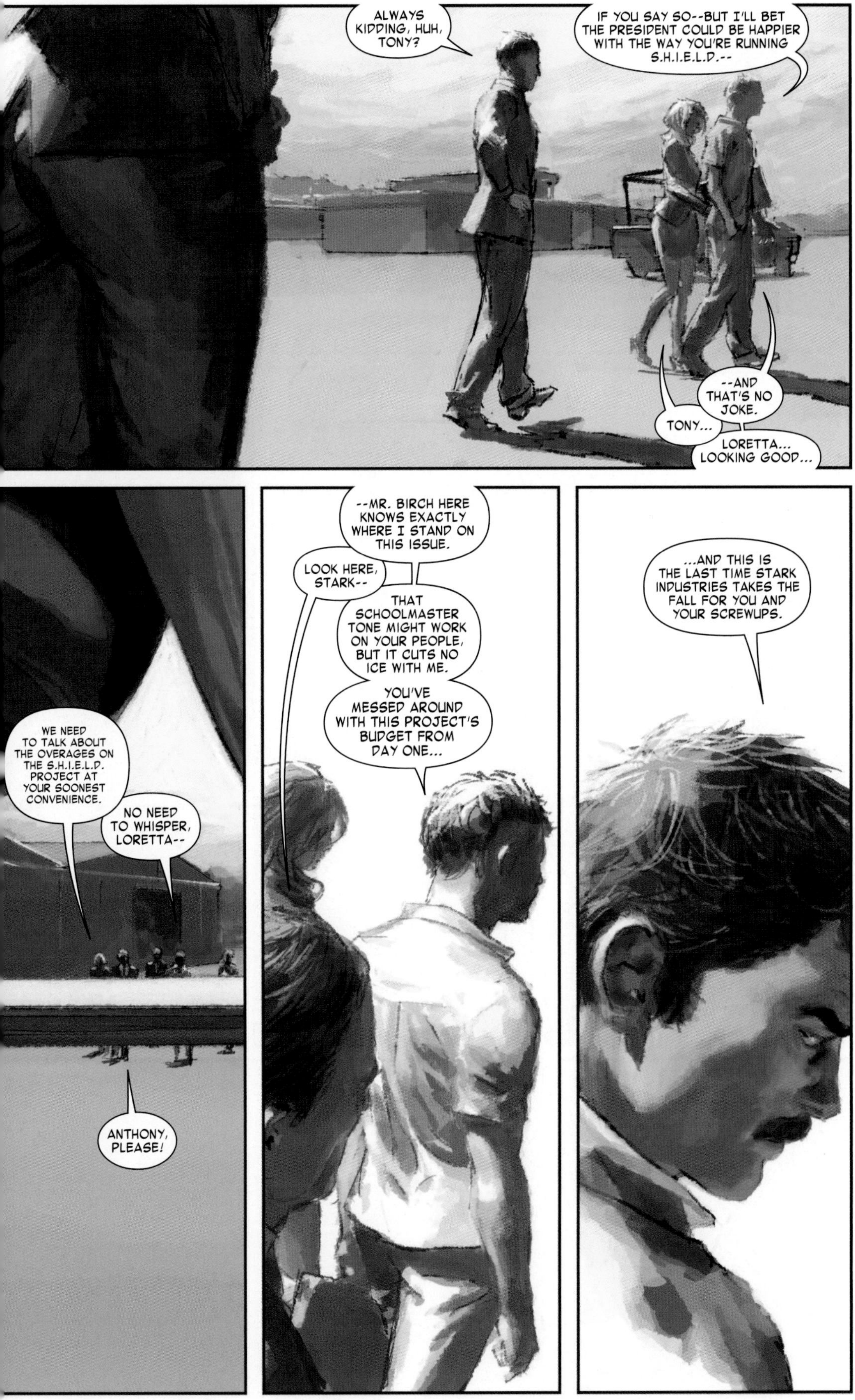
ALWAYS KIDDING, HUH, TONY?
IF YOU SAY SO--BUT I'LL BET THE PRESIDENT COULD BE HAPPIER WITH THE WAY YOU'RE RUNNING S.H.I.E.L.D.--
--AND THAT'S NO JOKE.
TONY...
LORETTA... LOOKING GOOD...
WE NEED TO TALK ABOUT THE OVERAGES ON THE S.H.I.E.L.D. PROJECT AT YOUR SOONEST CONVENIENCE.
NO NEED TO WHISPER, LORETTA--
ANTHONY, PLEASE!
--MR. BIRCH HERE KNOWS EXACTLY WHERE I STAND ON THIS ISSUE.
LOOK HERE, STARK--
THAT SCHOOLMASTER TONE MIGHT WORK ON YOUR PEOPLE, BUT IT CUTS NO ICE WITH ME.
YOU'VE MESSED AROUND WITH THIS PROJECT'S BUDGET FROM DAY ONE...
...AND THIS IS THE LAST TIME STARK INDUSTRIES TAKES THE FALL FOR YOU AND YOUR SCREWUPS.

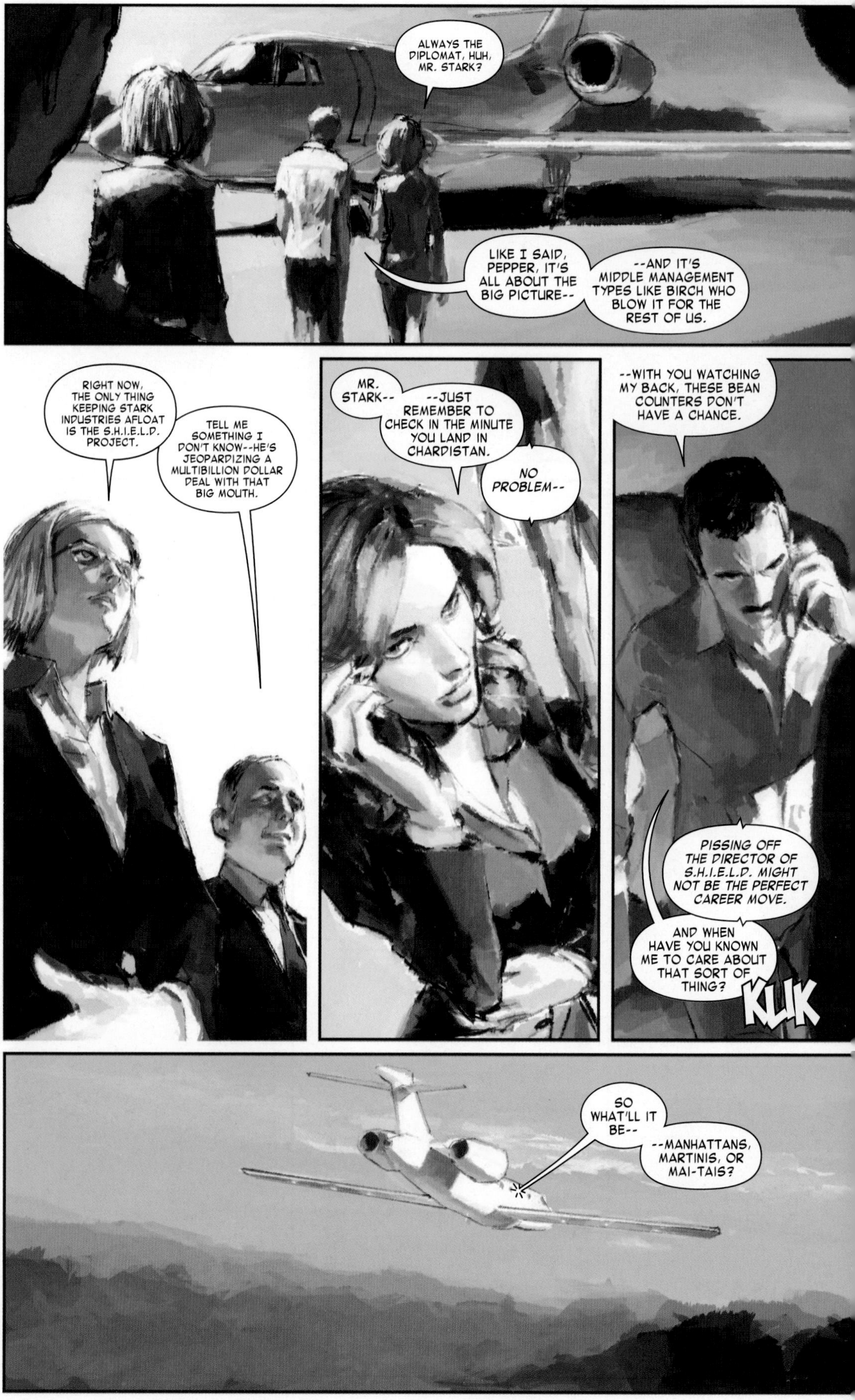
ALWAYS THE DIPLOMAT, HUH, MR. STARK?
LIKE I SAID, PEPPER, IT'S ALL ABOUT THE BIG PICTURE--
--AND IT'S MIDDLE MANAGEMENT TYPES LIKE BIRCH WHO BLOW IT FOR THE REST OF US.
RIGHT NOW, THE ONLY THING KEEPING STARK INDUSTRIES AFLOAT IS THE S.H.I.E.L.D. PROJECT.
TELL ME SOMETHING I DON'T KNOW--HE'S JEOPARDIZING A MULTIBILLION DOLLAR DEAL WITH THAT BIG MOUTH.
MR. STARK--
--JUST REMEMBER TO CHECK IN THE MINUTE YOU LAND IN CHARDISTAN.
NO PROBLEM--
--WITH YOU WATCHING MY BACK, THESE BEAN COUNTERS DON'T HAVE A CHANCE.
PISSING OFF THE DIRECTOR OF S.H.I.E.L.D. MIGHT NOT BE THE PERFECT CAREER MOVE.
AND WHEN HAVE YOU KNOWN ME TO CARE ABOUT THAT SORT OF THING?
KLIK
SO WHAT'LL IT BE--
--MANHATTANS, MARTINIS, OR MAI-TAIS?

THE OPTIMIST SEES THE GLASS IS HALF FULL...

...THE PESSIMIST SEES THE GLASS AS HALF EMPTY...

...BUT I'M A REALIST...

...AND A REALIST DOESN'T GIVE A DAMN WHETHER A GLASS IS HALF FULL OR HALF EMPTY...

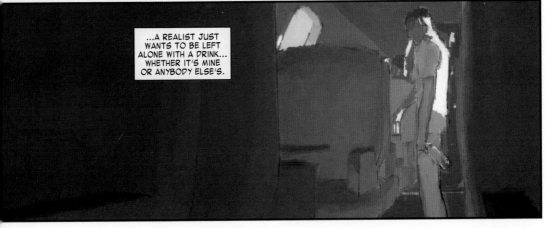
...A REALIST JUST WANTS TO BE LEFT ALONE WITH A DRINK... WHETHER IT'S MINE OR ANYBODY ELSE'S.

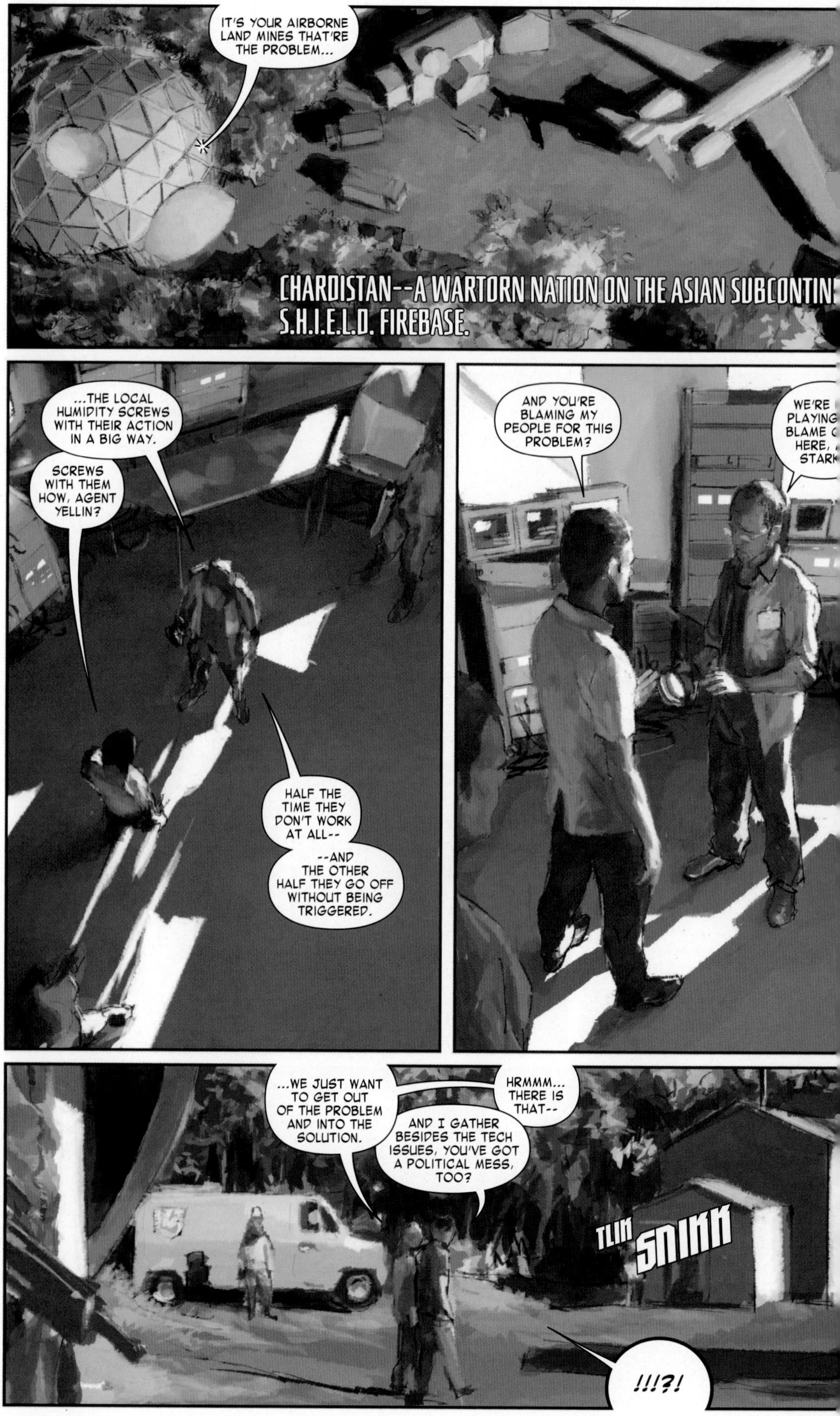
IT'S YOUR AIRBORNE LAND MINES THAT'RE THE PROBLEM...
CHARDISTAN--A WARTORN NATION ON THE ASIAN SUBCONTIN
S.H.I.E.L.D. FIREBASE.
...THE LOCAL HUMIDITY SCREWS WITH THEIR ACTION IN A BIG WAY.
SCREWS WITH THEM HOW, AGENT YELLIN?
HALF THE TIME THEY DON'T WORK AT ALL--
--AND THE OTHER HALF THEY GO OFF WITHOUT BEING TRIGGERED.
AND YOU'RE BLAMING MY PEOPLE FOR THIS PROBLEM?
WE'RE PLAYING BLAME HERE, STARK
...WE JUST WANT TO GET OUT OF THE PROBLEM AND INTO THE SOLUTION.
HRMMM... THERE IS THAT--
AND I GATHER BESIDES THE TECH ISSUES, YOU'VE GOT A POLITICAL MESS, TOO?
TLIK SNIKK
!!!?!

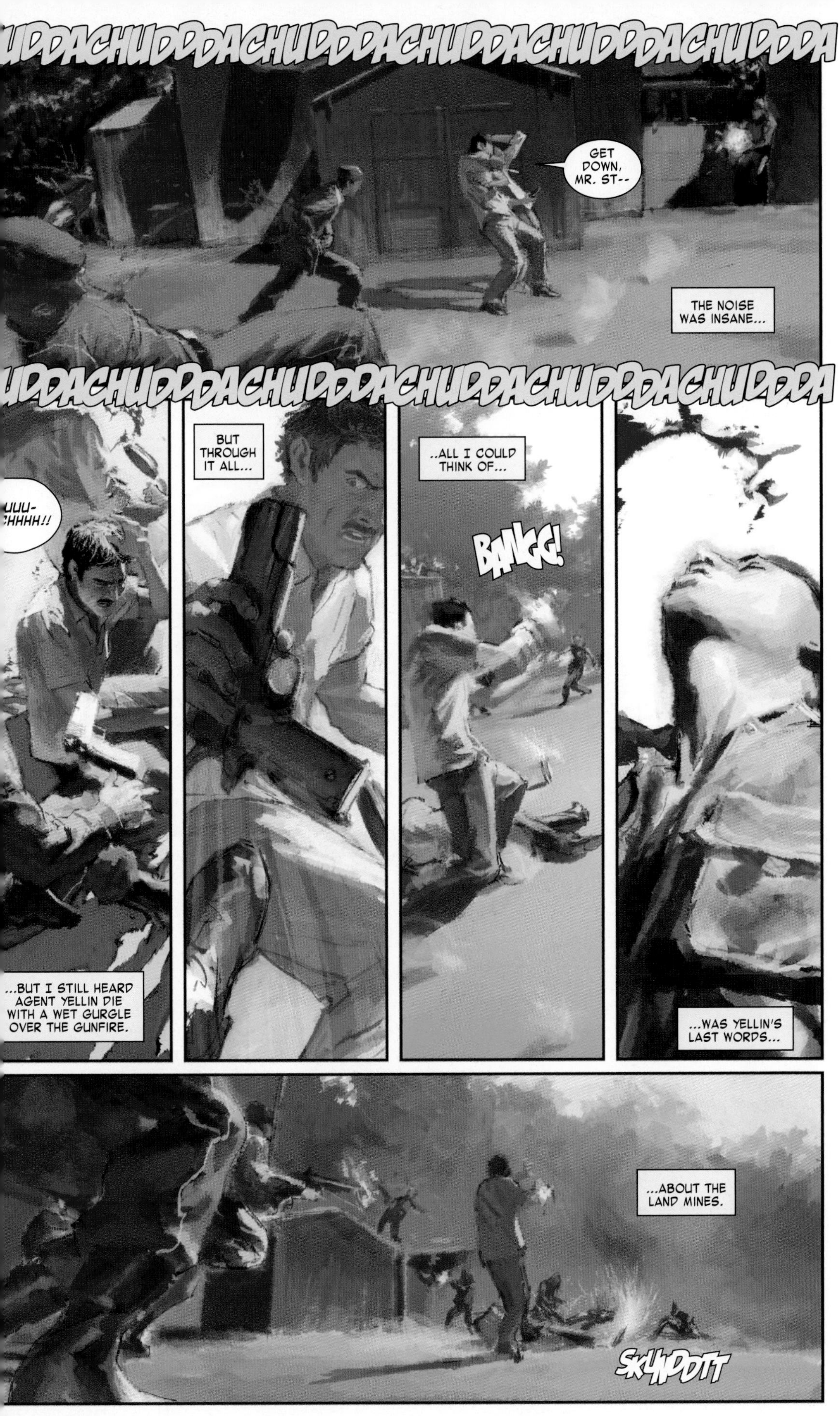

UDDACHUDDDACHUDDDACHUDDACHUDDDACHUDDDA
GET DOWN, MR. ST--
THE NOISE WAS INSANE...
UDDACHUDDDACHUDDDACHUDDDACHUDDDACHUDDDA
UUU-CHHHH!!
...BUT I STILL HEARD AGENT YELLIN DIE WITH A WET GURGLE OVER THE GUNFIRE.
BUT THROUGH IT ALL...
..ALL I COULD THINK OF...
BANGG!
...WAS YELLIN'S LAST WORDS...
...ABOUT THE LAND MINES.
SKUDDTT

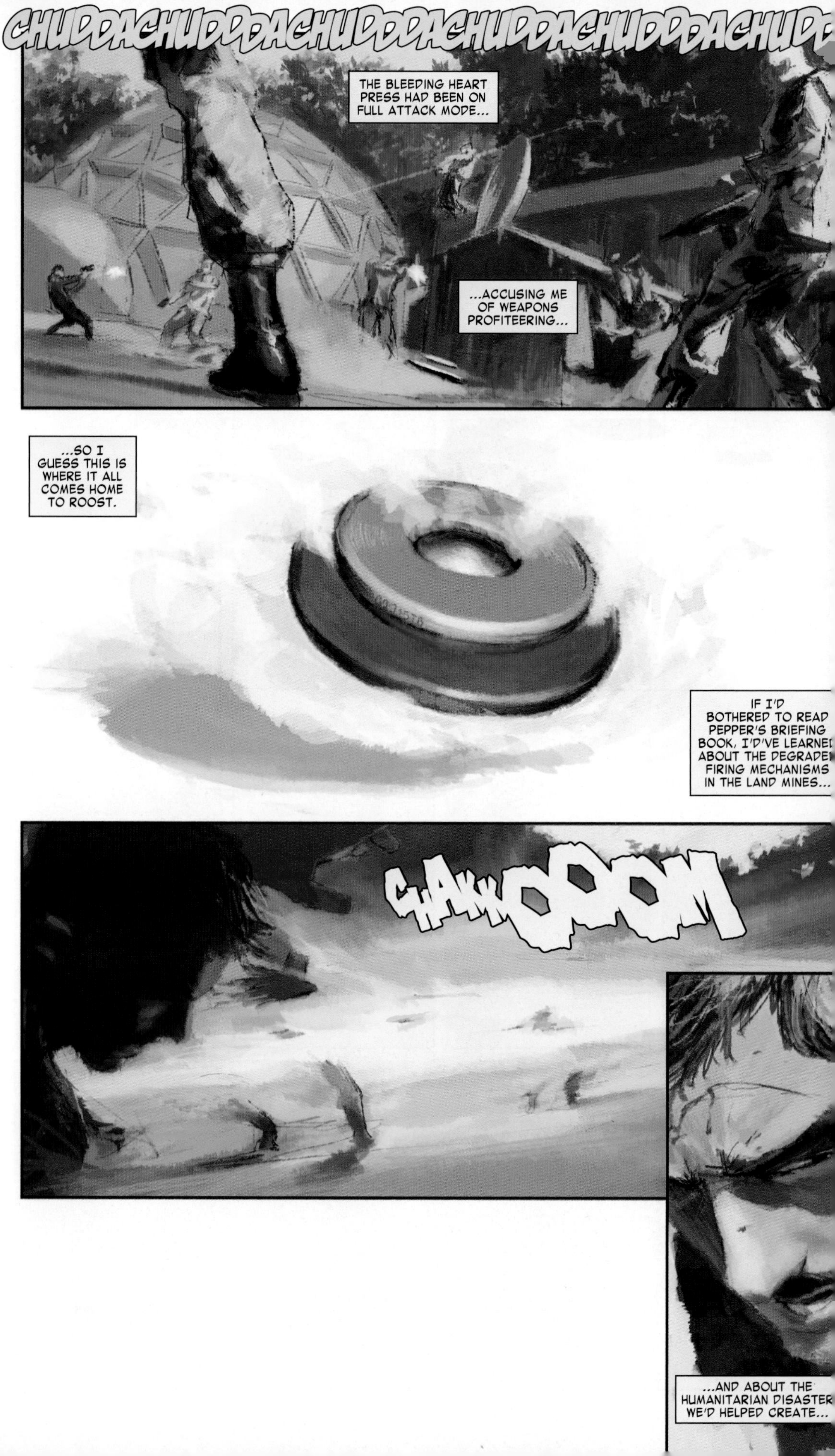

CHUDDACHUDDDACHUDDDACHUDDACHUDDDACHUDD
THE BLEEDING HEART PRESS HAD BEEN ON FULL ATTACK MODE...
...ACCUSING ME OF WEAPONS PROFITEERING...
...SO I GUESS THIS IS WHERE IT ALL COMES HOME TO ROOST.
IF I'D BOTHERED TO READ PEPPER'S BRIEFING BOOK, I'D'VE LEARNED ABOUT THE DEGRADED FIRING MECHANISMS IN THE LAND MINES...
CHAKKOOOM
...AND ABOUT THE HUMANITARIAN DISASTER WE'D HELPED CREATE...

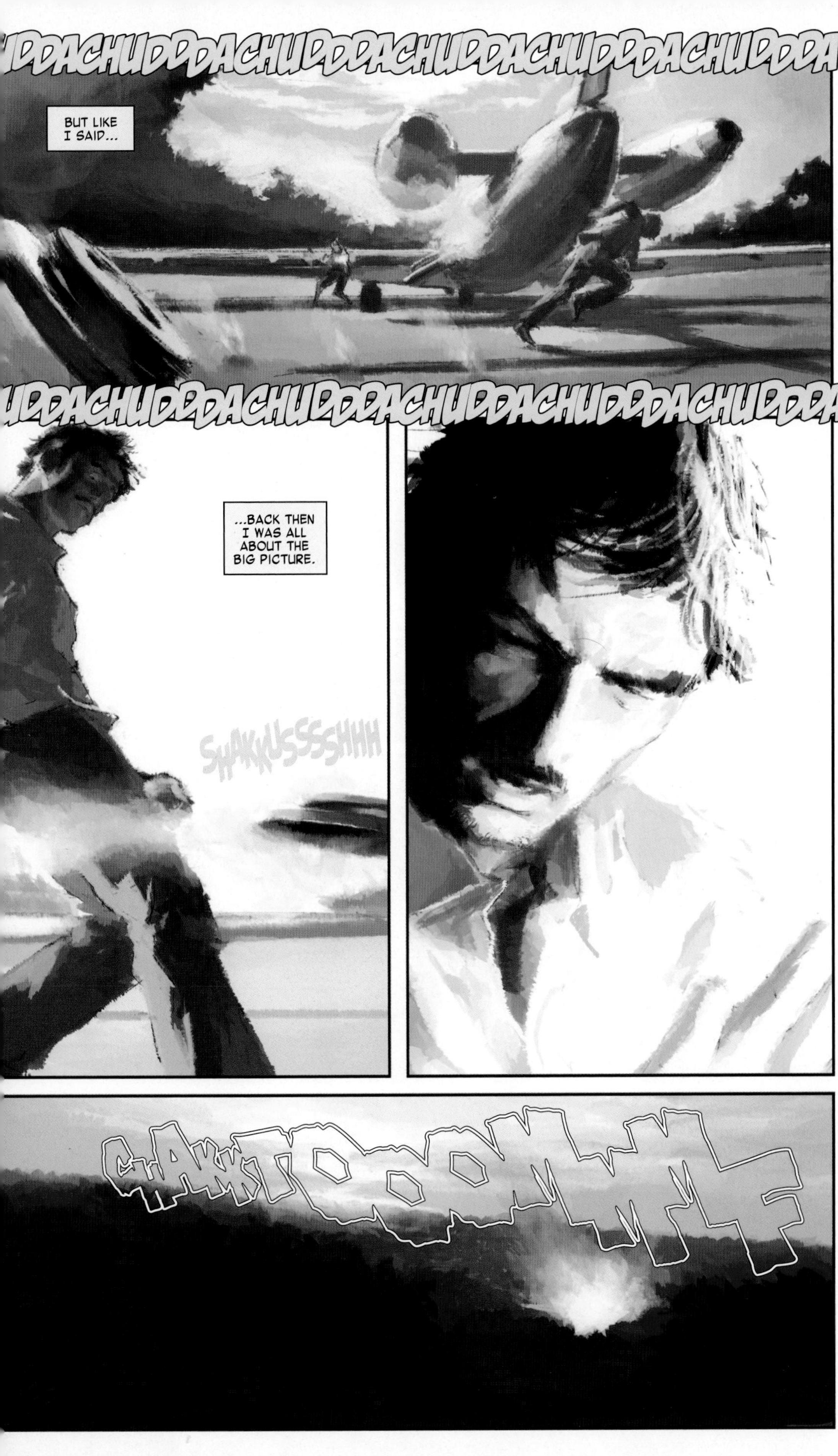
DDACHUDDACHUDDACHUDDACHUDDACHUDDA
BUT LIKE I SAID...
DDACHUDDACHUDDACHUDDACHUDDACHUDDA
...BACK THEN I WAS ALL ABOUT THE BIG PICTURE.
SHAKKUSSSSHHH

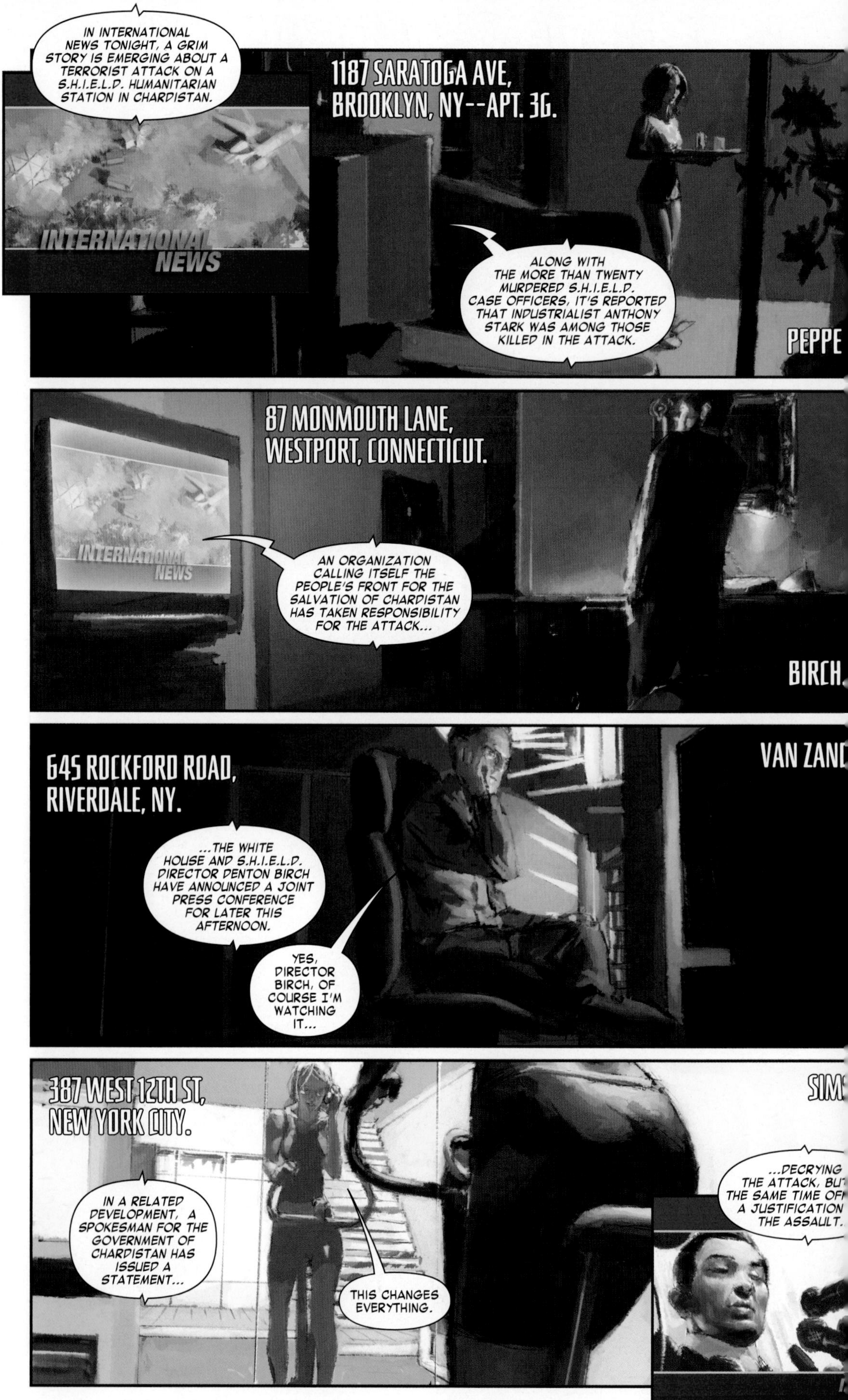

IN INTERNATIONAL NEWS TONIGHT, A GRIM STORY IS EMERGING ABOUT A TERRORIST ATTACK ON A S.H.I.E.L.D. HUMANITARIAN STATION IN CHARDISTAN.
INTERNATIONAL NEWS
1187 SARATOGA AVE, BROOKLYN, NY--APT. 3G.
ALONG WITH THE MORE THAN TWENTY MURDERED S.H.I.E.L.D. CASE OFFICERS, IT'S REPORTED THAT INDUSTRIALIST ANTHONY STARK WAS AMONG THOSE KILLED IN THE ATTACK.
PEPPE
87 MONMOUTH LANE, WESTPORT, CONNECTICUT.
INTERNATIONAL NEWS
AN ORGANIZATION CALLING ITSELF THE PEOPLE'S FRONT FOR THE SALVATION OF CHARDISTAN HAS TAKEN RESPONSIBILITY FOR THE ATTACK...
BIRCH
645 ROCKFORD ROAD, RIVERDALE, NY.
VAN ZAND
...THE WHITE HOUSE AND S.H.I.E.L.D. DIRECTOR DENTON BIRCH HAVE ANNOUNCED A JOINT PRESS CONFERENCE FOR LATER THIS AFTERNOON.
YES, DIRECTOR BIRCH, OF COURSE I'M WATCHING IT...
387 WEST 12TH ST, NEW YORK CITY.
SIM
IN A RELATED DEVELOPMENT, A SPOKESMAN FOR THE GOVERNMENT OF CHARDISTAN HAS ISSUED A STATEMENT...
THIS CHANGES EVERYTHING.
...DECRYING THE ATTACK, BU THE SAME TIME OF A JUSTIFICATION THE ASSAULT.

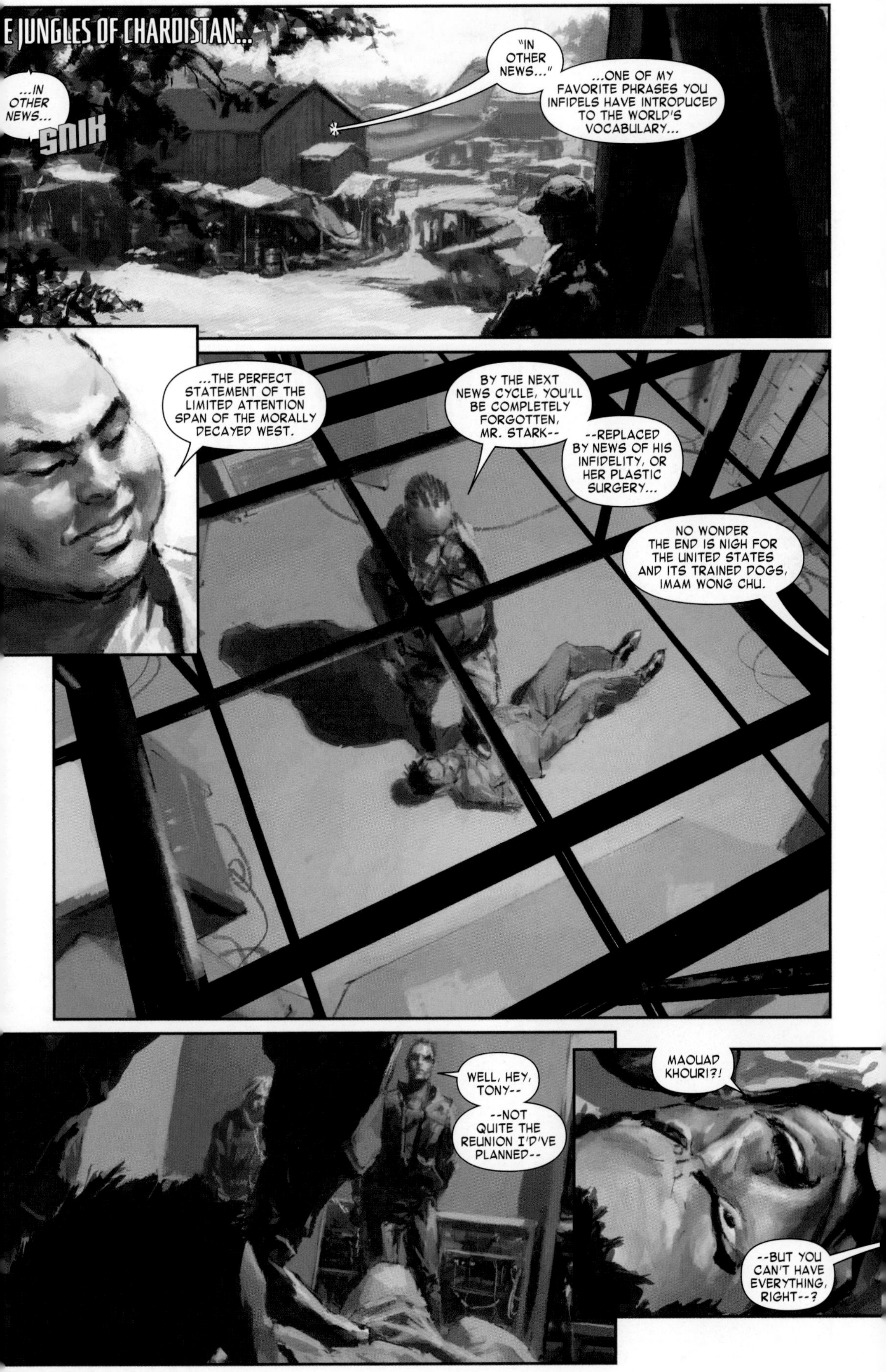
E JUNGLES OF CHARDISTAN...
...IN OTHER NEWS...
SNIK
"IN OTHER NEWS..."
...ONE OF MY FAVORITE PHRASES YOU INFIDELS HAVE INTRODUCED TO THE WORLD'S VOCABULARY...
...THE PERFECT STATEMENT OF THE LIMITED ATTENTION SPAN OF THE MORALLY DECAYED WEST.
BY THE NEXT NEWS CYCLE, YOU'LL BE COMPLETELY FORGOTTEN, MR. STARK--
--REPLACED BY NEWS OF HIS INFIDELITY, OR HER PLASTIC SURGERY...
NO WONDER THE END IS NIGH FOR THE UNITED STATES AND ITS TRAINED DOGS, IMAM WONG CHU.
WELL, HEY, TONY--
--NOT QUITE THE REUNION I'D'VE PLANNED--
MAOUAD KHOURI?!
--BUT YOU CAN'T HAVE EVERYTHING, RIGHT--?

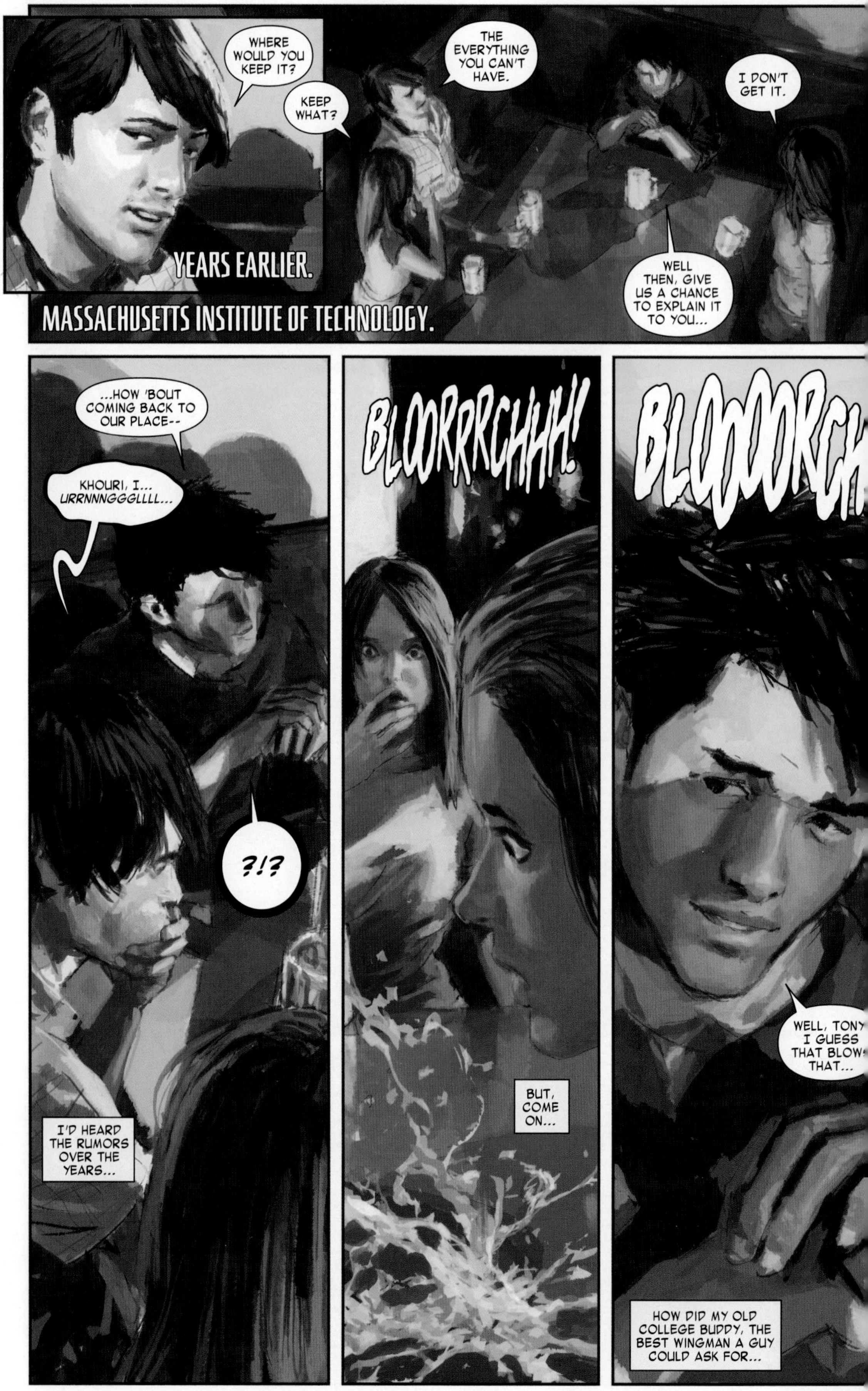

WHERE WOULD YOU KEEP IT?
KEEP WHAT?
THE EVERYTHING YOU CAN'T HAVE.
I DON'T GET IT.
YEARS EARLIER.
MASSACHUSETTS INSTITUTE OF TECHNOLOGY.
WELL THEN, GIVE US A CHANCE TO EXPLAIN IT TO YOU...
...HOW 'BOUT COMING BACK TO OUR PLACE--
KHOURI, I... URRNNNGGGLLLL...
?!?
I'D HEARD THE RUMORS OVER THE YEARS...
BLOORRRCHHH!
BUT, COME ON...
BLOOOORCH
WELL, TONY I GUESS THAT BLOWS THAT...
HOW DID MY OLD COLLEGE BUDDY, THE BEST WINGMAN A GUY COULD ASK FOR...

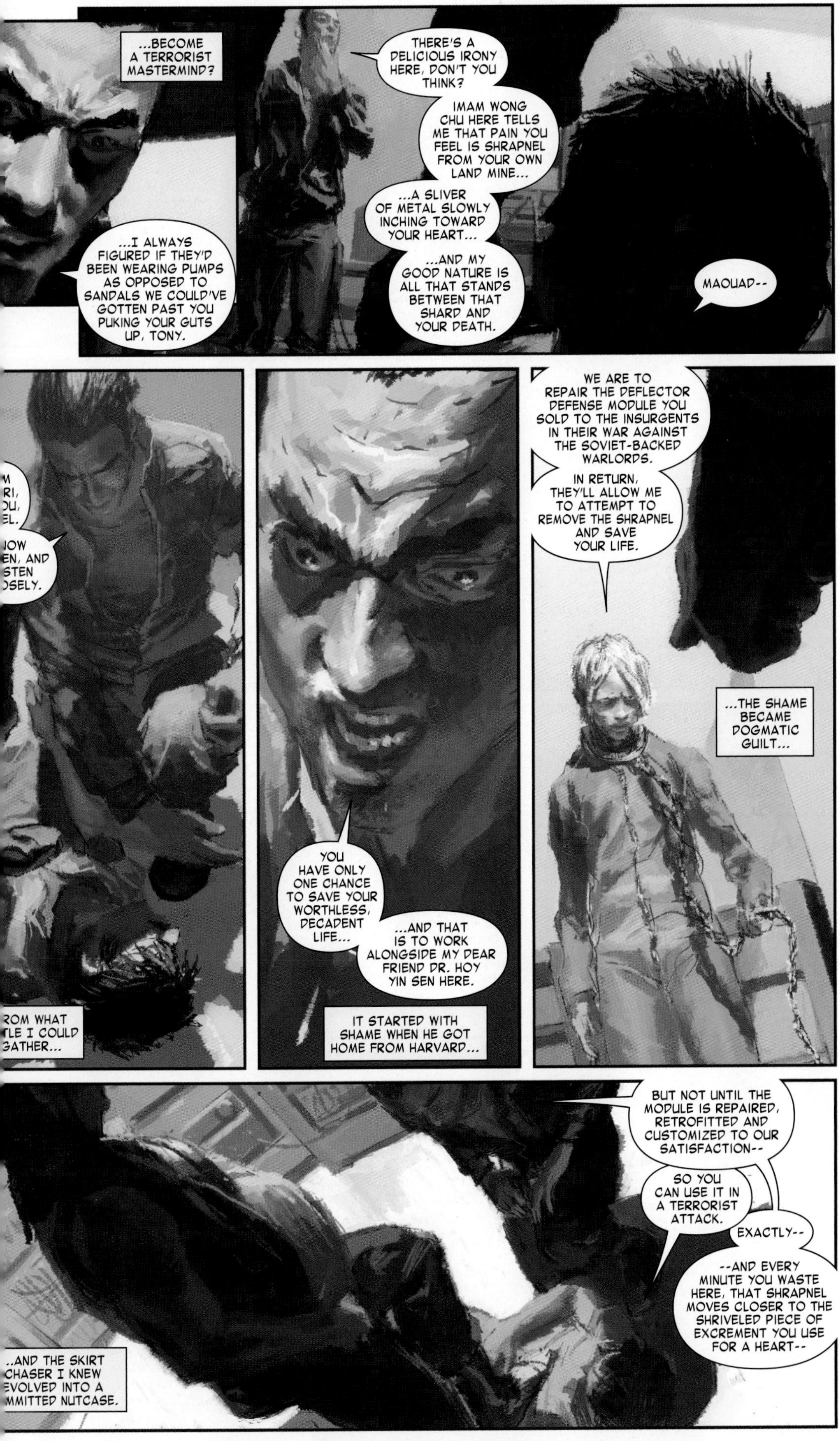
...BECOME A TERRORIST MASTERMIND?
...I ALWAYS FIGURED IF THEY'D BEEN WEARING PUMPS AS OPPOSED TO SANDALS WE COULD'VE GOTTEN PAST YOU PUKING YOUR GUTS UP, TONY.
THERE'S A DELICIOUS IRONY HERE, DON'T YOU THINK?
IMAM WONG CHU HERE TELLS ME THAT PAIN YOU FEEL IS SHRAPNEL FROM YOUR OWN LAND MINE...
...A SLIVER OF METAL SLOWLY INCHING TOWARD YOUR HEART...
...AND MY GOOD NATURE IS ALL THAT STANDS BETWEEN THAT SHARD AND YOUR DEATH.
MAOUAD--
M RI, OU, EL.
NOW EN, AND STEN OSELY.
ROM WHAT TLE I COULD GATHER...
YOU HAVE ONLY ONE CHANCE TO SAVE YOUR WORTHLESS, DECADENT LIFE...
...AND THAT IS TO WORK ALONGSIDE MY DEAR FRIEND DR. HOY YIN SEN HERE.
IT STARTED WITH SHAME WHEN HE GOT HOME FROM HARVARD...
WE ARE TO REPAIR THE DEFLECTOR DEFENSE MODULE YOU SOLD TO THE INSURGENTS IN THEIR WAR AGAINST THE SOVIET-BACKED WARLORDS.
IN RETURN, THEY'LL ALLOW ME TO ATTEMPT TO REMOVE THE SHRAPNEL AND SAVE YOUR LIFE.
...THE SHAME BECAME DOGMATIC GUILT...
..AND THE SKIRT CHASER I KNEW EVOLVED INTO A MMITTED NUTCASE.
BUT NOT UNTIL THE MODULE IS REPAIRED, RETROFITTED AND CUSTOMIZED TO OUR SATISFACTION--
SO YOU CAN USE IT IN A TERRORIST ATTACK.
EXACTLY--
--AND EVERY MINUTE YOU WASTE HERE, THAT SHRAPNEL MOVES CLOSER TO THE SHRIVELED PIECE OF EXCREMENT YOU USE FOR A HEART--

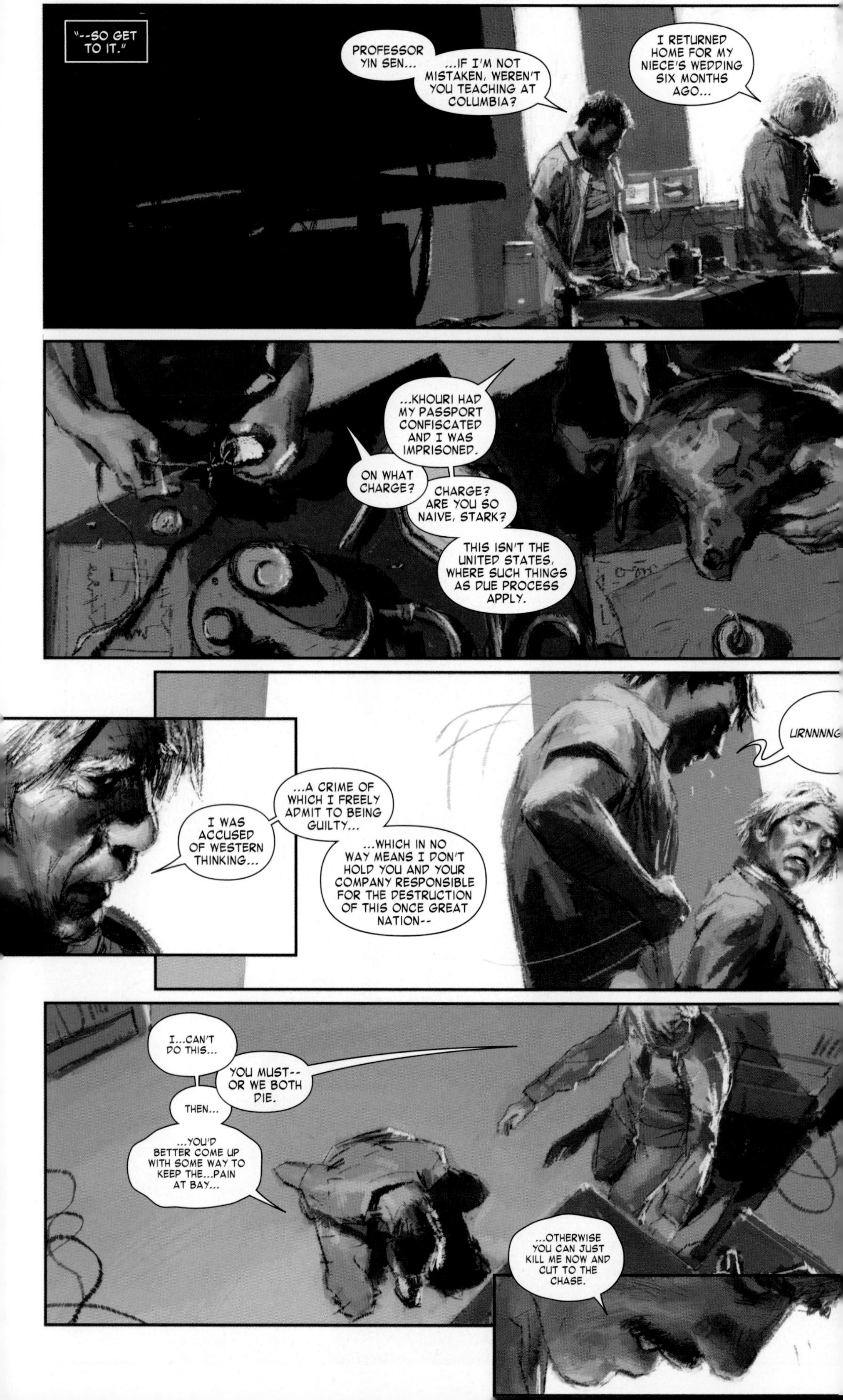
"--SO GET TO IT."
PROFESSOR YIN SEN...
...IF I'M NOT MISTAKEN, WEREN'T YOU TEACHING AT COLUMBIA?
I RETURNED HOME FOR MY NIECE'S WEDDING SIX MONTHS AGO...
...KHOURI HAD MY PASSPORT CONFISCATED AND I WAS IMPRISONED.
ON WHAT CHARGE?
CHARGE? ARE YOU SO NAIVE, STARK?
THIS ISN'T THE UNITED STATES, WHERE SUCH THINGS AS DUE PROCESS APPLY.
URNNNNG
I WAS ACCUSED OF WESTERN THINKING...
...A CRIME OF WHICH I FREELY ADMIT TO BEING GUILTY...
...WHICH IN NO WAY MEANS I DON'T HOLD YOU AND YOUR COMPANY RESPONSIBLE FOR THE DESTRUCTION OF THIS ONCE GREAT NATION--
I...CAN'T DO THIS...
YOU MUST--OR WE BOTH DIE.
THEN...
...YOU'D BETTER COME UP WITH SOME WAY TO KEEP THE...PAIN AT BAY...
...OTHERWISE YOU CAN JUST KILL ME NOW AND CUT TO THE CHASE.

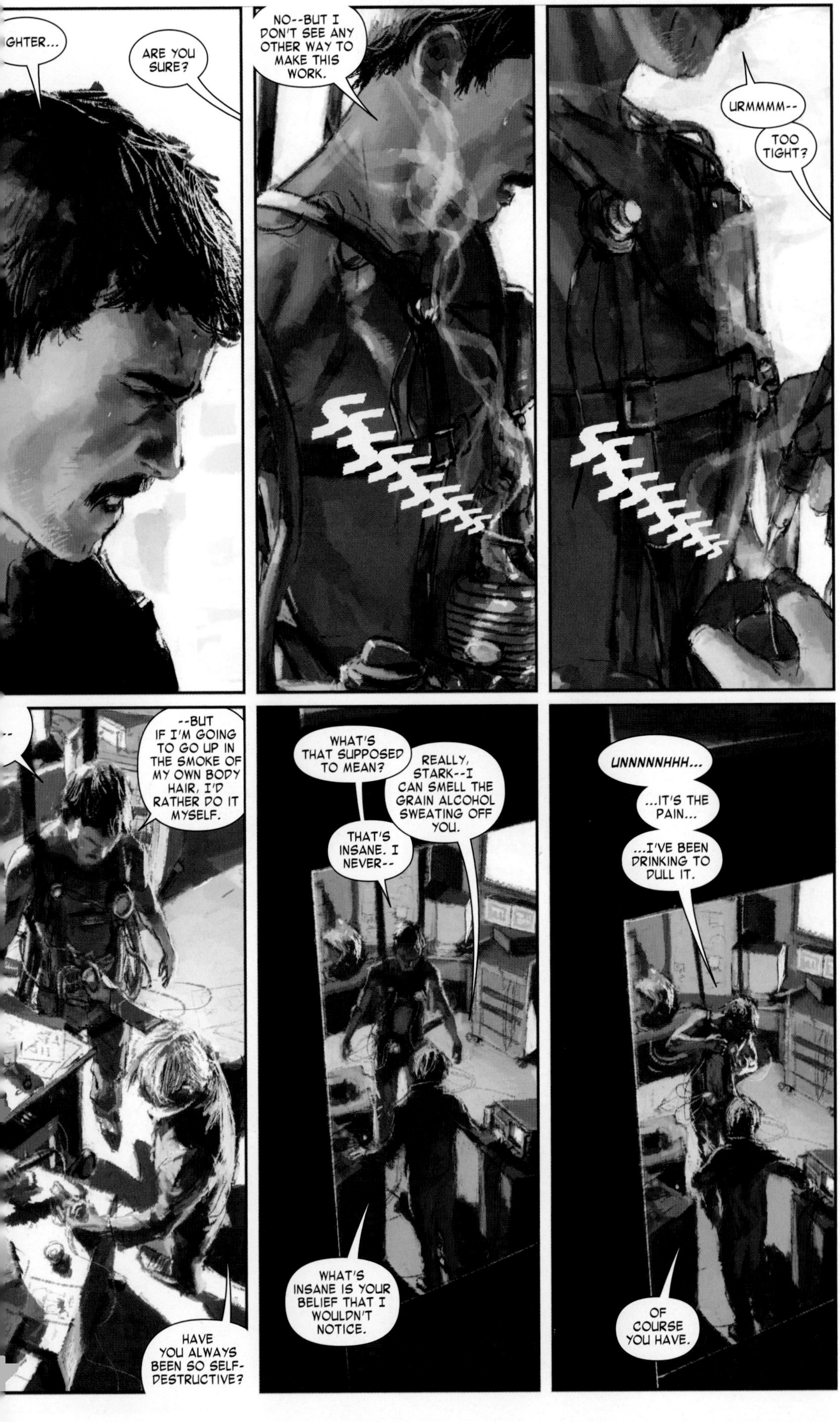
GHTER...
ARE YOU SURE?
NO--BUT I DON'T SEE ANY OTHER WAY TO MAKE THIS WORK.
SSSSSSSSS
SSSSSSSSS
URMMMM--
TOO TIGHT?
--BUT IF I'M GOING TO GO UP IN THE SMOKE OF MY OWN BODY HAIR, I'D RATHER DO IT MYSELF.
HAVE YOU ALWAYS BEEN SO SELF-DESTRUCTIVE?
WHAT'S THAT SUPPOSED TO MEAN?
REALLY, STARK--I CAN SMELL THE GRAIN ALCOHOL SWEATING OFF YOU.
THAT'S INSANE. I NEVER--
WHAT'S INSANE IS YOUR BELIEF THAT I WOULDN'T NOTICE.
UNNNNNHHH...
...IT'S THE PAIN...
...I'VE BEEN DRINKING TO DULL IT.
OF COURSE YOU HAVE.

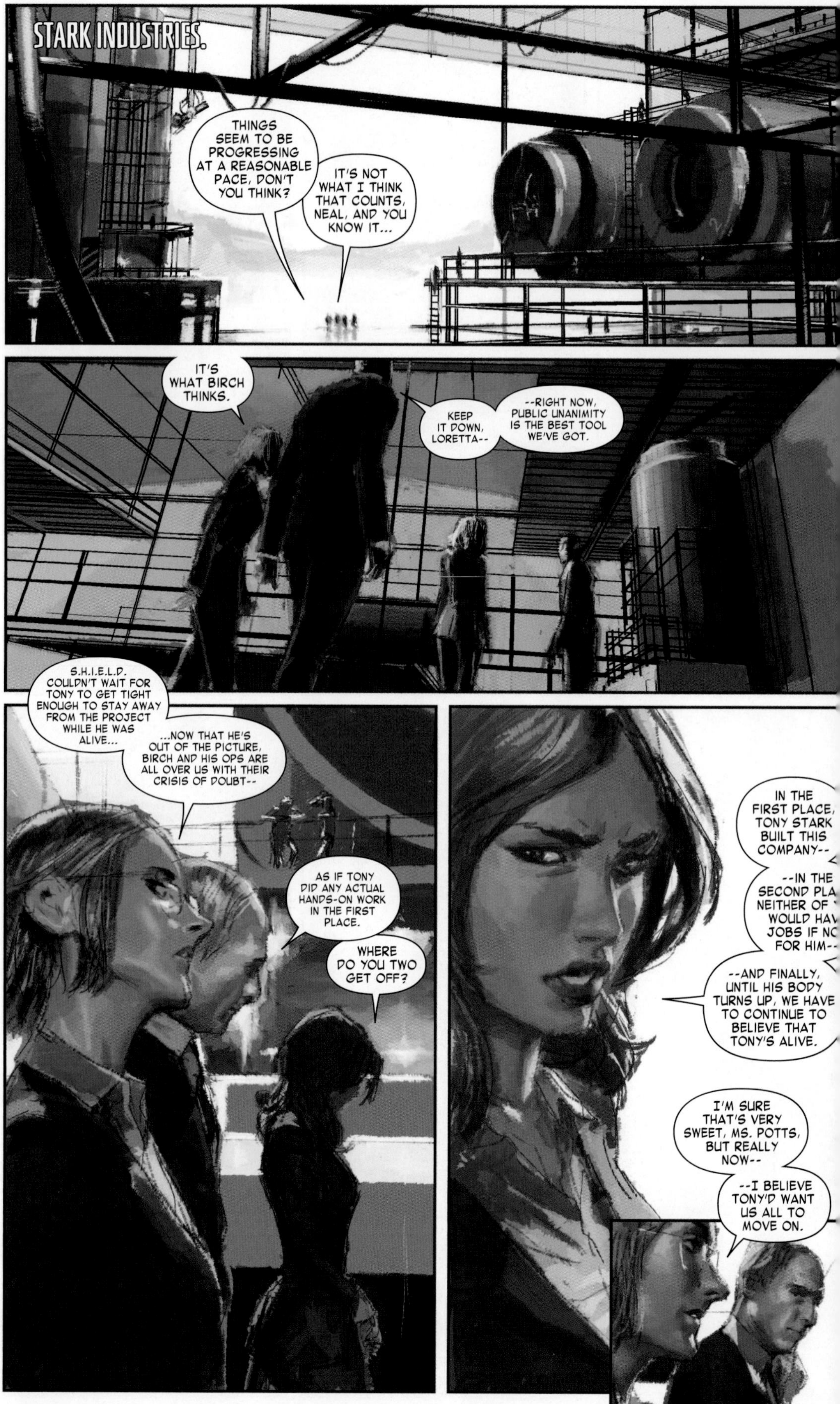
STARK INDUSTRIES.
THINGS SEEM TO BE PROGRESSING AT A REASONABLE PACE, DON'T YOU THINK?
IT'S NOT WHAT I THINK THAT COUNTS, NEAL, AND YOU KNOW IT...
IT'S WHAT BIRCH THINKS.
KEEP IT DOWN, LORETTA--
--RIGHT NOW, PUBLIC UNANIMITY IS THE BEST TOOL WE'VE GOT.
S.H.I.E.L.D. COULDN'T WAIT FOR TONY TO GET TIGHT ENOUGH TO STAY AWAY FROM THE PROJECT WHILE HE WAS ALIVE...
...NOW THAT HE'S OUT OF THE PICTURE, BIRCH AND HIS OPS ARE ALL OVER US WITH THEIR CRISIS OF DOUBT--
AS IF TONY DID ANY ACTUAL HANDS-ON WORK IN THE FIRST PLACE.
WHERE DO YOU TWO GET OFF?
IN THE FIRST PLACE, TONY STARK BUILT THIS COMPANY--
--AND FINALLY, UNTIL HIS BODY TURNS UP, WE HAVE TO CONTINUE TO BELIEVE THAT TONY'S ALIVE.
I'M SURE THAT'S VERY SWEET, MS. POTTS, BUT REALLY NOW--
--I BELIEVE TONY'D WANT US ALL TO MOVE ON.

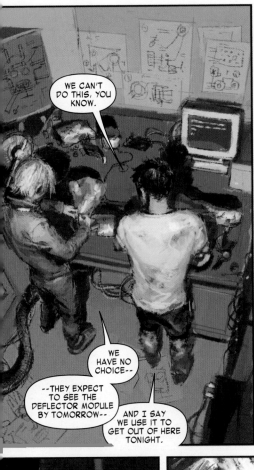

WE CAN'T DO THIS, YOU KNOW.

WE HAVE NO CHOICE--

--THEY EXPECT TO SEE THE DEFLECTOR MODULE BY TOMORROW--

AND I SAY WE USE IT TO GET OUT OF HERE TONIGHT.

BUT--

I'VE BEEN THINKING ABOUT THIS BREASTPLATE.

YES--?

THE PAIN IS GONE-- OR AT LEAST ABATED...

I DID NOTICE WE WEREN'T RUNNING OUT OF GRAIN ALCOHOL QUITE SO SWIFTLY.

SO WHY NOT [AP]PLY THE SAME [D]EFLECTOR [T]ECHNOLOGY TO THIS?

YOU WANT TO USE THIS-- THIS SUIT TO ESCAPE?

I'VE ASSEMBLED MOST OF THE COMPONENTS--

I'M TERRIBLY DISAPPOINTED.

NOT IN YOU, STARK--

--ONE MUST ASSUME YOU'VE ALWAYS BEEN SPIRITUALLY BANKRUPT.

BUT DR. YIN SEN...

...I HAD HOPED YOUR PATRIOTIC REEDUCATION WOULD HAVE SAVED YOU FROM YOUR PAST DECADENT EXCESSES.

THE LAW OF UNINTENDED CONSEQUENCES.

BLAMM

THE DEFLECTOR DEFENSE MODULE REPELLED WONG CH BULLET, SAVING MY LIFE--

--KILLING DR. YIN SEN INSTANTLY.

I NEVER MEANT TO KILL WONG CHU...

SHKRUMMPPPFFF

I REVERSED THE DEFLECTOR DEFENSIVELY...

...AIMING A KHOURI...

...BUT WONG C TOOK THE HIT

OOOEEOOEEOOOEEOOOEEOOEEOOEEOOEEOOEEOOOEEOOEEOOOEEOOOEEOOEEOO

I RAN OUT OF THE CAMP, INTO THE UNDERBRUSH, AND INTENDED TO KEEP RUNNING...

...UNTI I JUST STOPPED

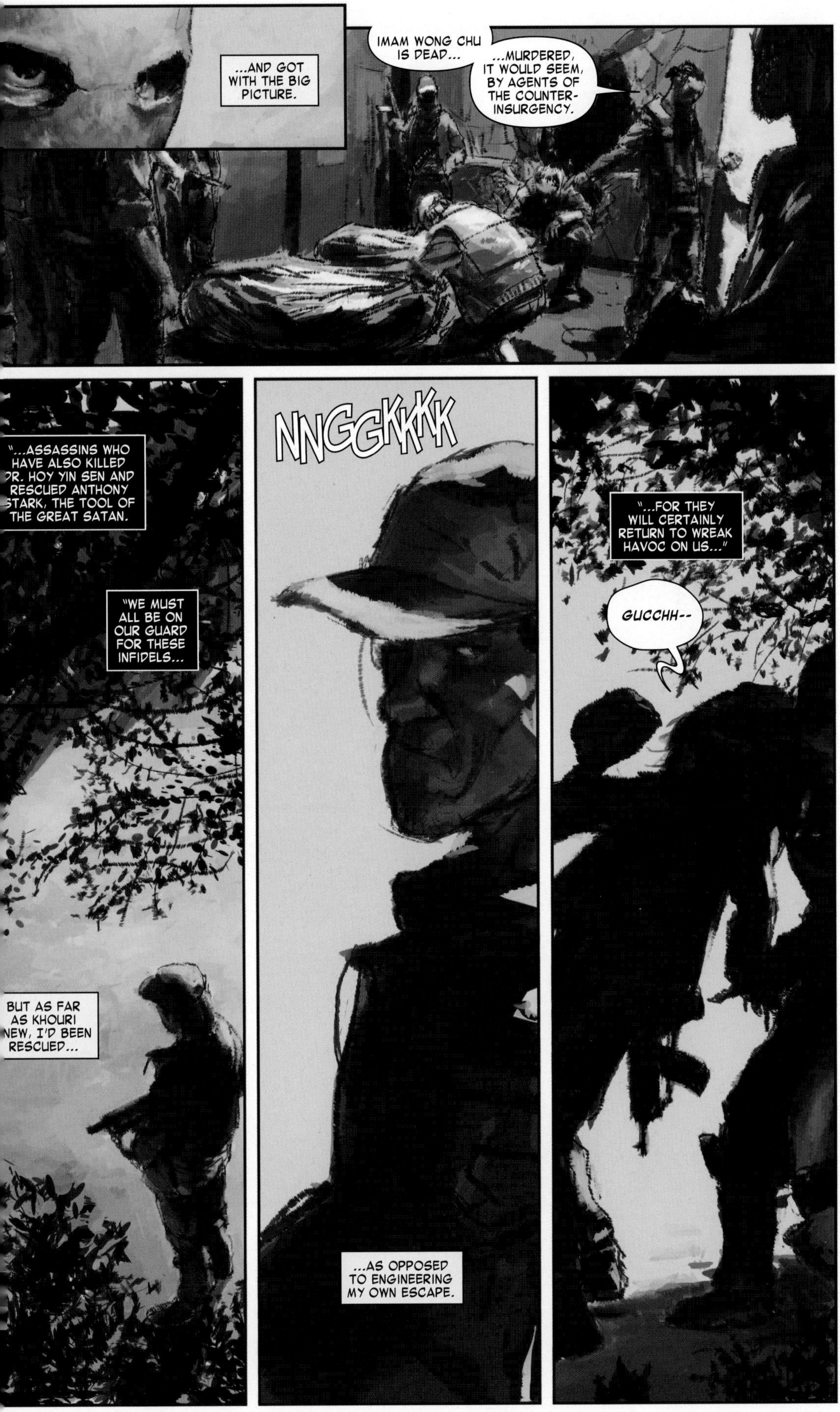
...AND GOT WITH THE BIG PICTURE.
IMAM WONG CHU IS DEAD...
...MURDERED, IT WOULD SEEM, BY AGENTS OF THE COUNTER-INSURGENCY.
"...ASSASSINS WHO HAVE ALSO KILLED DR. HOY YIN SEN AND RESCUED ANTHONY STARK, THE TOOL OF THE GREAT SATAN.
"WE MUST ALL BE ON OUR GUARD FOR THESE INFIDELS...
BUT AS FAR AS KHOURI KNEW, I'D BEEN RESCUED...
NNGGKKKK
...AS OPPOSED TO ENGINEERING MY OWN ESCAPE.
"...FOR THEY WILL CERTAINLY RETURN TO WREAK HAVOC ON US..."
GUCCHH--

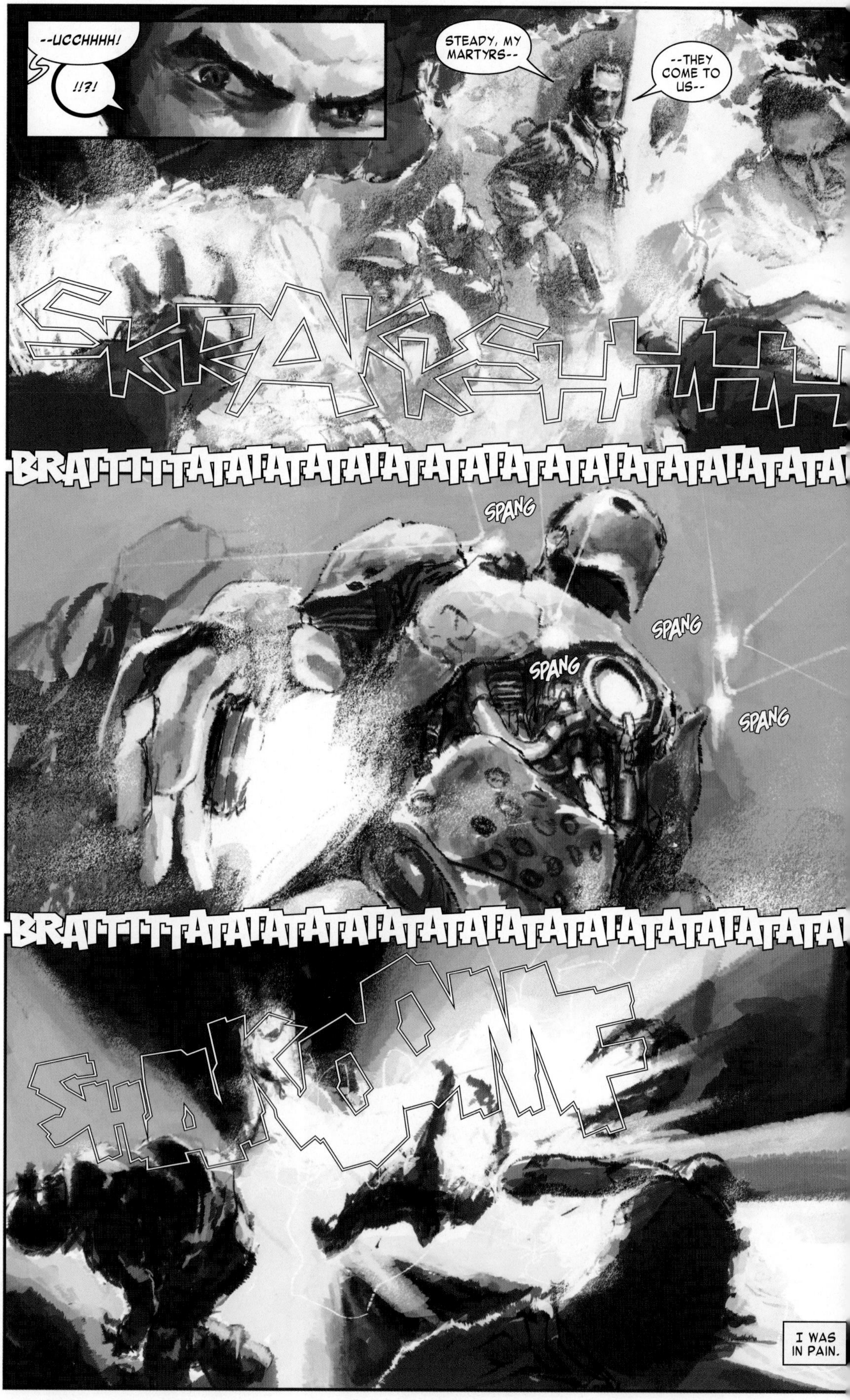
--UCCHHHH!
!!?!
STEADY, MY MARTYRS--
--THEY COME TO US--
SKRAKASHHHH
BRATTTTTATATATATATATATATATATATATATATATATATAT
SPANG
SPANG
SPANG
SPANG
BRATTTTTATATATATATATATATATATATATATATATATATAT
SHAKOOMF
I WAS IN PAIN.

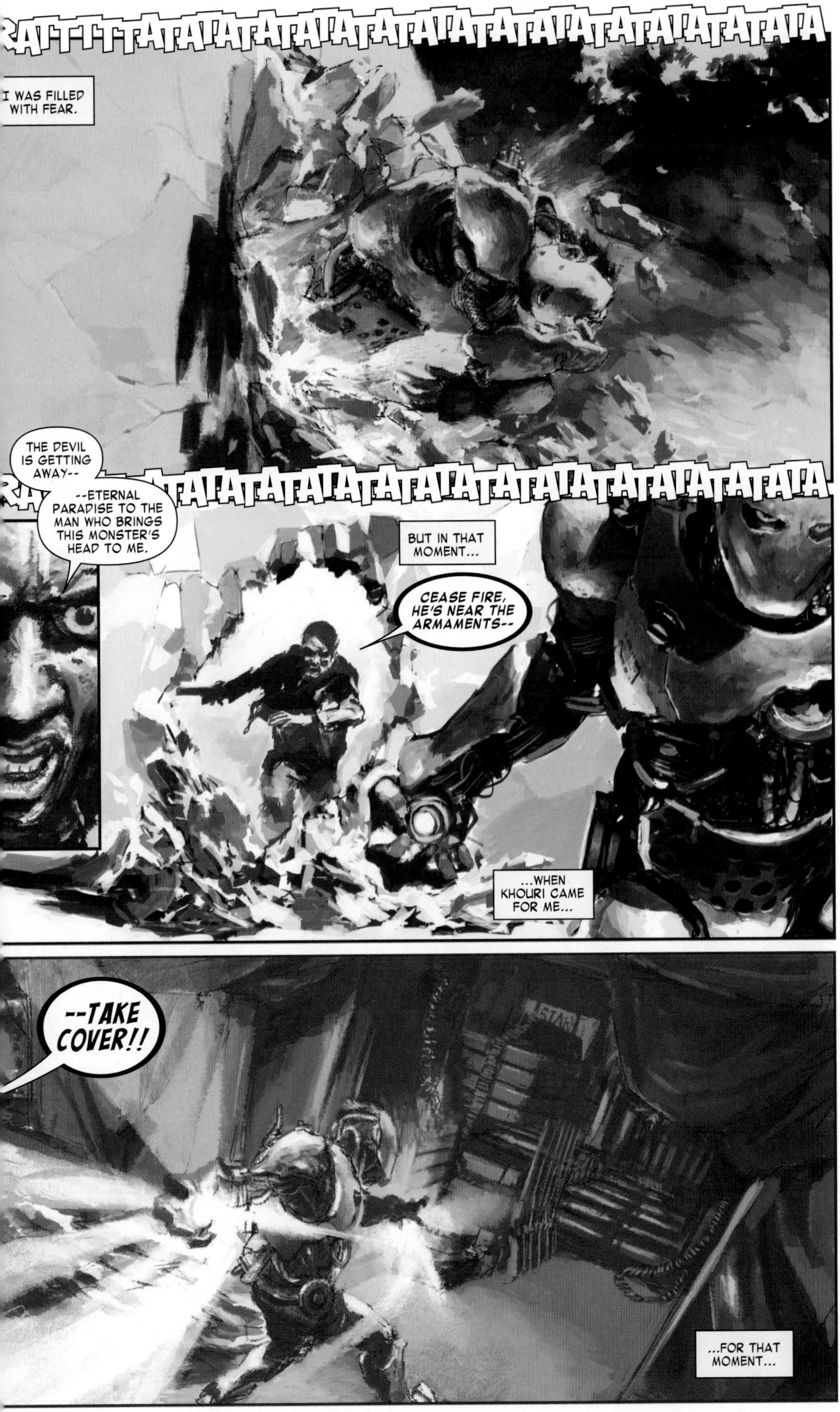
RATTTTTATATATATATATATATATATATATATATATATATATA
I WAS FILLED WITH FEAR.
THE DEVIL IS GETTING AWAY--
--ETERNAL PARADISE TO THE MAN WHO BRINGS THIS MONSTER'S HEAD TO ME.
BUT IN THAT MOMENT...
CEASE FIRE, HE'S NEAR THE ARMAMENTS--
...WHEN KHOURI CAME FOR ME...
--TAKE COVER!!
...FOR THAT MOMENT...

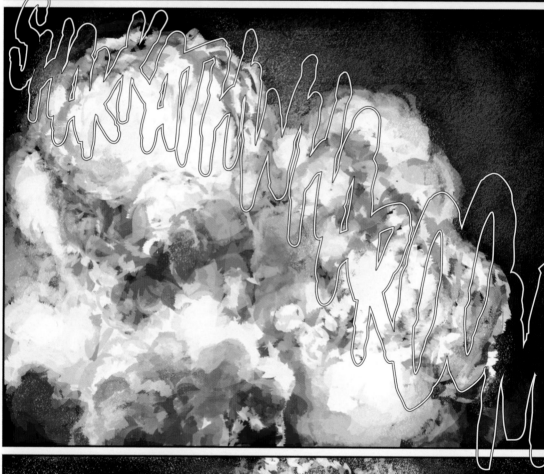

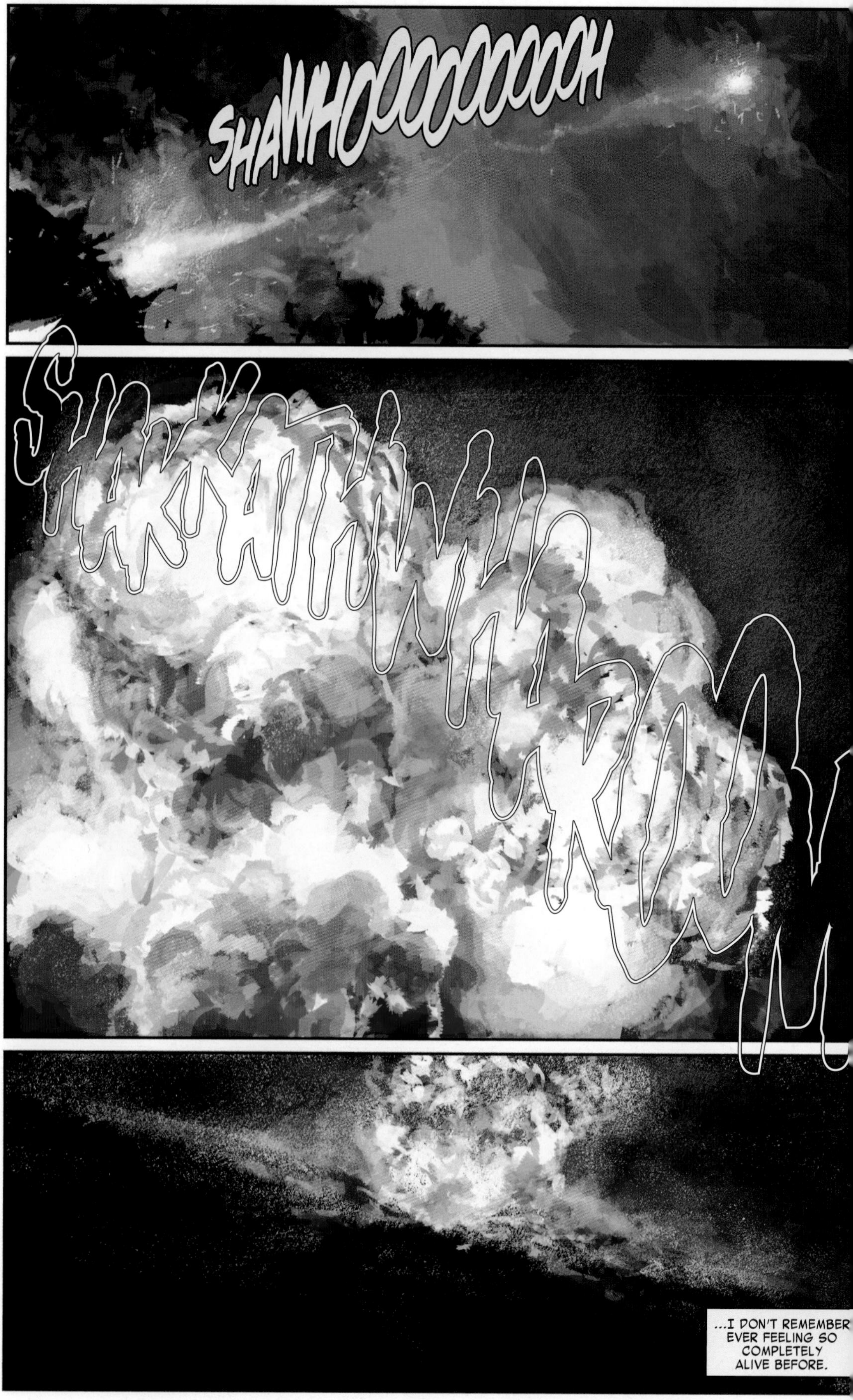

...I DON'T REMEMBER EVER FEELING SO COMPLETELY ALIVE BEFORE.

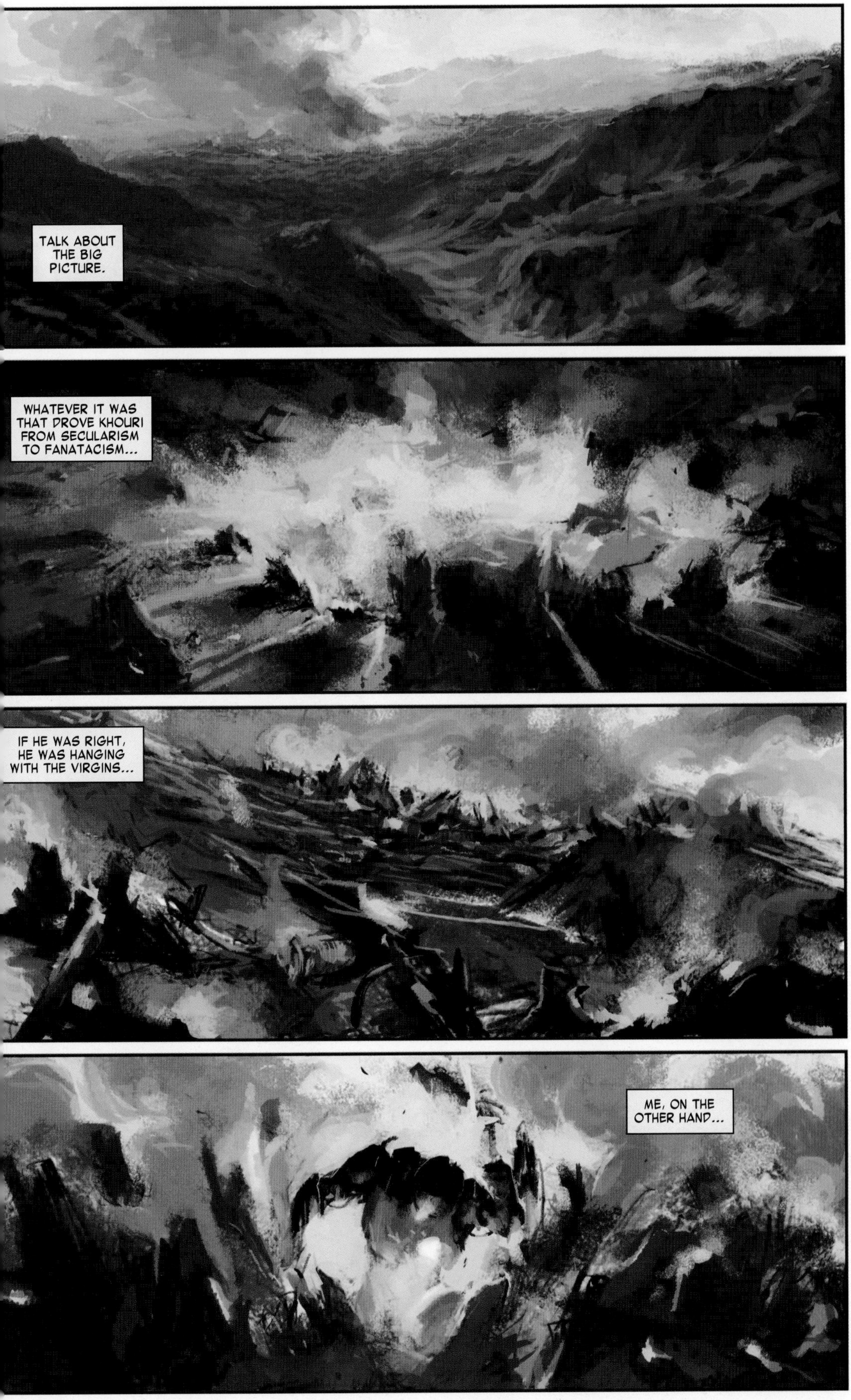
TALK ABOUT THE BIG PICTURE.
WHATEVER IT WAS THAT DROVE KHOURI FROM SECULARISM TO FANATACISM...
IF HE WAS RIGHT, HE WAS HANGING WITH THE VIRGINS...
ME, ON THE OTHER HAND...

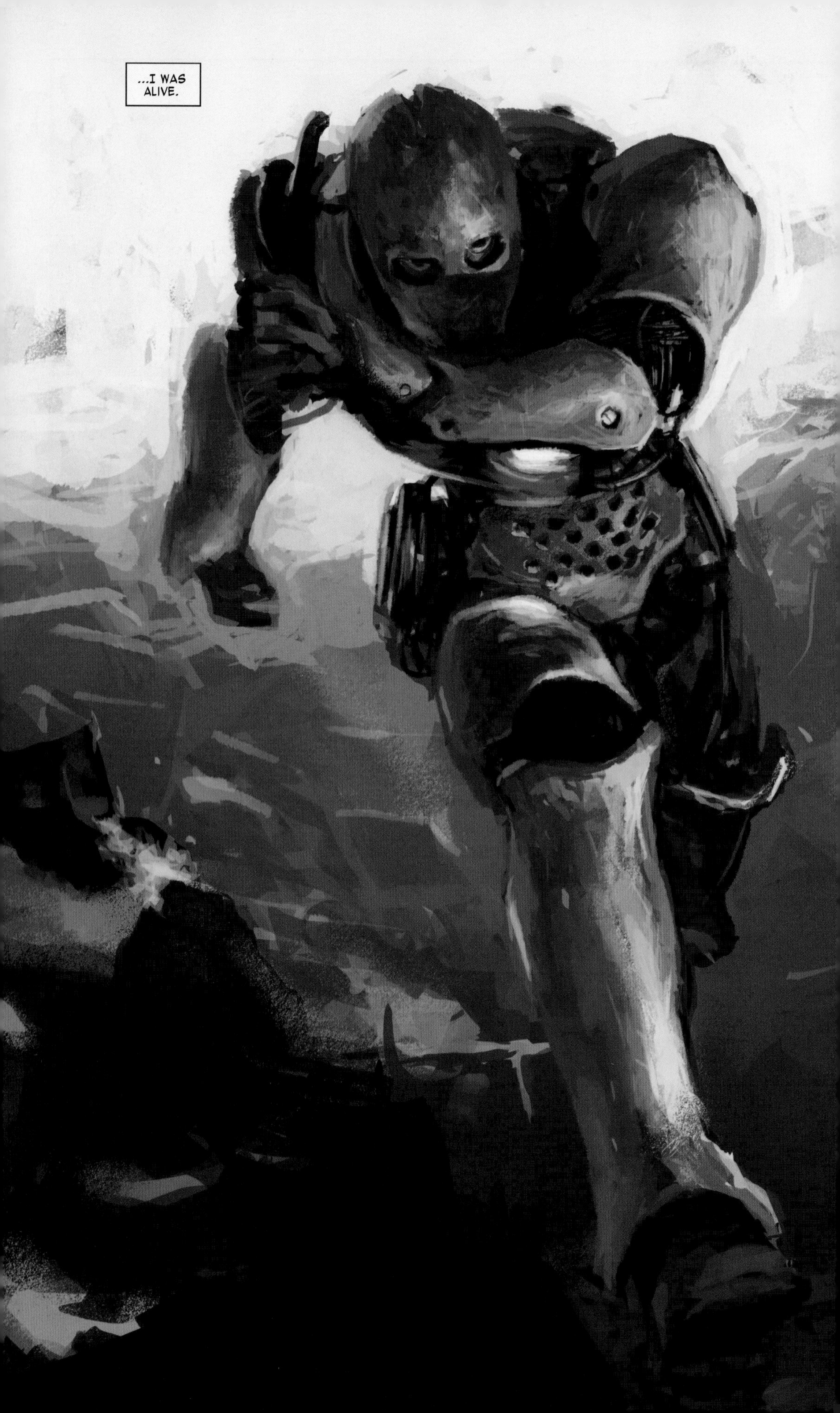
...I WAS ALIVE.

WHEN I WAS A KID, MAYBE EIGHT OR NINE...

...MY DAD TOOK ME ALONG ON A BUSINESS TRIP TO ONE OF HIS HOLDINGS...

...A MEAT PROCESSING PLANT OUT IN EAST ELEPHANT'S BREATH IOWA OR SOME PLACE.

THAT WAS THE LAST TIME I REMEMBER SMELLING ANYTHING LIKE THIS...

...BLOOD, FLESH, FECES...

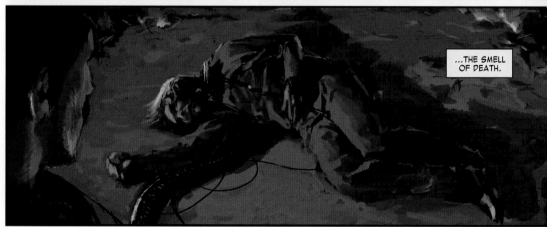

...THE SMELL OF DEATH.

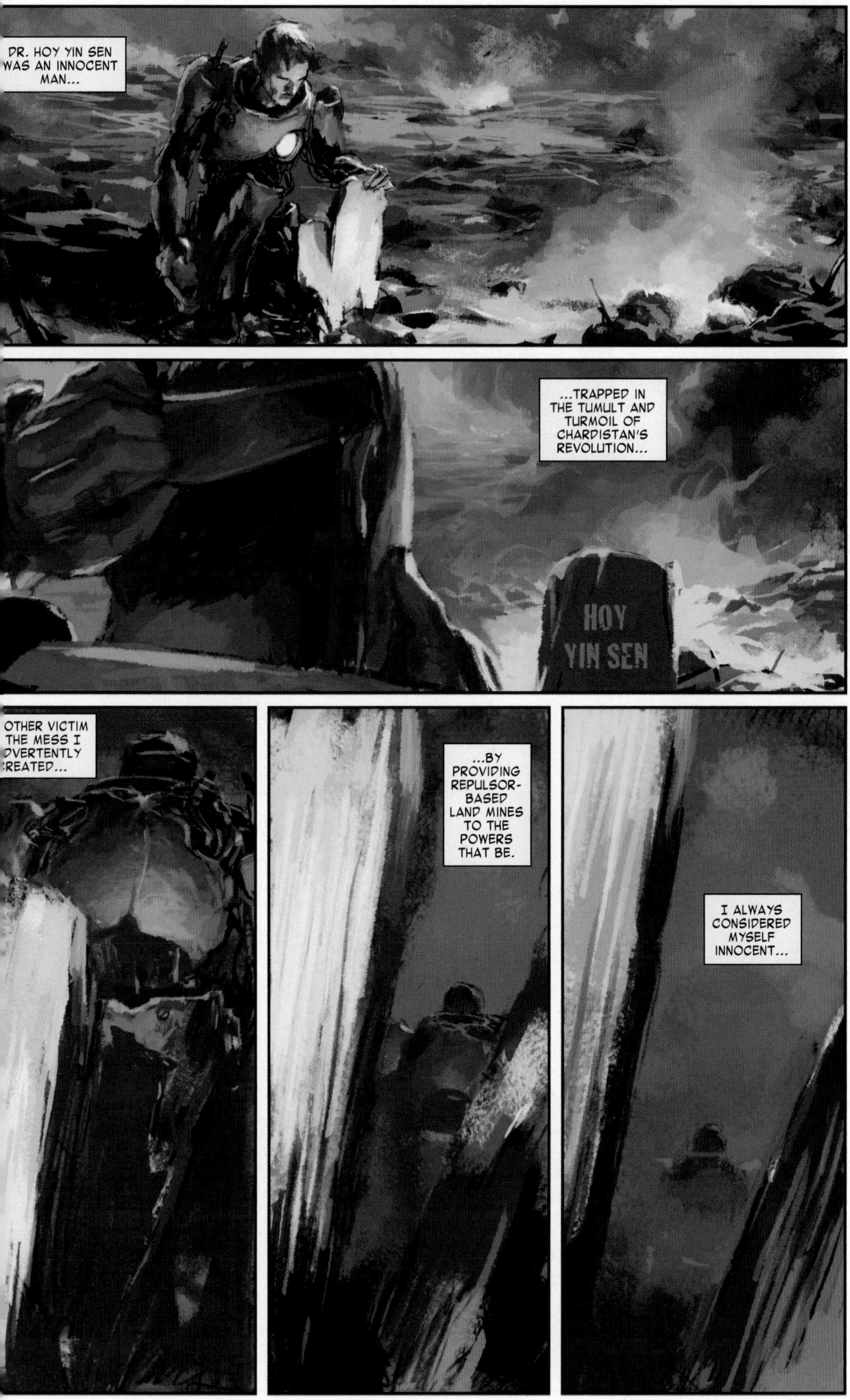
DR. HOY YIN SEN WAS AN INNOCENT MAN...
...TRAPPED IN THE TUMULT AND TURMOIL OF CHARDISTAN'S REVOLUTION...
HOY YIN SEN
OTHER VICTIM THE MESS I DVERTENTLY CREATED...
...BY PROVIDING REPULSOR-BASED LAND MINES TO THE POWERS THAT BE.
I ALWAYS CONSIDERED MYSELF INNOCENT...

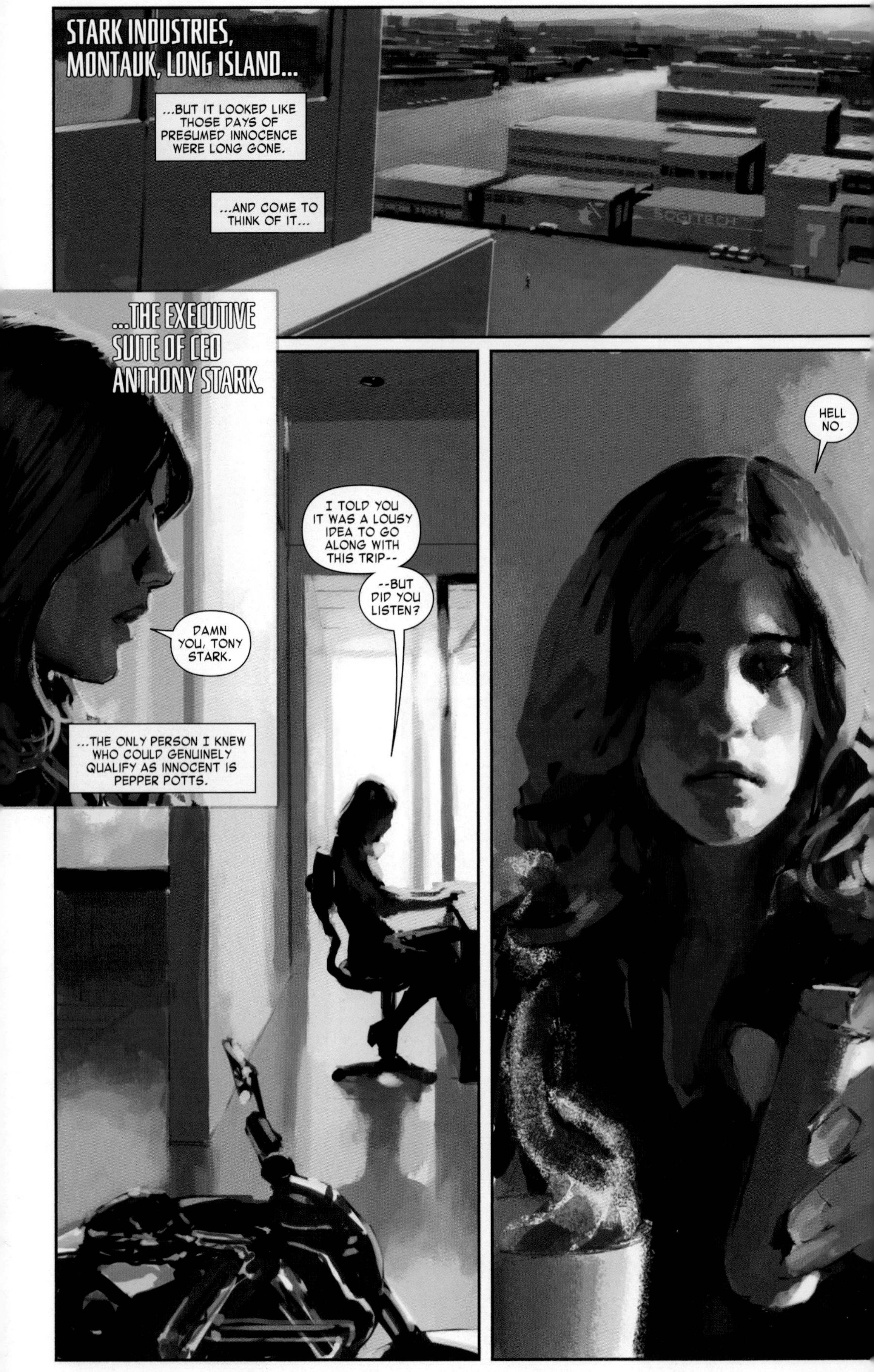
STARK INDUSTRIES, MONTAUK, LONG ISLAND...
...BUT IT LOOKED LIKE THOSE DAYS OF PRESUMED INNOCENCE WERE LONG GONE.
...AND COME TO THINK OF IT...
...THE EXECUTIVE SUITE OF CEO ANTHONY STARK.
DAMN YOU, TONY STARK.
...THE ONLY PERSON I KNEW WHO COULD GENUINELY QUALIFY AS INNOCENT IS PEPPER POTTS.
I TOLD YOU IT WAS A LOUSY IDEA TO GO ALONG WITH THIS TRIP--
--BUT DID YOU LISTEN?
HELL NO.

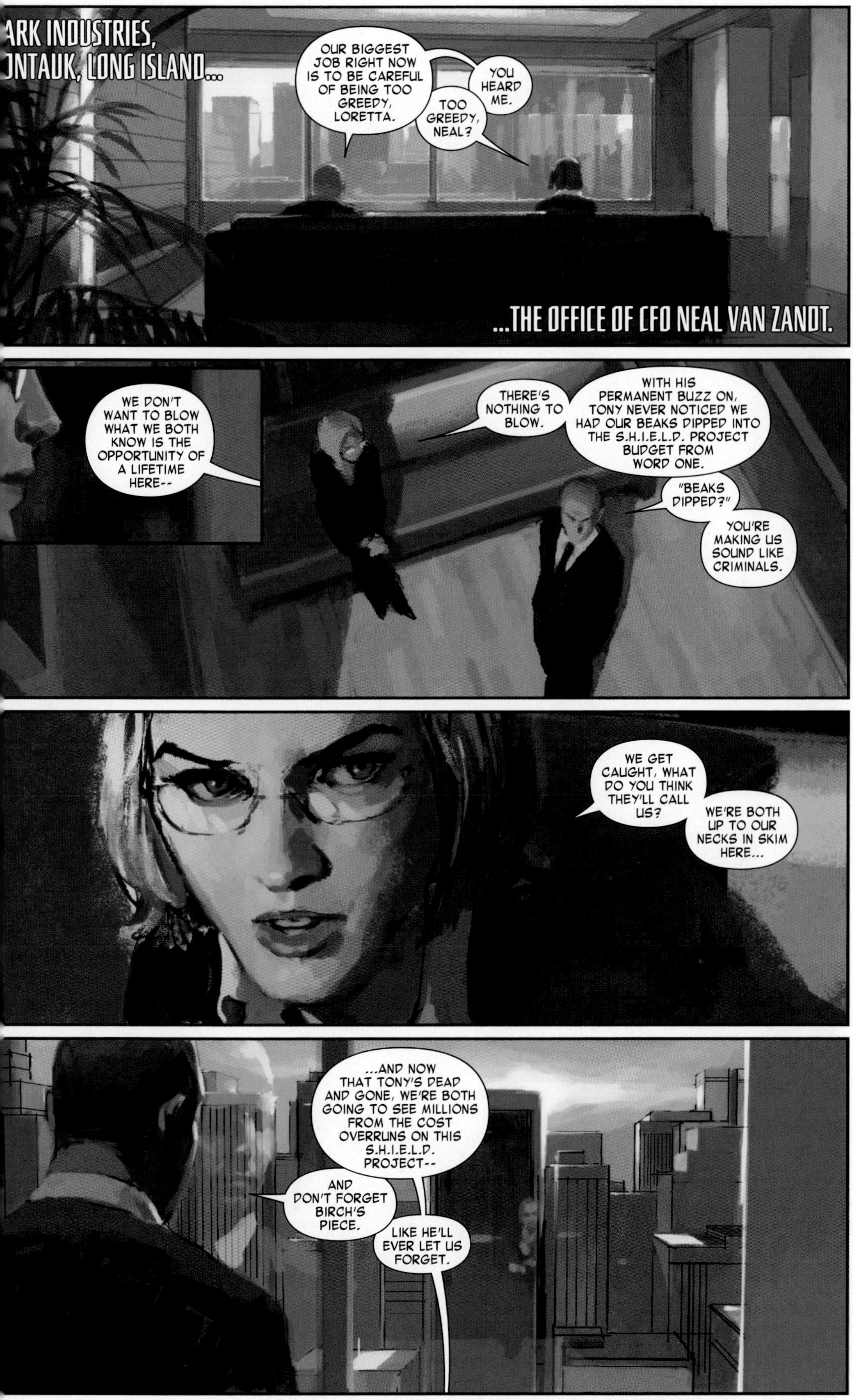
ARK INDUSTRIES,
NTAUK, LONG ISLAND...
OUR BIGGEST JOB RIGHT NOW IS TO BE CAREFUL OF BEING TOO GREEDY, LORETTA.
TOO GREEDY, NEAL?
YOU HEARD ME.
...THE OFFICE OF CFO NEAL VAN ZANDT.
WE DON'T WANT TO BLOW WHAT WE BOTH KNOW IS THE OPPORTUNITY OF A LIFETIME HERE--
THERE'S NOTHING TO BLOW.
WITH HIS PERMANENT BUZZ ON, TONY NEVER NOTICED WE HAD OUR BEAKS DIPPED INTO THE S.H.I.E.L.D. PROJECT BUDGET FROM WORD ONE.
"BEAKS DIPPED?"
YOU'RE MAKING US SOUND LIKE CRIMINALS.
WE GET CAUGHT, WHAT DO YOU THINK THEY'LL CALL US?
WE'RE BOTH UP TO OUR NECKS IN SKIM HERE...
...AND NOW THAT TONY'S DEAD AND GONE, WE'RE BOTH GOING TO SEE MILLIONS FROM THE COST OVERRUNS ON THIS S.H.I.E.L.D. PROJECT--
AND DON'T FORGET BIRCH'S PIECE.
LIKE HE'LL EVER LET US FORGET.

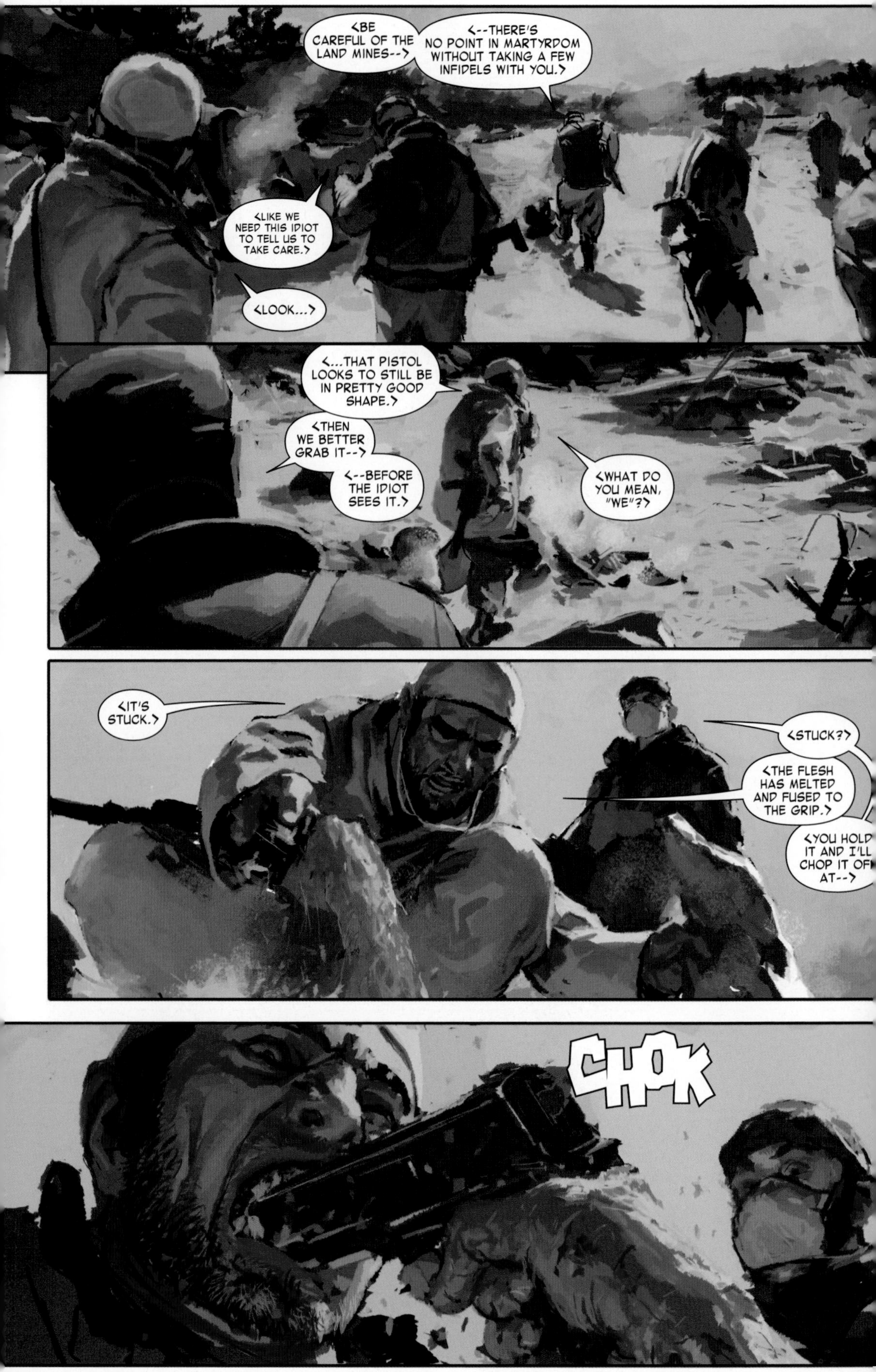
<BE CAREFUL OF THE LAND MINES-->
<--THERE'S NO POINT IN MARTYRDOM WITHOUT TAKING A FEW INFIDELS WITH YOU.>
<LIKE WE NEED THIS IDIOT TO TELL US TO TAKE CARE.>
<LOOK...>
<...THAT PISTOL LOOKS TO STILL BE IN PRETTY GOOD SHAPE.>
<THEN WE BETTER GRAB IT-->
<--BEFORE THE IDIOT SEES IT.>
<WHAT DO YOU MEAN, "WE"?>
<IT'S STUCK.>
<STUCK?>
<THE FLESH HAS MELTED AND FUSED TO THE GRIP.>
<YOU HOLD IT AND I'LL CHOP IT OF AT-->
CHOK

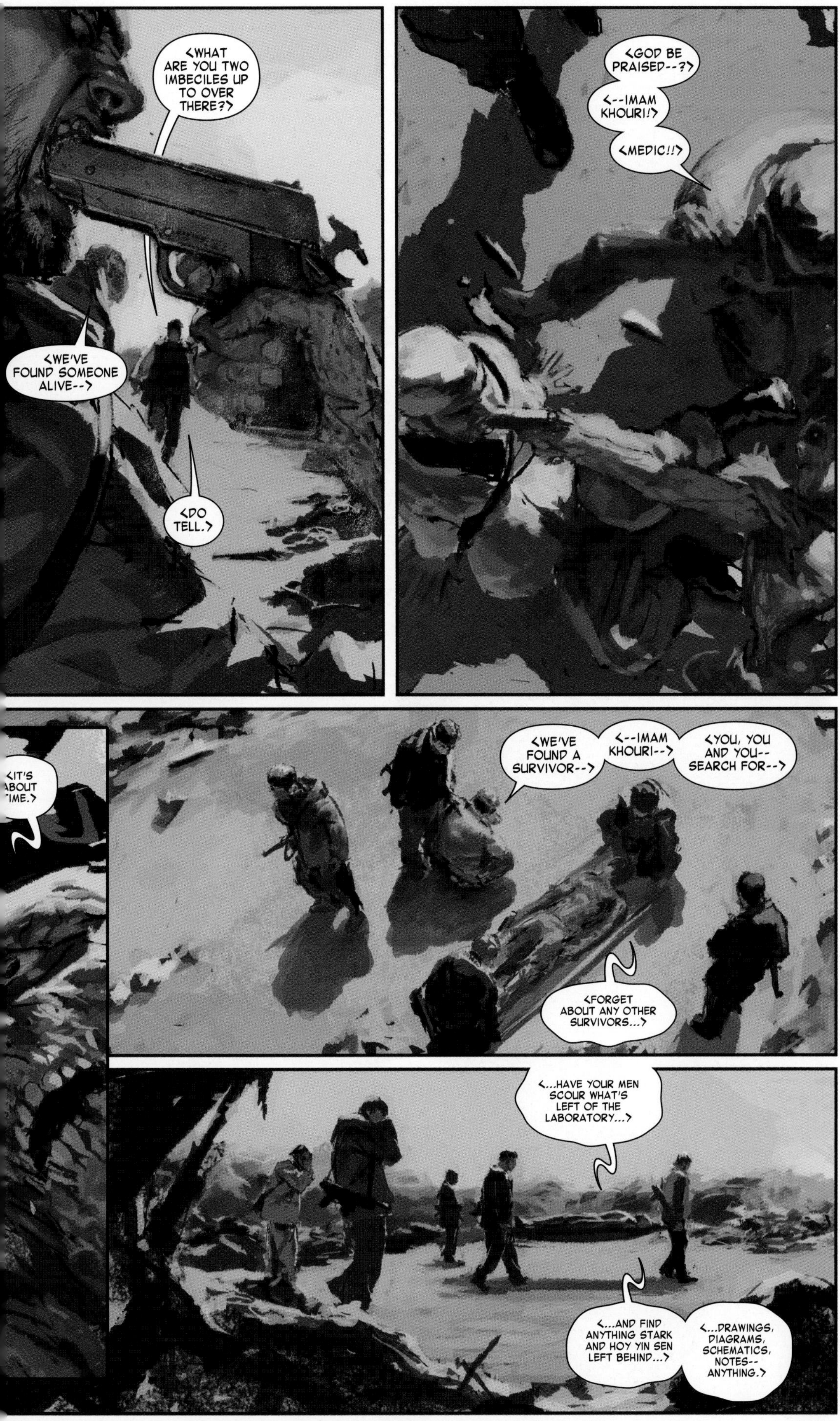
<WHAT ARE YOU TWO IMBECILES UP TO OVER THERE?>
<WE'VE FOUND SOMEONE ALIVE-->
<DO TELL.>
<GOD BE PRAISED--?>
<--IMAM KHOURI!>
<MEDIC!!>
<IT'S ABOUT IME.>
<WE'VE FOUND A SURVIVOR-->
<--IMAM KHOURI-->
<YOU, YOU AND YOU--SEARCH FOR-->
<FORGET ABOUT ANY OTHER SURVIVORS...>
<...HAVE YOUR MEN SCOUR WHAT'S LEFT OF THE LABORATORY...>
<...AND FIND ANYTHING STARK AND HOY YIN SEN LEFT BEHIND...>
<...DRAWINGS, DIAGRAMS, SCHEMATICS, NOTES--ANYTHING.>

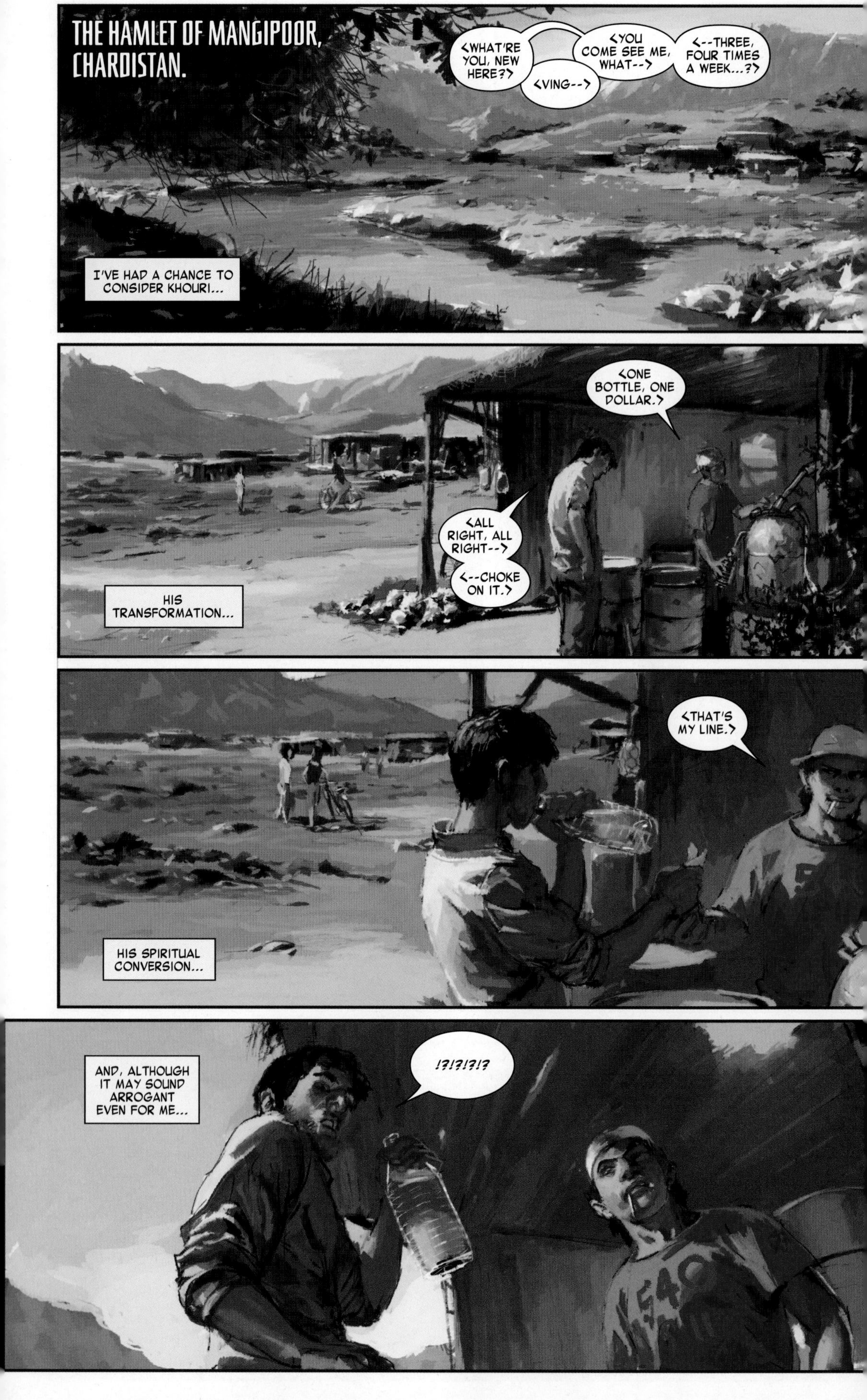

THE HAMLET OF MANGIPOOR, CHARDISTAN.
<WHAT'RE YOU, NEW HERE?>
<VING-->
<YOU COME SEE ME, WHAT-->
<--THREE, FOUR TIMES A WEEK...?>
I'VE HAD A CHANCE TO CONSIDER KHOURI...
<ONE BOTTLE, ONE DOLLAR.>
<ALL RIGHT, ALL RIGHT-->
<--CHOKE ON IT.>
HIS TRANSFORMATION...
<THAT'S MY LINE.>
HIS SPIRITUAL CONVERSION...
AND, ALTHOUGH IT MAY SOUND ARROGANT EVEN FOR ME...
!?!?!?!?

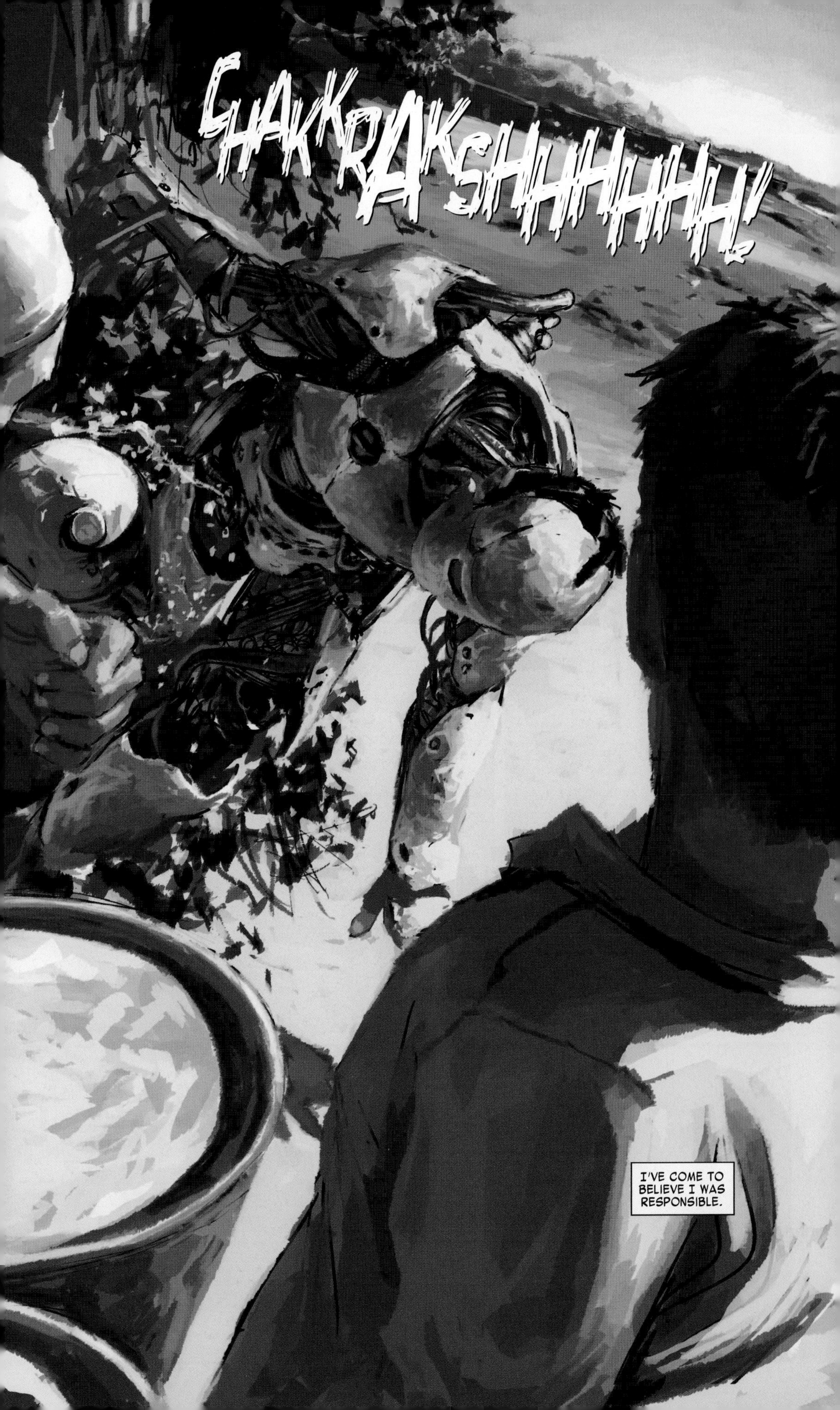
CHAKRAKSHHHHHH!
I'VE COME TO BELIEVE I WAS RESPONSIBLE.

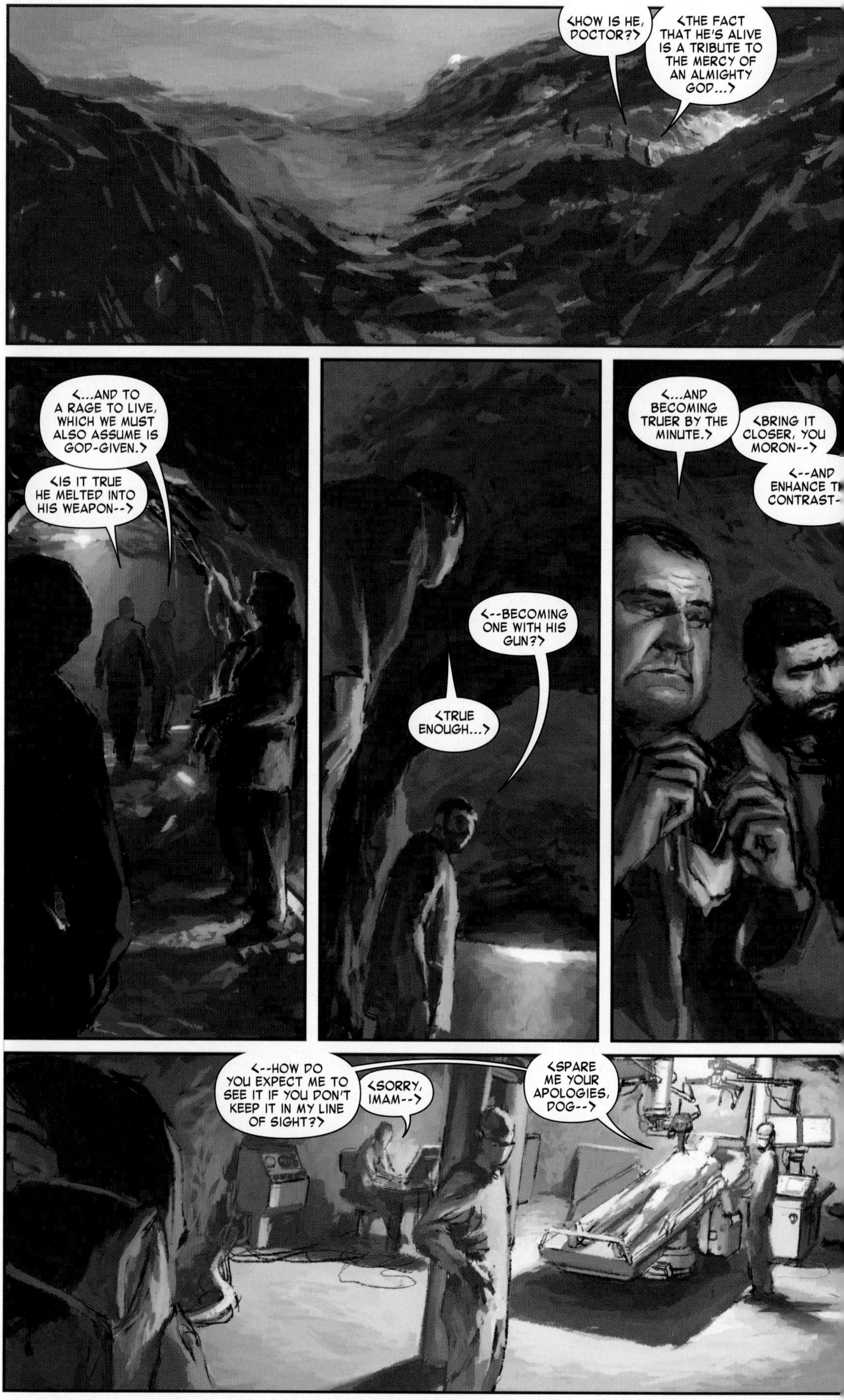

<HOW IS HE, DOCTOR?>
<THE FACT THAT HE'S ALIVE IS A TRIBUTE TO THE MERCY OF AN ALMIGHTY GOD...>
<...AND TO A RAGE TO LIVE, WHICH WE MUST ALSO ASSUME IS GOD-GIVEN.>
<IS IT TRUE HE MELTED INTO HIS WEAPON-->
<--BECOMING ONE WITH HIS GUN?>
<TRUE ENOUGH...>
<...AND BECOMING TRUER BY THE MINUTE.>
<BRING IT CLOSER, YOU MORON-->
<--AND ENHANCE T
CONTRAST-
<--HOW DO YOU EXPECT ME TO SEE IT IF YOU DON'T KEEP IT IN MY LINE OF SIGHT?>
<SORRY, IMAM-->
<SPARE ME YOUR APOLOGIES, DOG-->

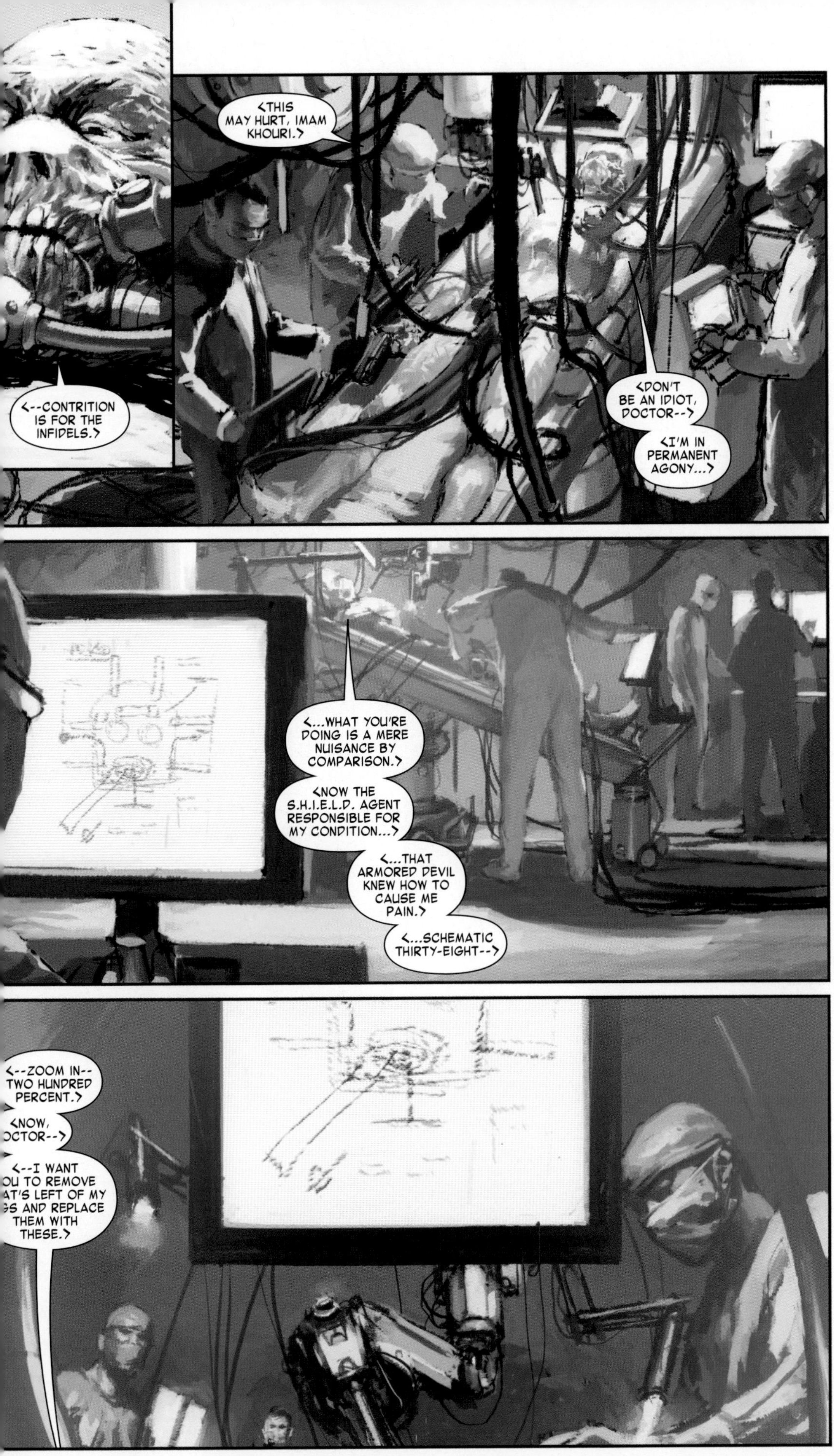
<--CONTRITION IS FOR THE INFIDELS.>
<THIS MAY HURT, IMAM KHOURI.>
<DON'T BE AN IDIOT, DOCTOR-->
<I'M IN PERMANENT AGONY...>
<...WHAT YOU'RE DOING IS A MERE NUISANCE BY COMPARISON.>
<NOW THE S.H.I.E.L.D. AGENT RESPONSIBLE FOR MY CONDITION...>
<...THAT ARMORED DEVIL KNEW HOW TO CAUSE ME PAIN.>
<...SCHEMATIC THIRTY-EIGHT-->
<--ZOOM IN-- TWO HUNDRED PERCENT.>
<NOW, OCTOR-->
<--I WANT OU TO REMOVE AT'S LEFT OF MY GS AND REPLACE THEM WITH THESE.>

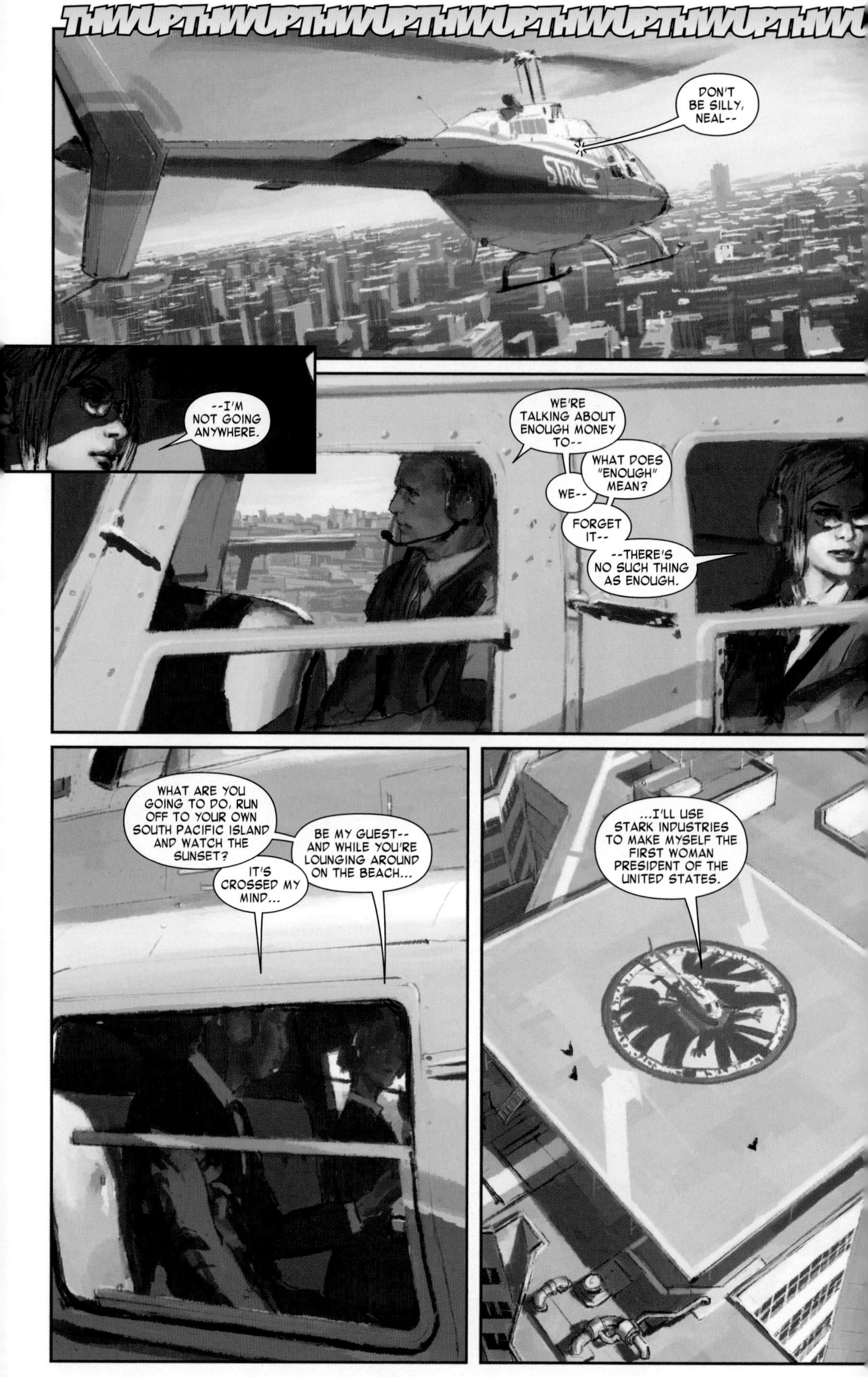
THWUPTHWUPTHWUPTHWUPTHWUPTHWUPTHWU
DON'T BE SILLY, NEAL--
--I'M NOT GOING ANYWHERE.
WE'RE TALKING ABOUT ENOUGH MONEY TO--
WE--
WHAT DOES "ENOUGH" MEAN?
FORGET IT--
--THERE'S NO SUCH THING AS ENOUGH.
WHAT ARE YOU GOING TO DO, RUN OFF TO YOUR OWN SOUTH PACIFIC ISLAND AND WATCH THE SUNSET?
IT'S CROSSED MY MIND...
BE MY GUEST-- AND WHILE YOU'RE LOUNGING AROUND ON THE BEACH...
...I'LL USE STARK INDUSTRIES TO MAKE MYSELF THE FIRST WOMAN PRESIDENT OF THE UNITED STATES.

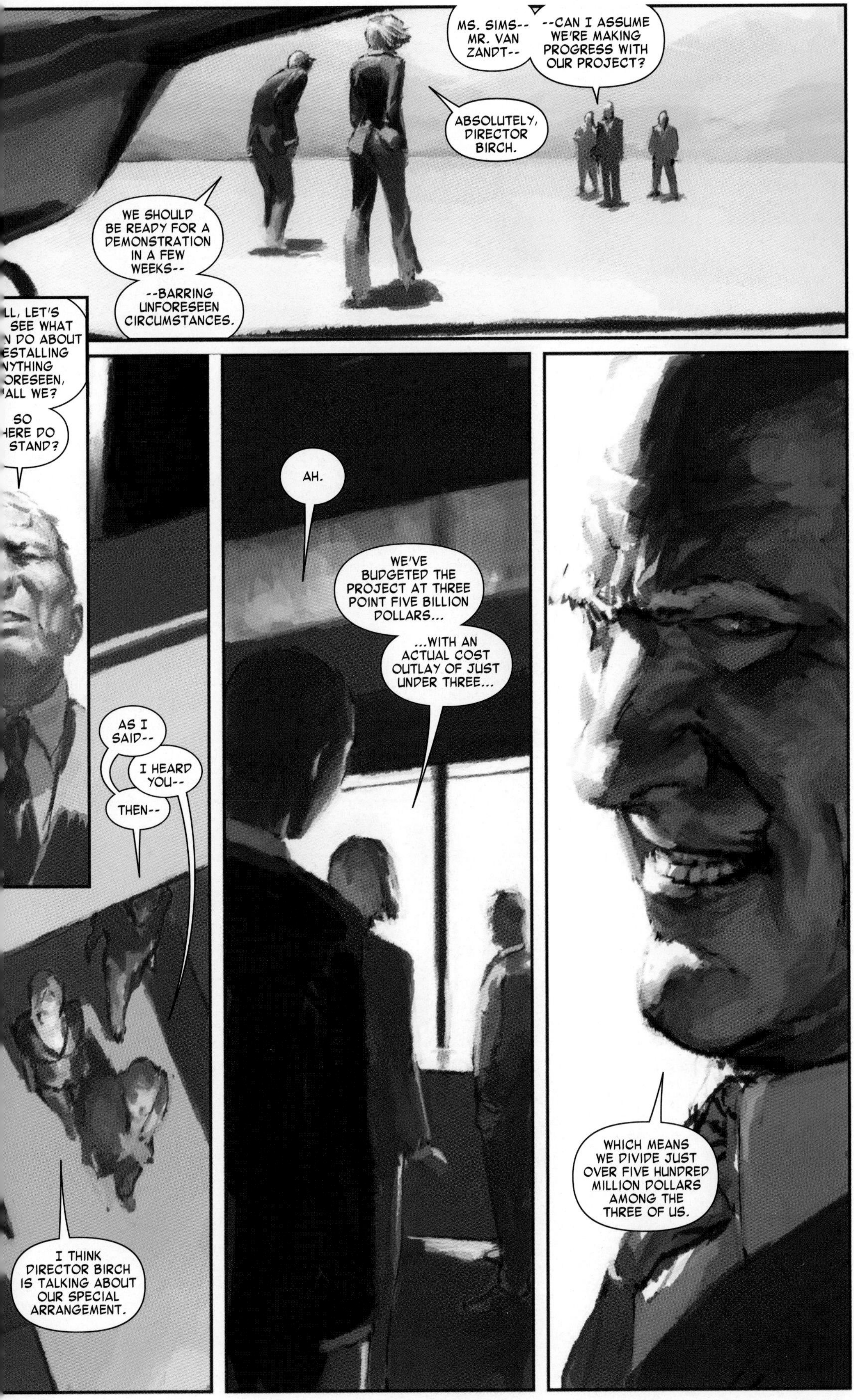
MS. SIMS-- MR. VAN ZANDT--
--CAN I ASSUME WE'RE MAKING PROGRESS WITH OUR PROJECT?
ABSOLUTELY, DIRECTOR BIRCH.
WE SHOULD BE READY FOR A DEMONSTRATION IN A FEW WEEKS--
--BARRING UNFORESEEN CIRCUMSTANCES.
LL, LET'S SEE WHAT N DO ABOUT ESTALLING NYTHING ORESEEN, ALL WE?
SO HERE DO STAND?
AS I SAID--
I HEARD YOU--
THEN--
I THINK DIRECTOR BIRCH IS TALKING ABOUT OUR SPECIAL ARRANGEMENT.
AH.
WE'VE BUDGETED THE PROJECT AT THREE POINT FIVE BILLION DOLLARS...
...WITH AN ACTUAL COST OUTLAY OF JUST UNDER THREE...
WHICH MEANS WE DIVIDE JUST OVER FIVE HUNDRED MILLION DOLLARS AMONG THE THREE OF US.

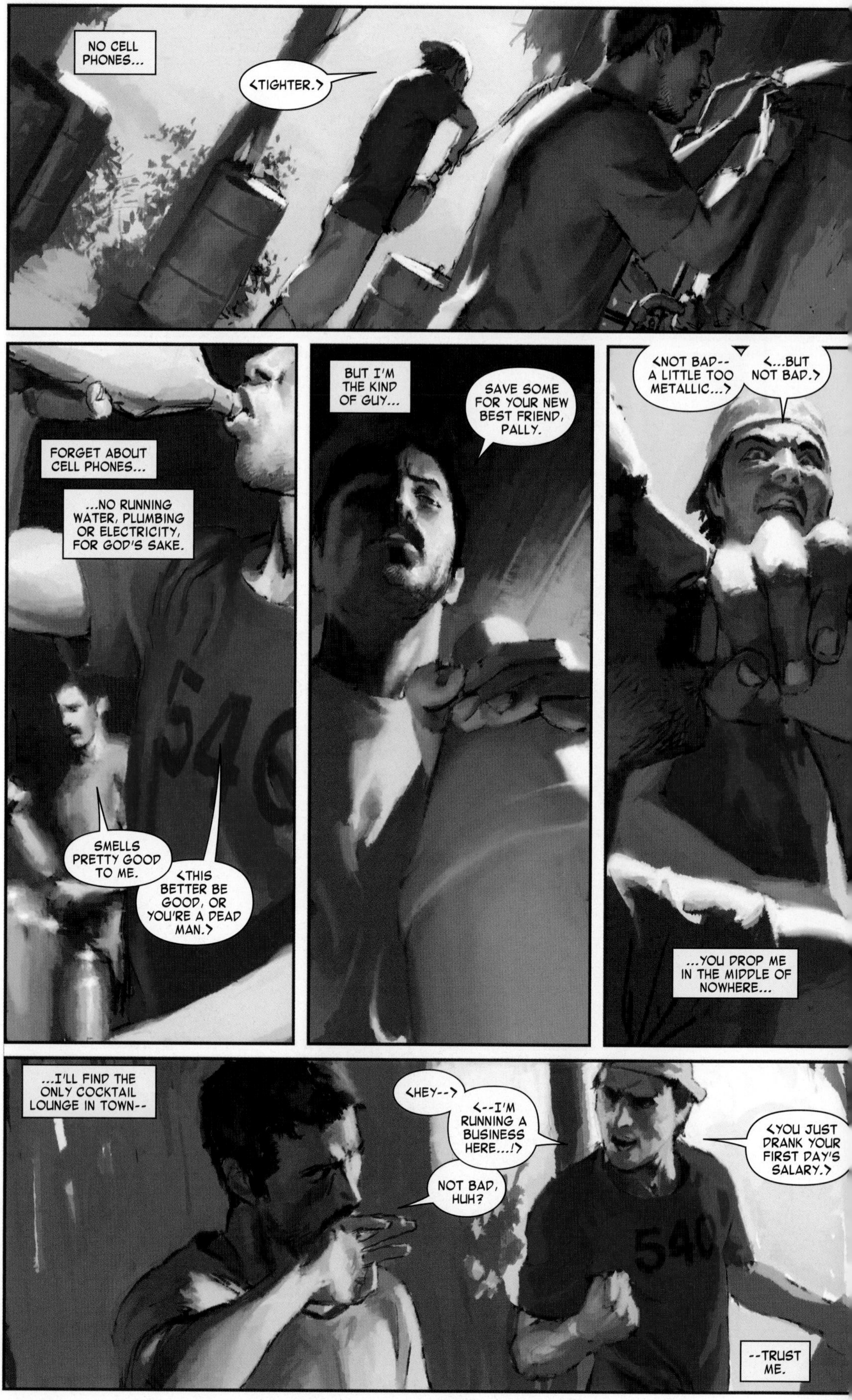
NO CELL PHONES...
<TIGHTER.>
FORGET ABOUT CELL PHONES...
...NO RUNNING WATER, PLUMBING OR ELECTRICITY, FOR GOD'S SAKE.
SMELLS PRETTY GOOD TO ME.
<THIS BETTER BE GOOD, OR YOU'RE A DEAD MAN.>
BUT I'M THE KIND OF GUY...
SAVE SOME FOR YOUR NEW BEST FRIEND, PALLY.
<NOT BAD-- A LITTLE TOO METALLIC...>
<...BUT NOT BAD.>
...YOU DROP ME IN THE MIDDLE OF NOWHERE...
...I'LL FIND THE ONLY COCKTAIL LOUNGE IN TOWN--
<HEY-->
<--I'M RUNNING A BUSINESS HERE...!>
NOT BAD, HUH?
<YOU JUST DRANK YOUR FIRST DAY'S SALARY.>
--TRUST ME.

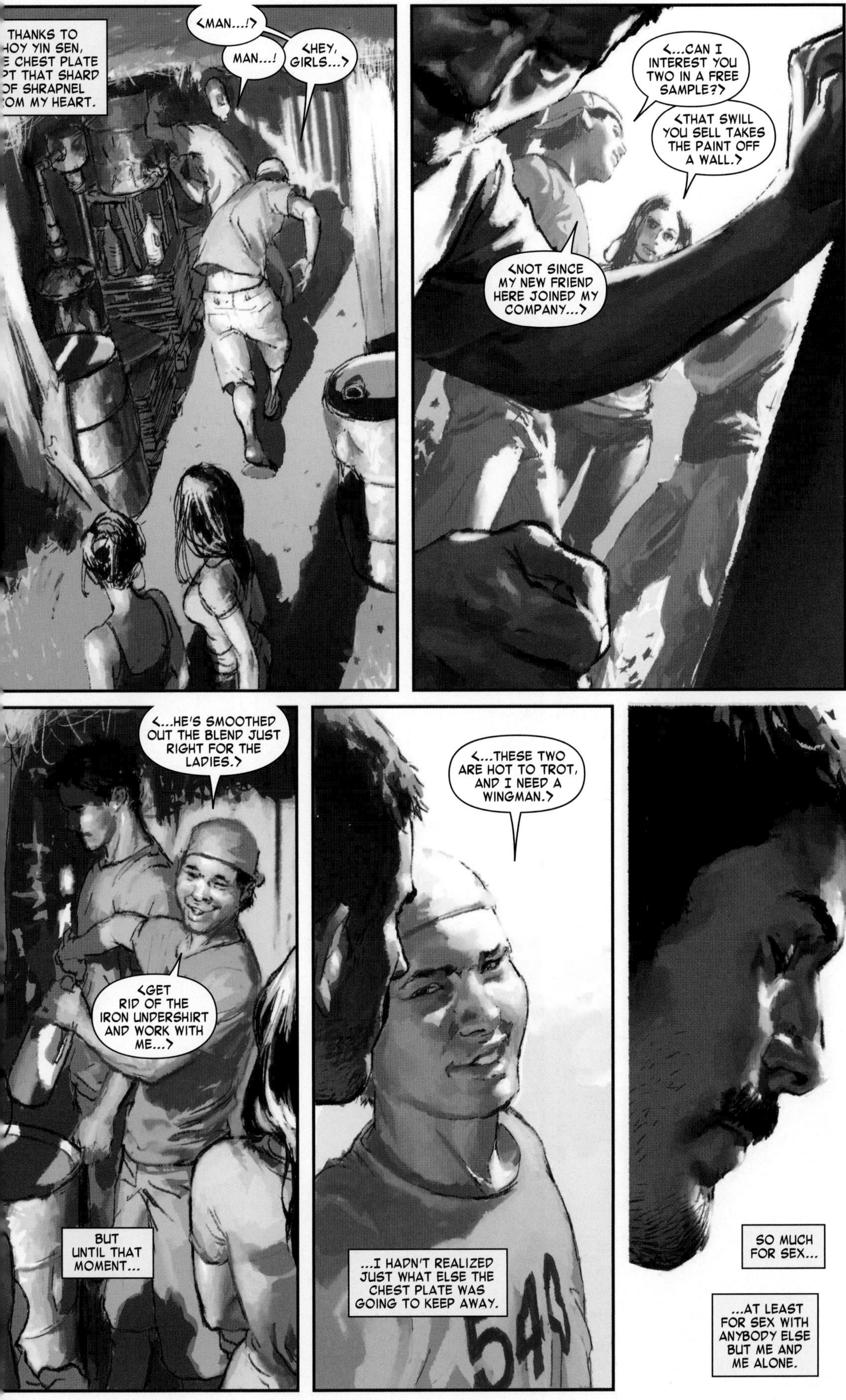
THANKS TO
HOY YIN SEN,
E CHEST PLATE
PT THAT SHARD
OF SHRAPNEL
OM MY HEART.
<MAN...!>
MAN...!
<HEY, GIRLS...>
<...CAN I INTEREST YOU TWO IN A FREE SAMPLE?>
<THAT SWILL YOU SELL TAKES THE PAINT OFF A WALL.>
<NOT SINCE MY NEW FRIEND HERE JOINED MY COMPANY...>
<...HE'S SMOOTHED OUT THE BLEND JUST RIGHT FOR THE LADIES.>
<GET RID OF THE IRON UNDERSHIRT AND WORK WITH ME...>
BUT UNTIL THAT MOMENT...
<...THESE TWO ARE HOT TO TROT, AND I NEED A WINGMAN.>
...I HADN'T REALIZED JUST WHAT ELSE THE CHEST PLATE WAS GOING TO KEEP AWAY.
540
SO MUCH FOR SEX...
...AT LEAST FOR SEX WITH ANYBODY ELSE BUT ME AND ME ALONE.

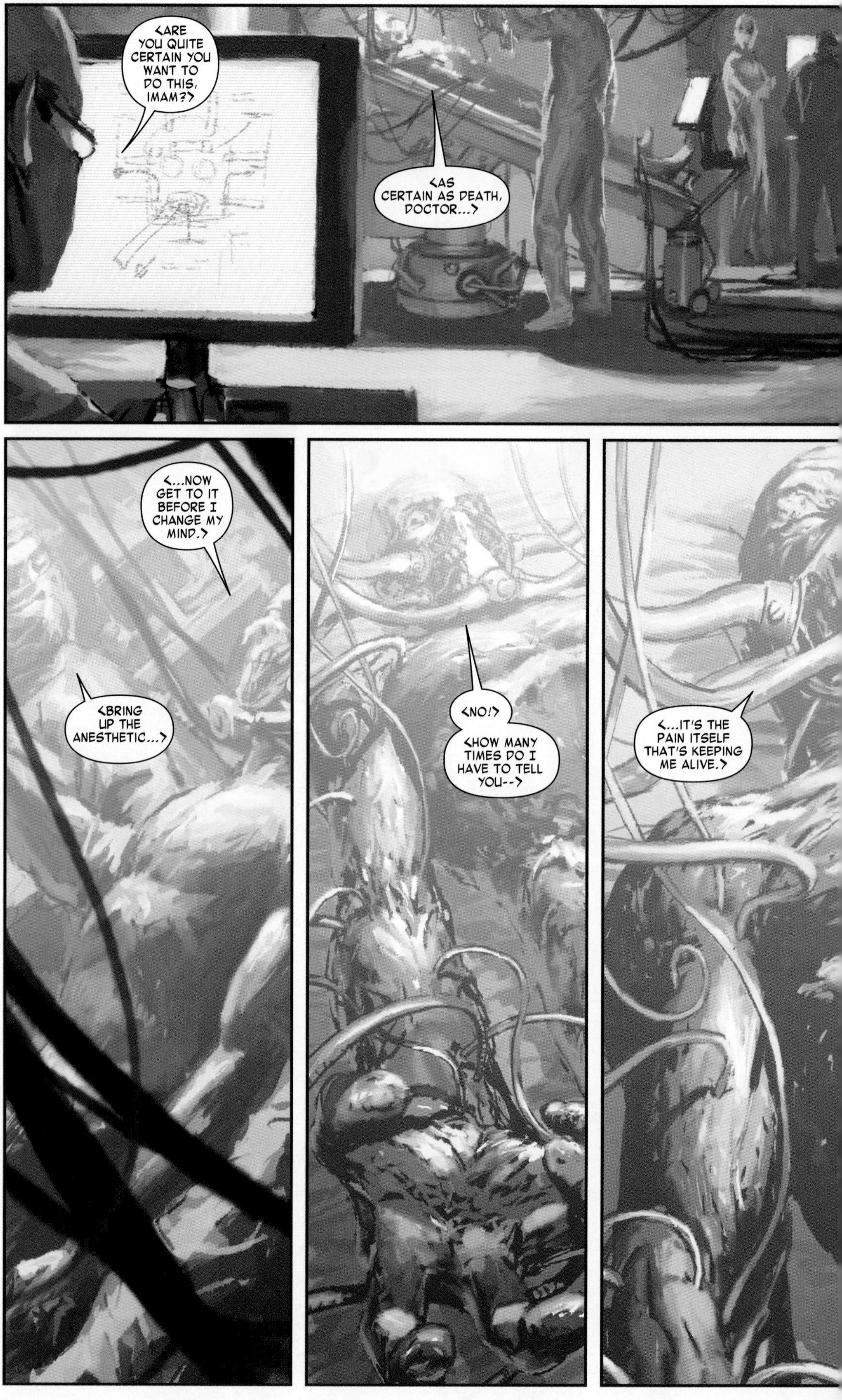
<ARE YOU QUITE CERTAIN YOU WANT TO DO THIS, IMAM?>
<AS CERTAIN AS DEATH, DOCTOR...>
<...NOW GET TO IT BEFORE I CHANGE MY MIND.>
<BRING UP THE ANESTHETIC...>
<NO!>
<HOW MANY TIMES DO I HAVE TO TELL YOU-->
<...IT'S THE PAIN ITSELF THAT'S KEEPING ME ALIVE.>

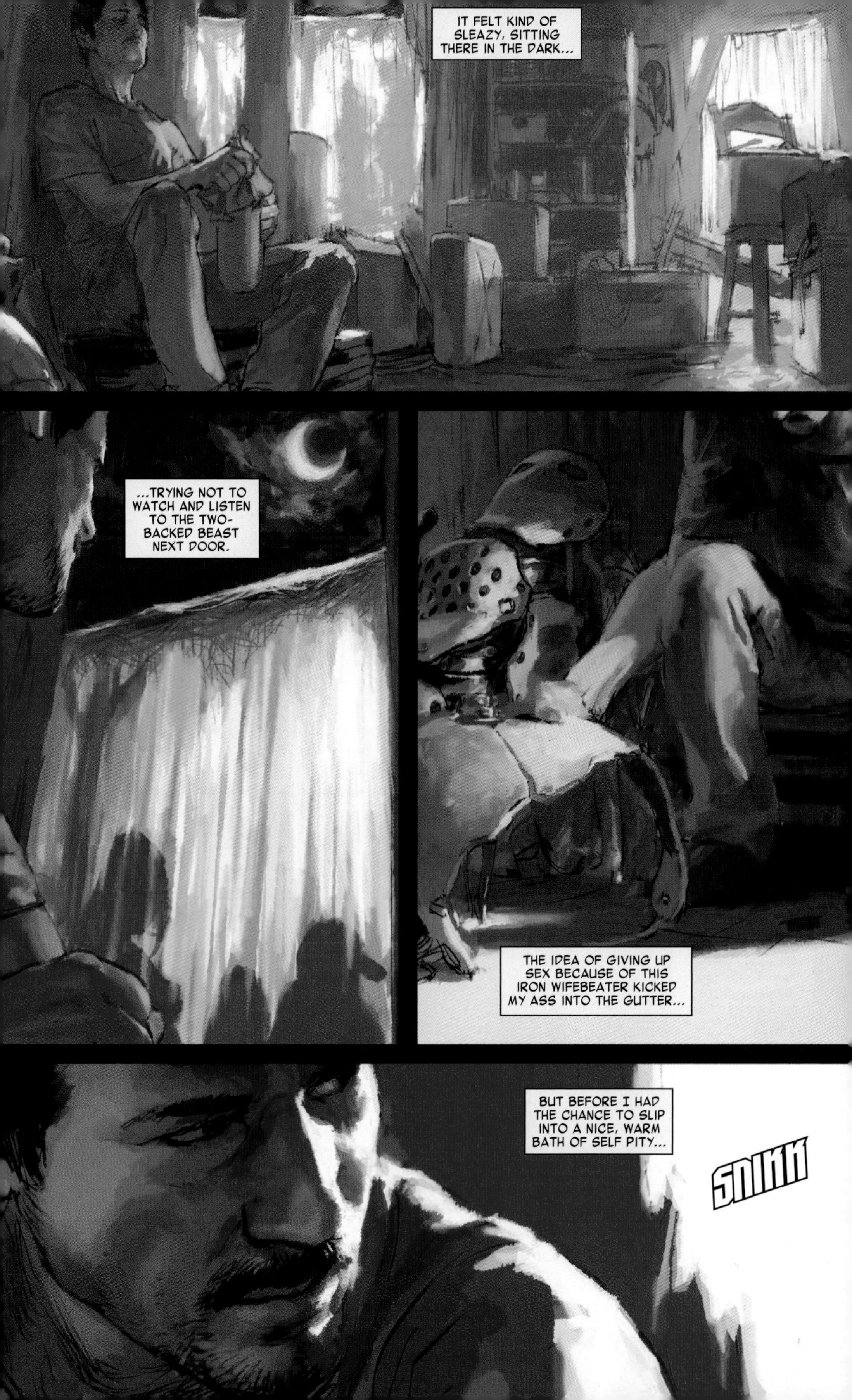
IT FELT KIND OF SLEAZY, SITTING THERE IN THE DARK...
...TRYING NOT TO WATCH AND LISTEN TO THE TWO-BACKED BEAST NEXT DOOR.
THE IDEA OF GIVING UP SEX BECAUSE OF THIS IRON WIFEBEATER KICKED MY ASS INTO THE GUTTER...
BUT BEFORE I HAD THE CHANCE TO SLIP INTO A NICE, WARM BATH OF SELF PITY...
SNIKT

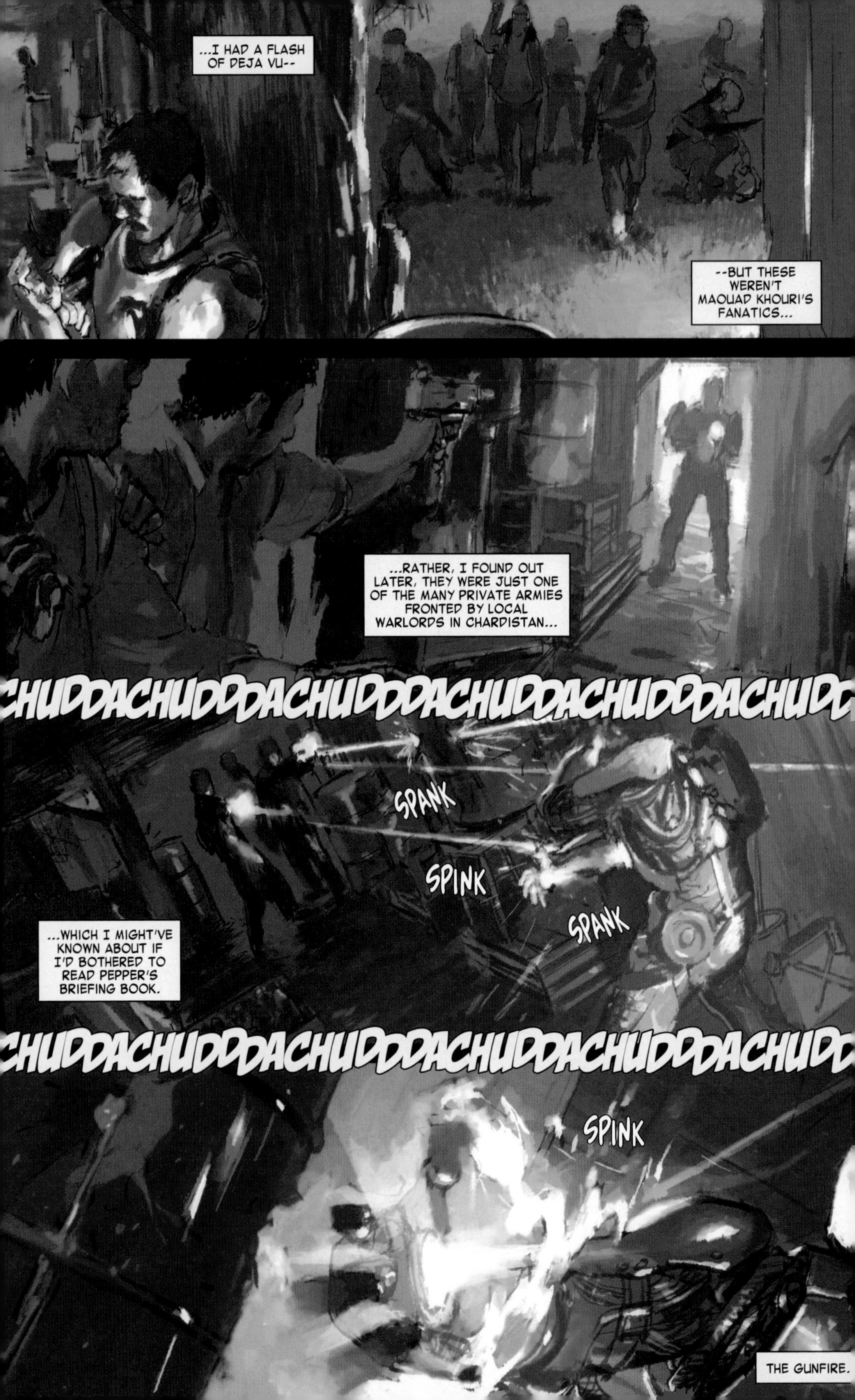

...I HAD A FLASH OF DEJA VU--
--BUT THESE WEREN'T MAOUAD KHOURI'S FANATICS...
...RATHER, I FOUND OUT LATER, THEY WERE JUST ONE OF THE MANY PRIVATE ARMIES FRONTED BY LOCAL WARLORDS IN CHARDISTAN...
CHUDDACHUDDDACHUDDDACHUDDACHUDDDACHUDD
SPANK
SPINK
SPANK
...WHICH I MIGHT'VE KNOWN ABOUT IF I'D BOTHERED TO READ PEPPER'S BRIEFING BOOK.
CHUDDACHUDDDACHUDDDACHUDDACHUDDDACHUDD
SPINK
THE GUNFIRE.

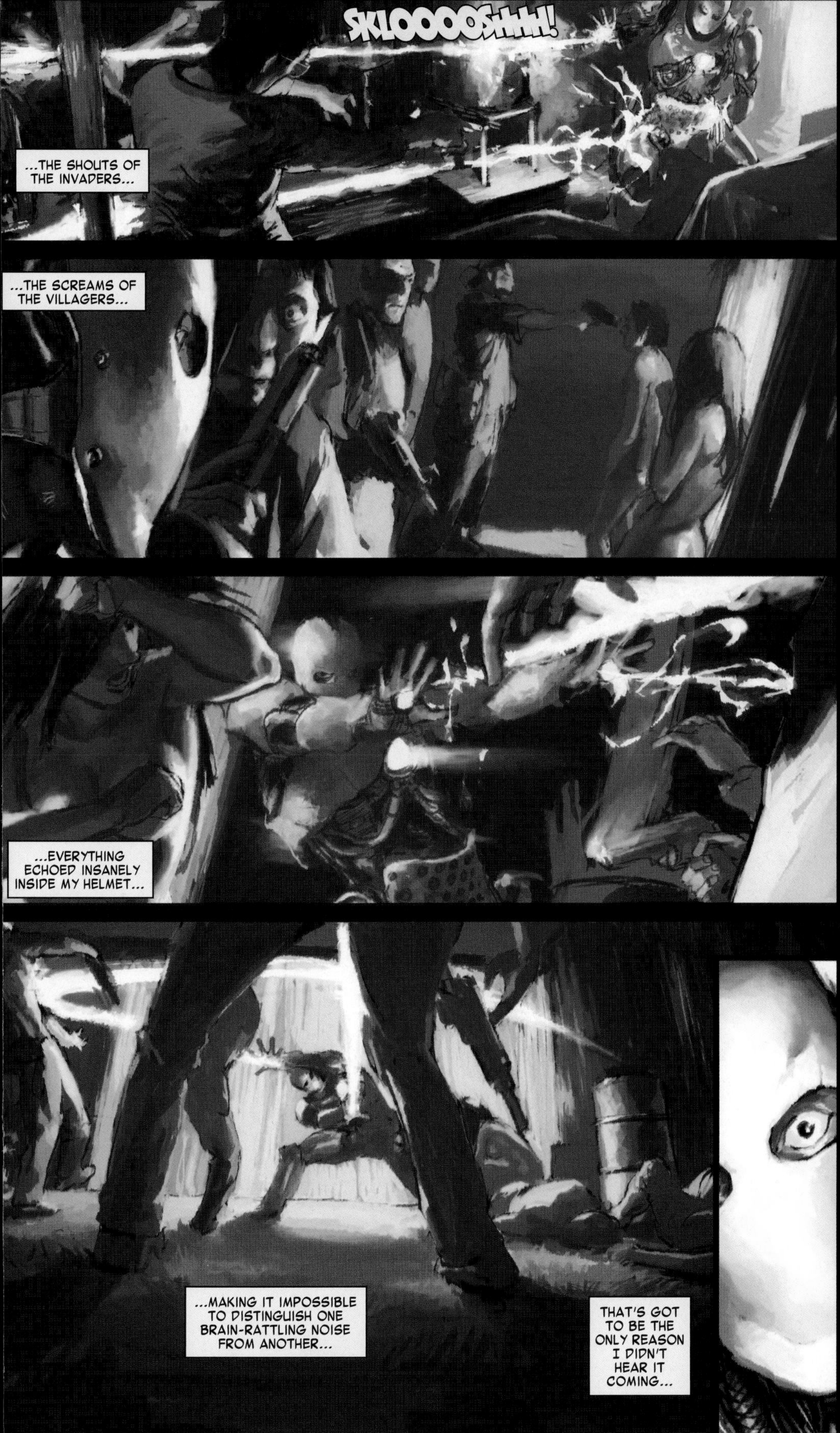
SKLOOOOSHHH!
...THE SHOUTS OF THE INVADERS...
...THE SCREAMS OF THE VILLAGERS...
...EVERYTHING ECHOED INSANELY INSIDE MY HELMET...
...MAKING IT IMPOSSIBLE TO DISTINGUISH ONE BRAIN-RATTLING NOISE FROM ANOTHER...
THAT'S GOT TO BE THE ONLY REASON I DIDN'T HEAR IT COMING...

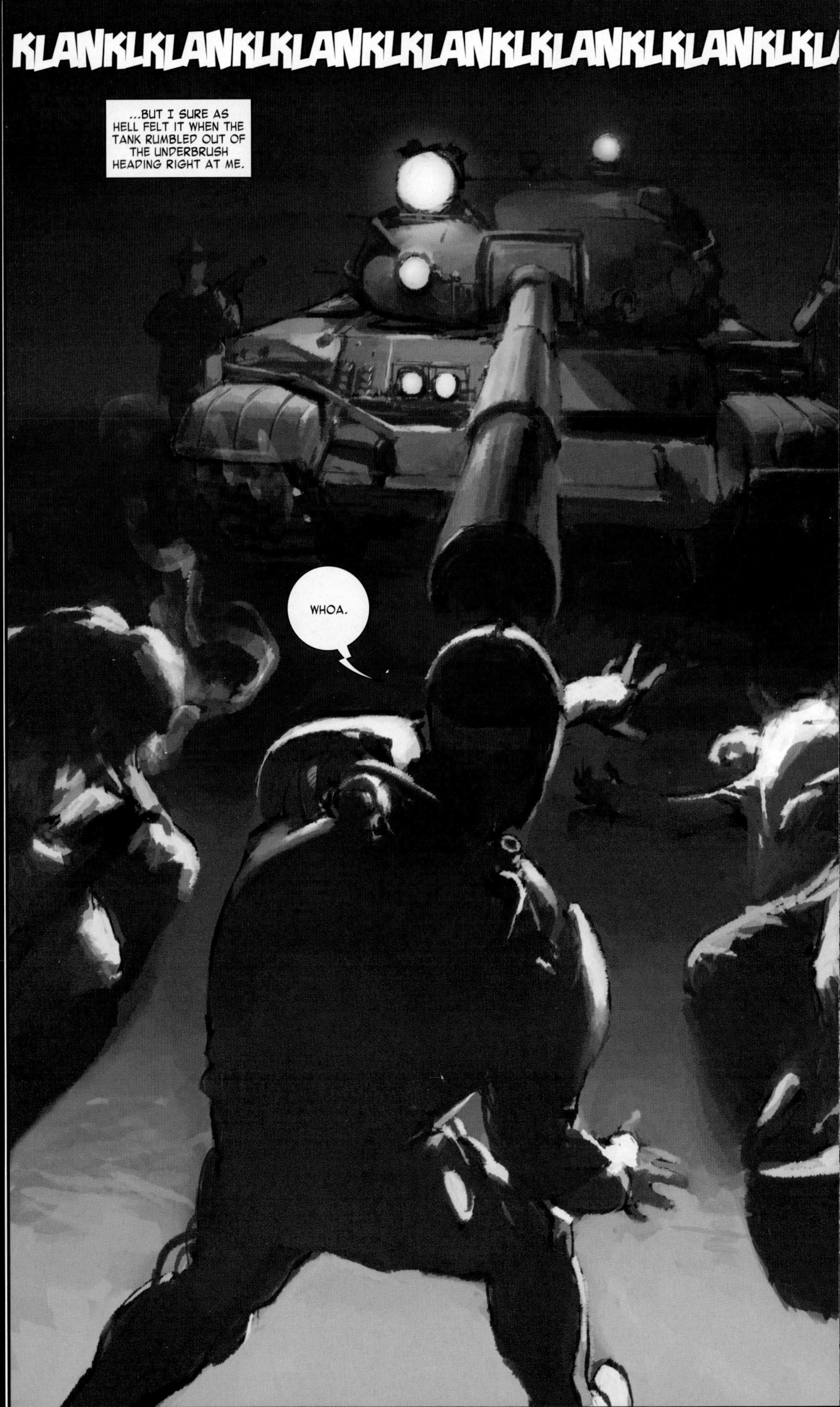

KLANKLKLANKLKLANKLKLANKLKLANKLKLANKLKL
...BUT I SURE AS HELL FELT IT WHEN THE TANK RUMBLED OUT OF THE UNDERBRUSH HEADING RIGHT AT ME.
WHOA.

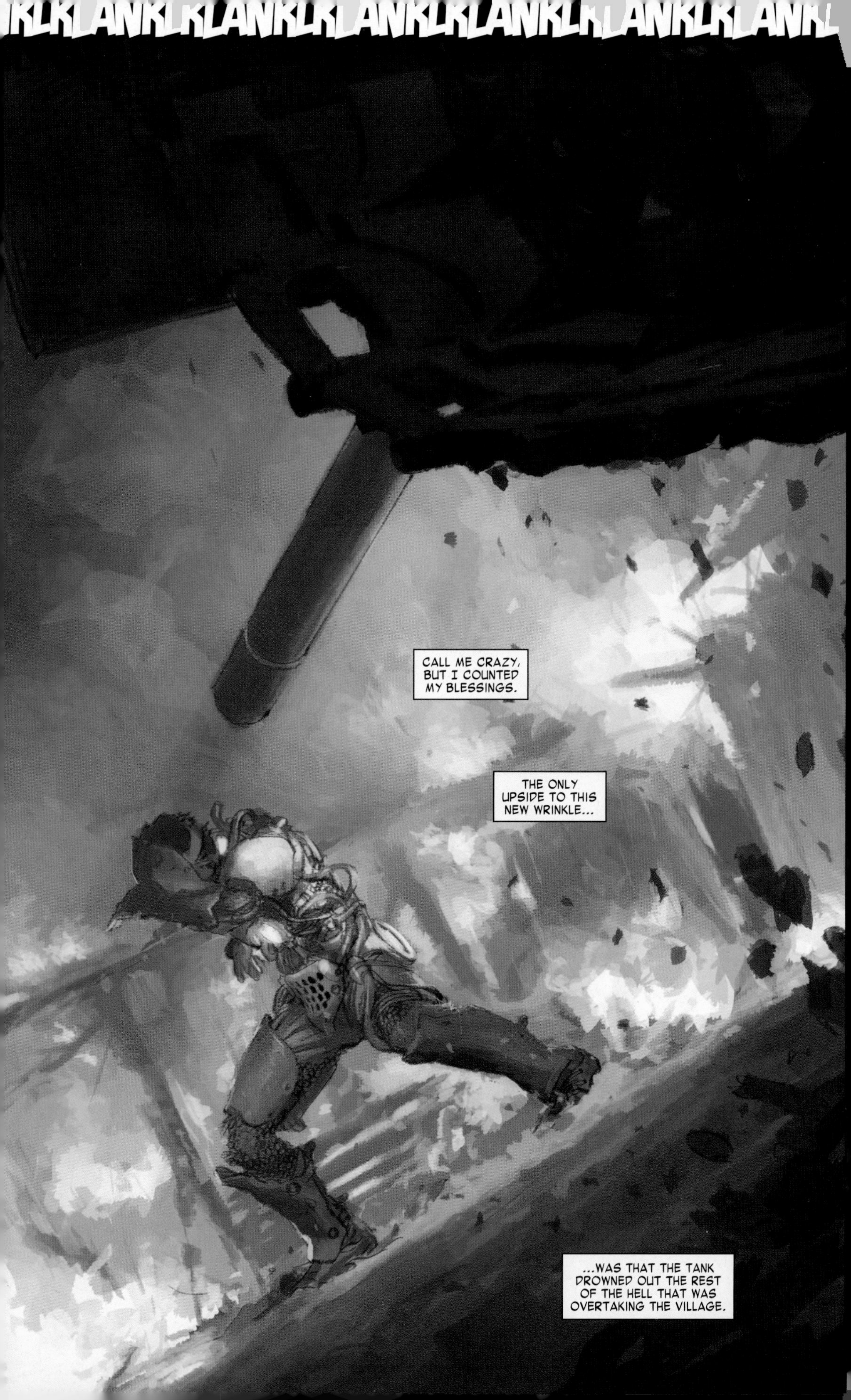
KLKLANKLKLANKLKLANKLKLANKLKLANKLKLANKL
CALL ME CRAZY, BUT I COUNTED MY BLESSINGS.
THE ONLY UPSIDE TO THIS NEW WRINKLE...
...WAS THAT THE TANK DROWNED OUT THE REST OF THE HELL THAT WAS OVERTAKING THE VILLAGE.

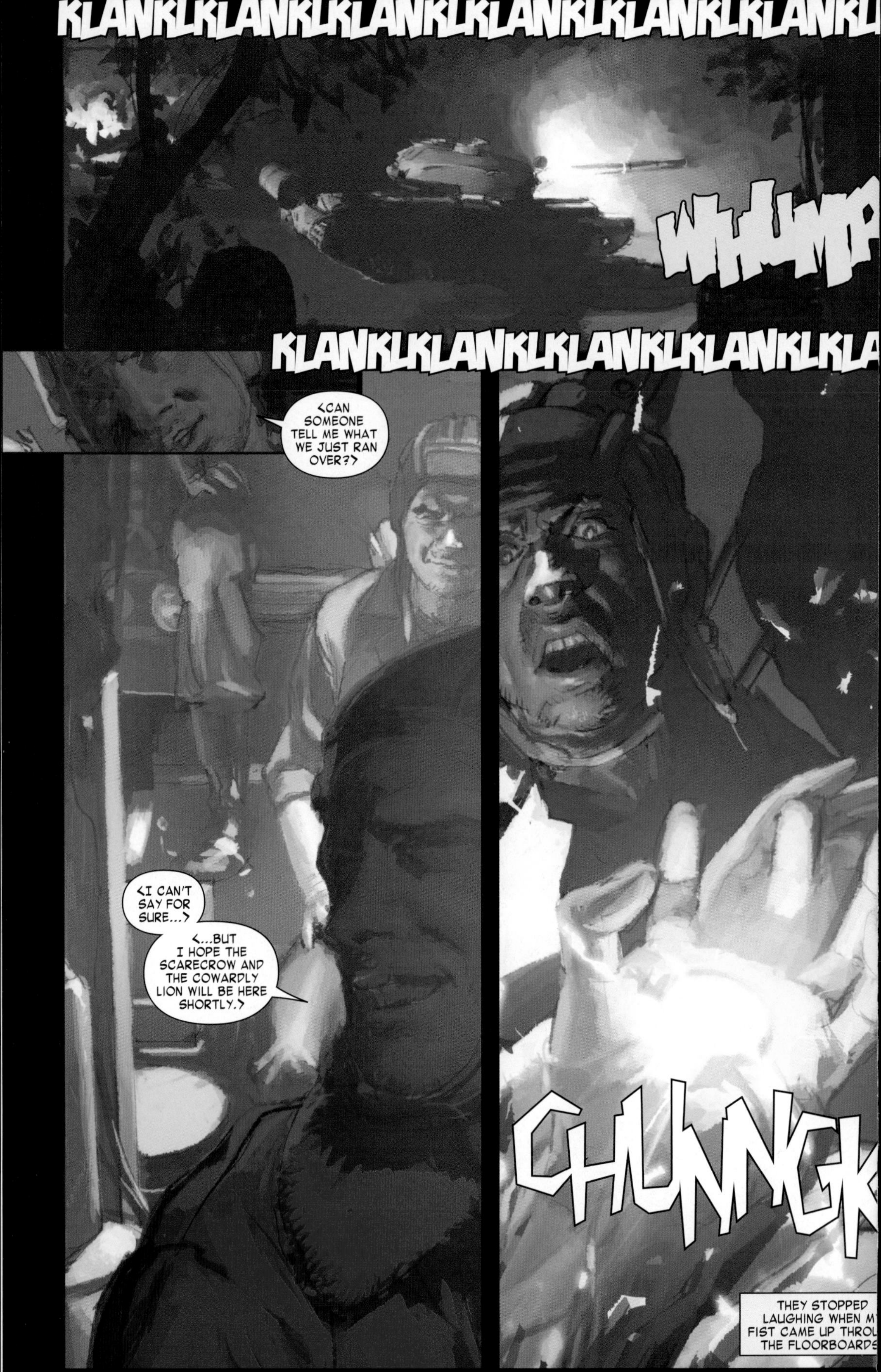

KLANKLKLANKLKLANKLKLANKLKLANKLKLANKL
WHUMP
KLANKLKLANKLKLANKLKLANKLKLA
<CAN SOMEONE TELL ME WHAT WE JUST RAN OVER?>
<I CAN'T SAY FOR SURE...>
<...BUT I HOPE THE SCARECROW AND THE COWARDLY LION WILL BE HERE SHORTLY.>
CHUNNGK
THEY STOPPED LAUGHING WHEN M
FIST CAME UP THROU
THE FLOORBOARDS

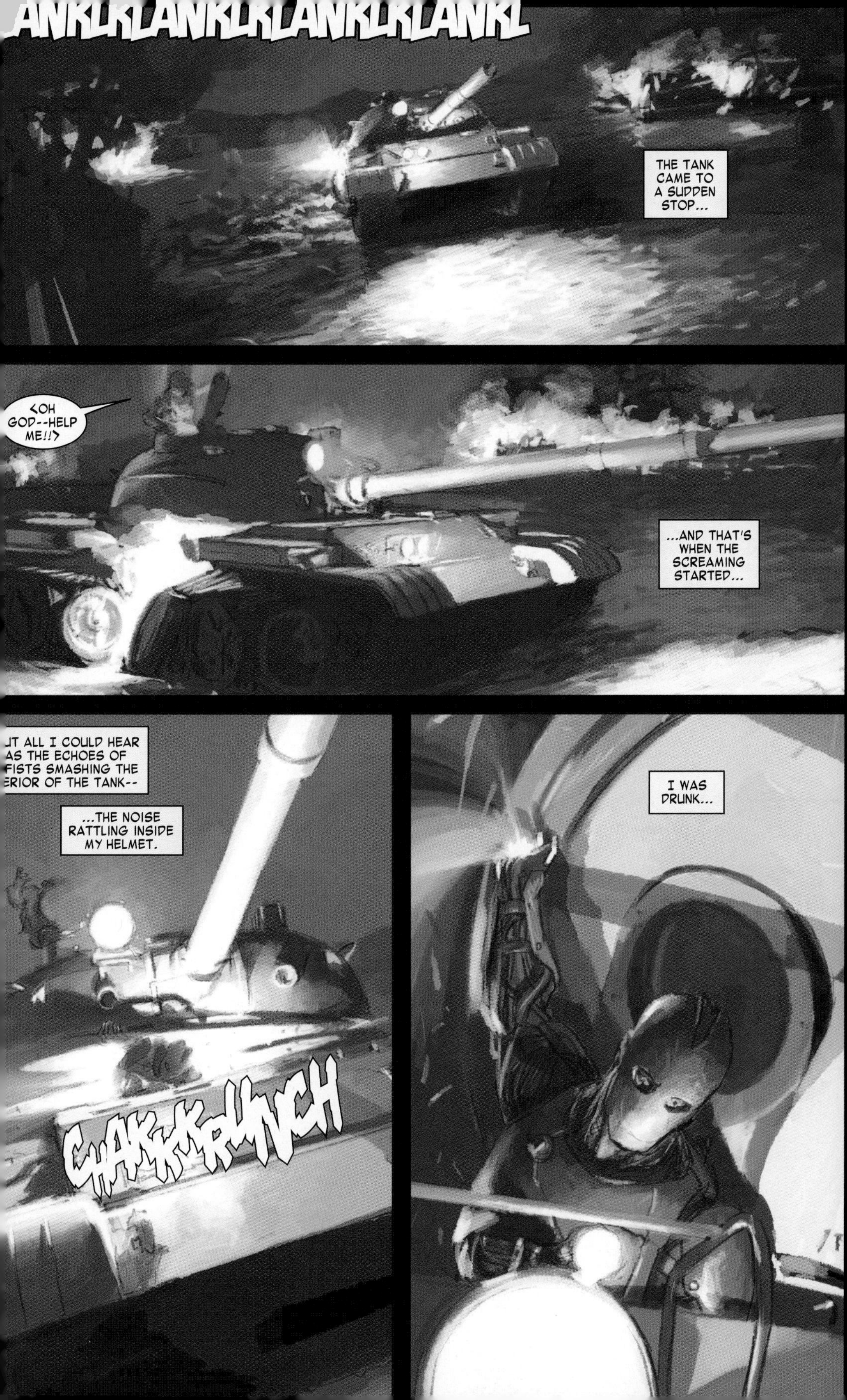
ANKLKLANKLKLANKLKLANKL
THE TANK CAME TO A SUDDEN STOP...
<OH GOD--HELP ME!!>
...AND THAT'S WHEN THE SCREAMING STARTED...
UT ALL I COULD HEAR AS THE ECHOES OF FISTS SMASHING THE ERIOR OF THE TANK--
...THE NOISE RATTLING INSIDE MY HELMET.
CHAKKKRUNCH
I WAS DRUNK...

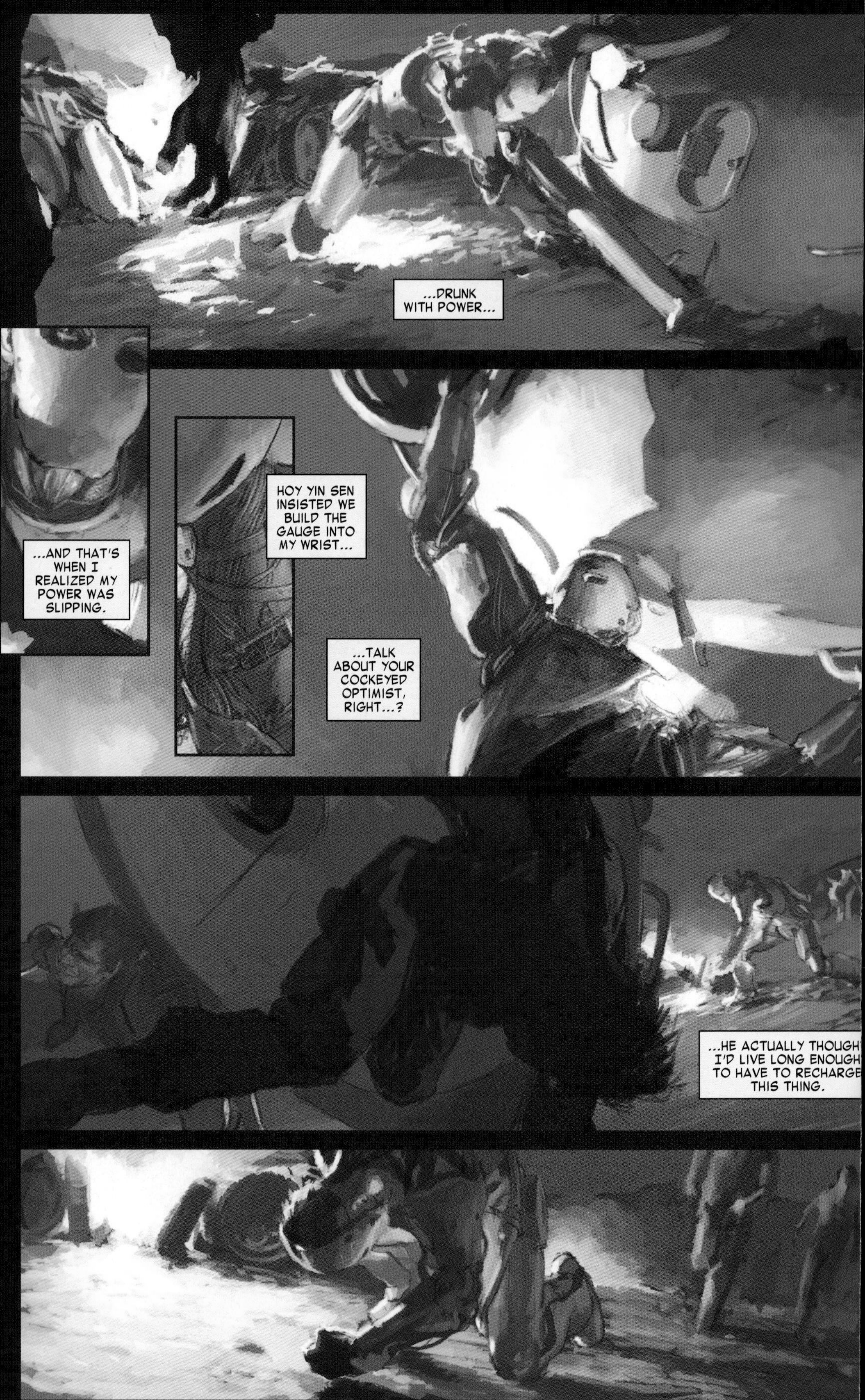
...DRUNK WITH POWER...
...AND THAT'S WHEN I REALIZED MY POWER WAS SLIPPING.
HOY YIN SEN INSISTED WE BUILD THE GAUGE INTO MY WRIST...
...TALK ABOUT YOUR COCKEYED OPTIMIST, RIGHT...?
...HE ACTUALLY THOUGHT I'D LIVE LONG ENOUGH TO HAVE TO RECHARGE THIS THING.

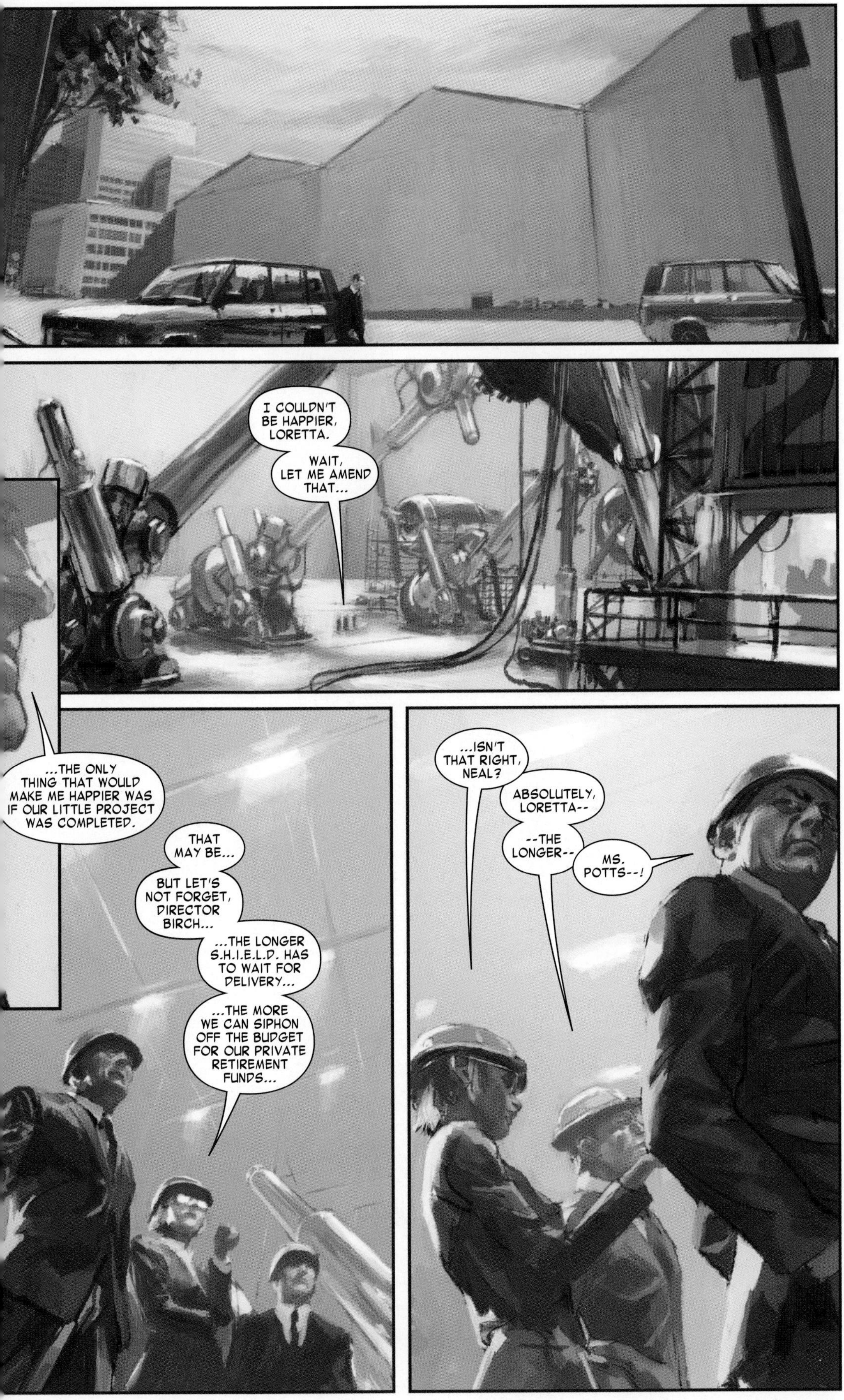
I COULDN'T BE HAPPIER, LORETTA.
WAIT, LET ME AMEND THAT...
...THE ONLY THING THAT WOULD MAKE ME HAPPIER WAS IF OUR LITTLE PROJECT WAS COMPLETED.
THAT MAY BE...
BUT LET'S NOT FORGET, DIRECTOR BIRCH...
...THE LONGER S.H.I.E.L.D. HAS TO WAIT FOR DELIVERY...
...THE MORE WE CAN SIPHON OFF THE BUDGET FOR OUR PRIVATE RETIREMENT FUNDS...
...ISN'T THAT RIGHT, NEAL?
ABSOLUTELY, LORETTA--
--THE LONGER--
MS. POTTS--!

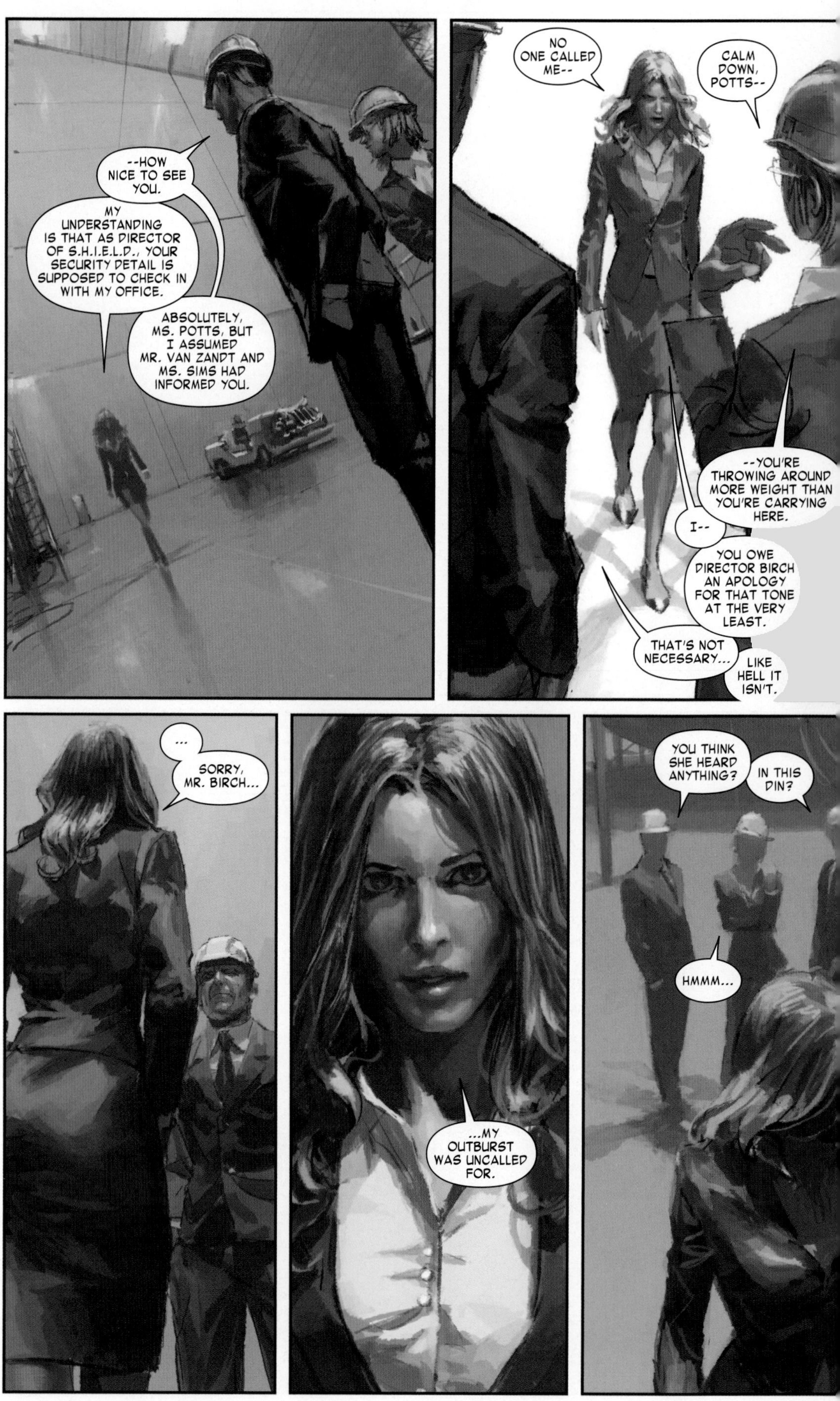
--HOW NICE TO SEE YOU.
MY UNDERSTANDING IS THAT AS DIRECTOR OF S.H.I.E.L.D., YOUR SECURITY DETAIL IS SUPPOSED TO CHECK IN WITH MY OFFICE.
ABSOLUTELY, MS. POTTS, BUT I ASSUMED MR. VAN ZANDT AND MS. SIMS HAD INFORMED YOU.
NO ONE CALLED ME--
CALM DOWN, POTTS--
--YOU'RE THROWING AROUND MORE WEIGHT THAN YOU'RE CARRYING HERE.
I--
YOU OWE DIRECTOR BIRCH AN APOLOGY FOR THAT TONE AT THE VERY LEAST.
THAT'S NOT NECESSARY...
LIKE HELL IT ISN'T.
...
SORRY, MR. BIRCH...
...MY OUTBURST WAS UNCALLED FOR.
YOU THINK SHE HEARD ANYTHING?
IN THIS DIN?
HMMM...

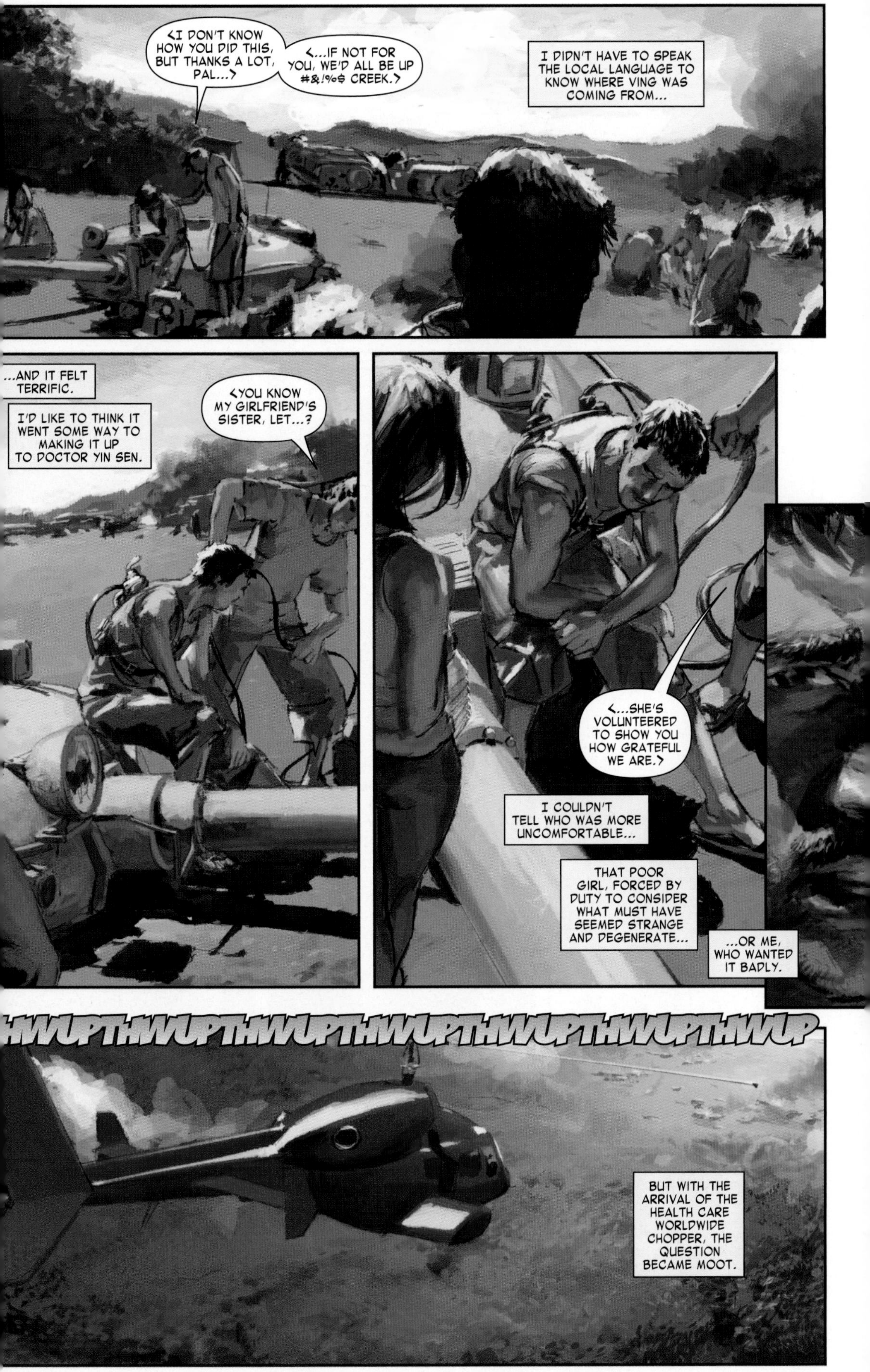
<I DON'T KNOW HOW YOU DID THIS, BUT THANKS A LOT, PAL...>
<...IF NOT FOR YOU, WE'D ALL BE UP #&!%$ CREEK.>
I DIDN'T HAVE TO SPEAK THE LOCAL LANGUAGE TO KNOW WHERE VING WAS COMING FROM...
...AND IT FELT TERRIFIC.
I'D LIKE TO THINK IT WENT SOME WAY TO MAKING IT UP TO DOCTOR YIN SEN.
<YOU KNOW MY GIRLFRIEND'S SISTER, LET...?
<...SHE'S VOLUNTEERED TO SHOW YOU HOW GRATEFUL WE ARE.>
I COULDN'T TELL WHO WAS MORE UNCOMFORTABLE...
THAT POOR GIRL, FORCED BY DUTY TO CONSIDER WHAT MUST HAVE SEEMED STRANGE AND DEGENERATE...
...OR ME, WHO WANTED IT BADLY.
HWUPTHWUPTHWUPTHWUPTHWUPTHWUPTHWUPTHWUP
BUT WITH THE ARRIVAL OF THE HEALTH CARE WORLDWIDE CHOPPER, THE QUESTION BECAME MOOT.

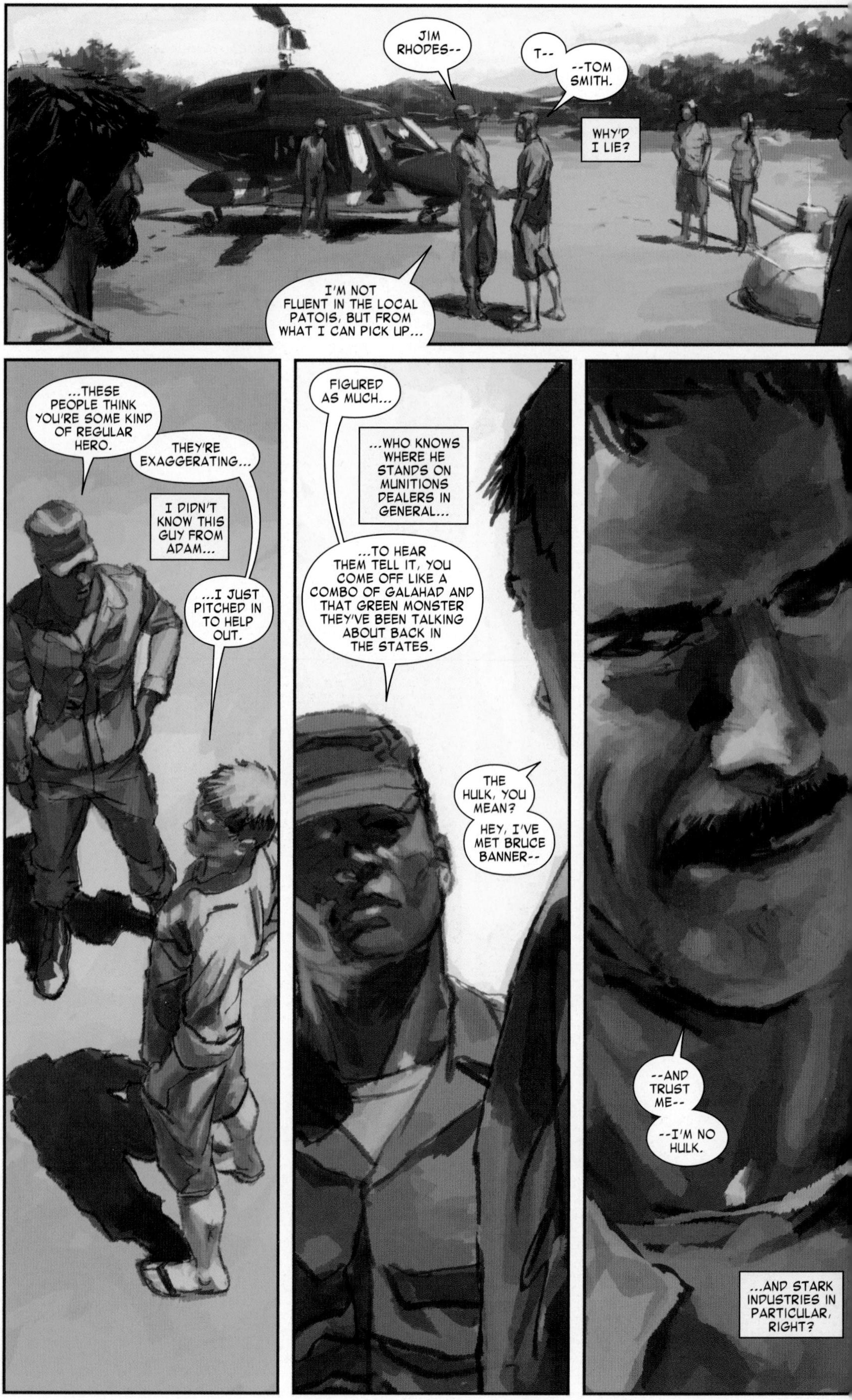
JIM RHODES--
T--
--TOM SMITH.
WHY'D I LIE?
I'M NOT FLUENT IN THE LOCAL PATOIS, BUT FROM WHAT I CAN PICK UP...
...THESE PEOPLE THINK YOU'RE SOME KIND OF REGULAR HERO.
THEY'RE EXAGGERATING...
I DIDN'T KNOW THIS GUY FROM ADAM...
...I JUST PITCHED IN TO HELP OUT.
FIGURED AS MUCH...
...WHO KNOWS WHERE HE STANDS ON MUNITIONS DEALERS IN GENERAL...
...TO HEAR THEM TELL IT, YOU COME OFF LIKE A COMBO OF GALAHAD AND THAT GREEN MONSTER THEY'VE BEEN TALKING ABOUT BACK IN THE STATES.
THE HULK, YOU MEAN?
HEY, I'VE MET BRUCE BANNER--
--AND TRUST ME--
--I'M NO HULK.
...AND STARK INDUSTRIES IN PARTICULAR, RIGHT?

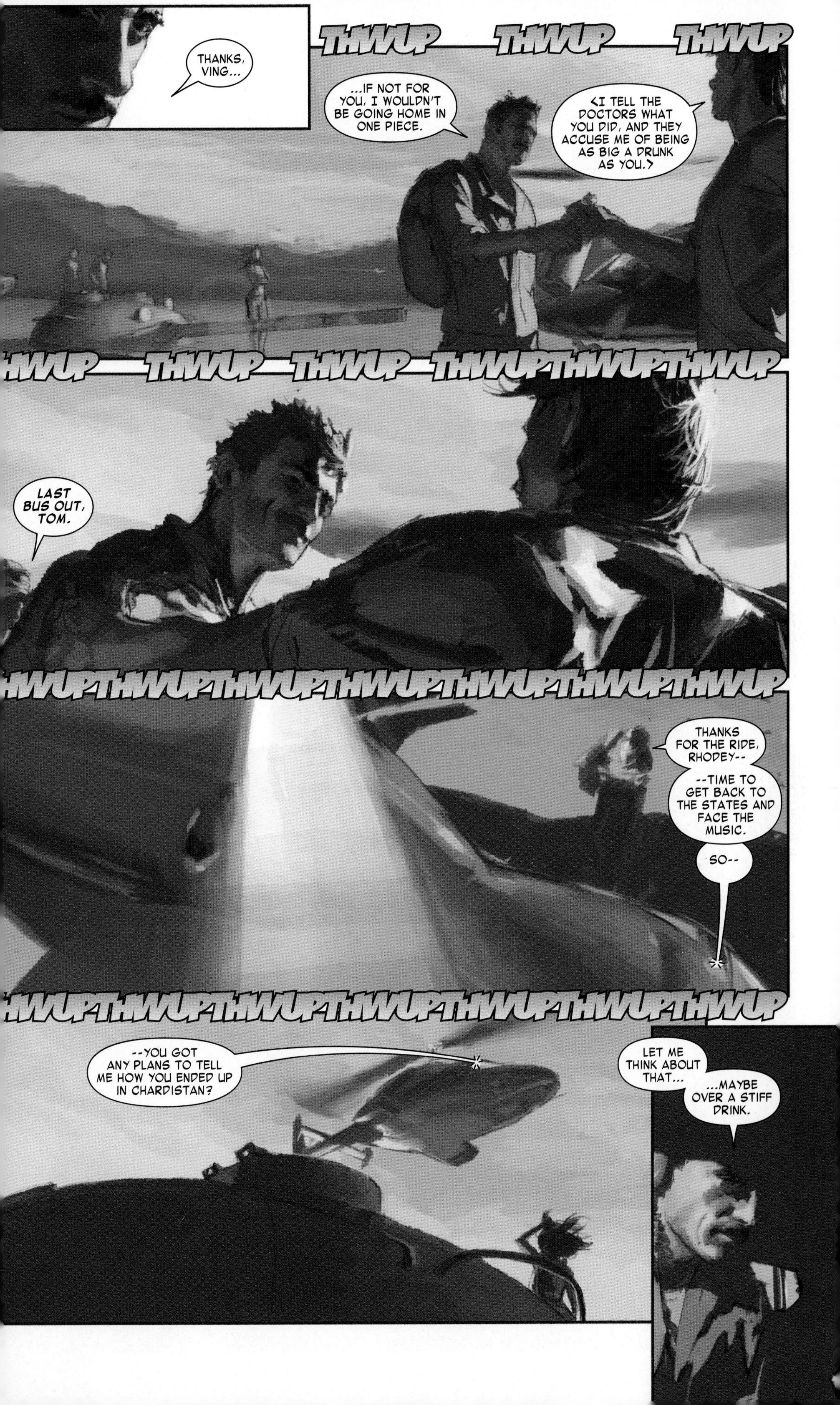
THANKS, VING...
THWUP THWUP THWUP
...IF NOT FOR YOU, I WOULDN'T BE GOING HOME IN ONE PIECE.
<I TELL THE DOCTORS WHAT YOU DID, AND THEY ACCUSE ME OF BEING AS BIG A DRUNK AS YOU.>
THWUP THWUP THWUP THWUPTHWUPTHWUP
LAST BUS OUT, TOM.
THWUPTHWUPTHWUPTHWUPTHWUPTHWUP
THANKS FOR THE RIDE, RHODEY--
--TIME TO GET BACK TO THE STATES AND FACE THE MUSIC.
SO--
THWUPTHWUPTHWUPTHWUPTHWUPTHWUP
--YOU GOT ANY PLANS TO TELL ME HOW YOU ENDED UP IN CHARDISTAN?
LET ME THINK ABOUT THAT...
...MAYBE OVER A STIFF DRINK.

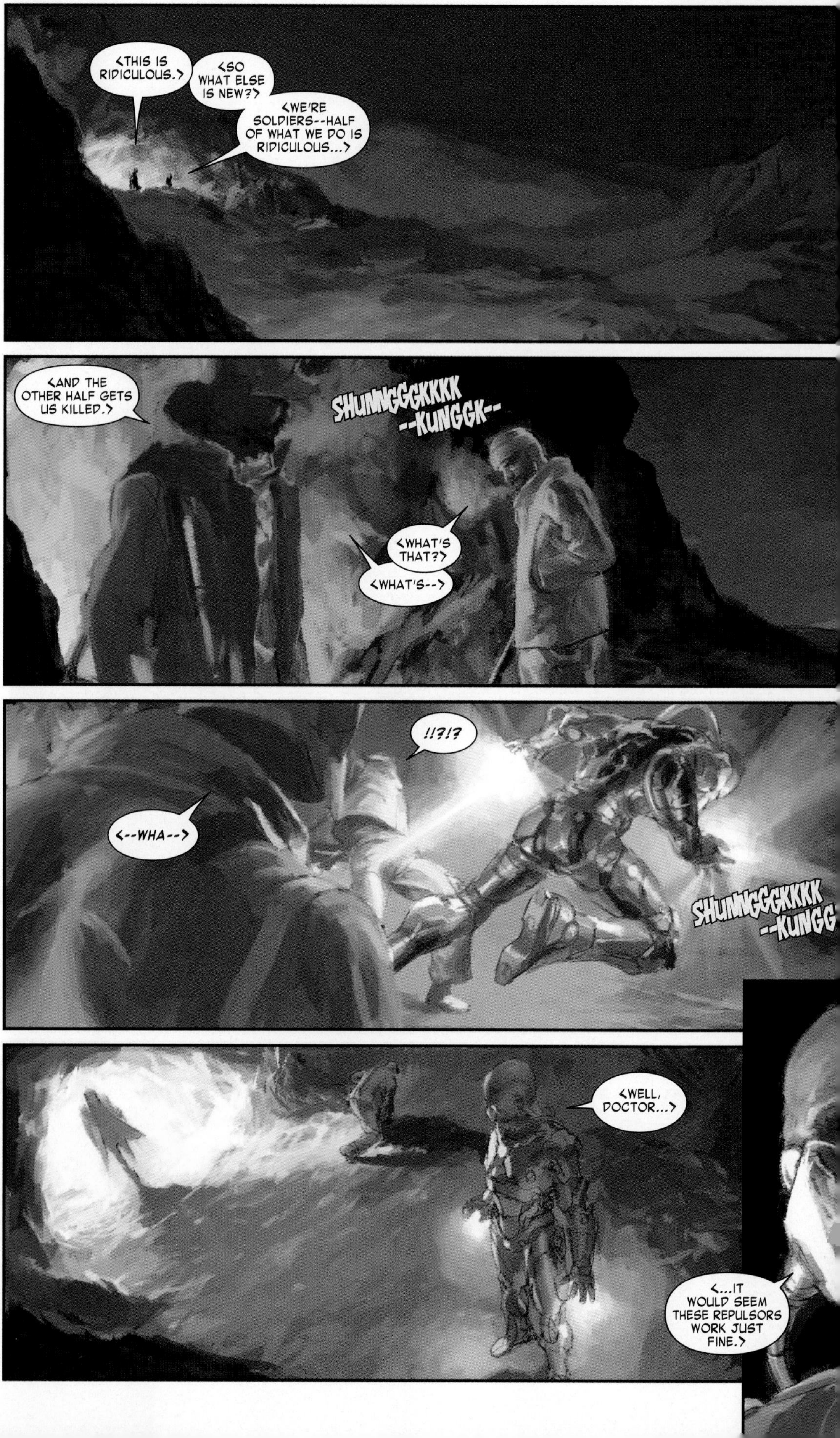
<THIS IS RIDICULOUS.>
<SO WHAT ELSE IS NEW?>
<WE'RE SOLDIERS--HALF OF WHAT WE DO IS RIDICULOUS...>
<AND THE OTHER HALF GETS US KILLED.>
SHUNNGGGKKKK --KUNGGK--
<WHAT'S THAT?>
<WHAT'S-->
!!?!?
<--WHA-->
SHUNNGGGKKKK --KUNGG
<WELL, DOCTOR...>
<...IT WOULD SEEM THESE REPULSORS WORK JUST FINE.>

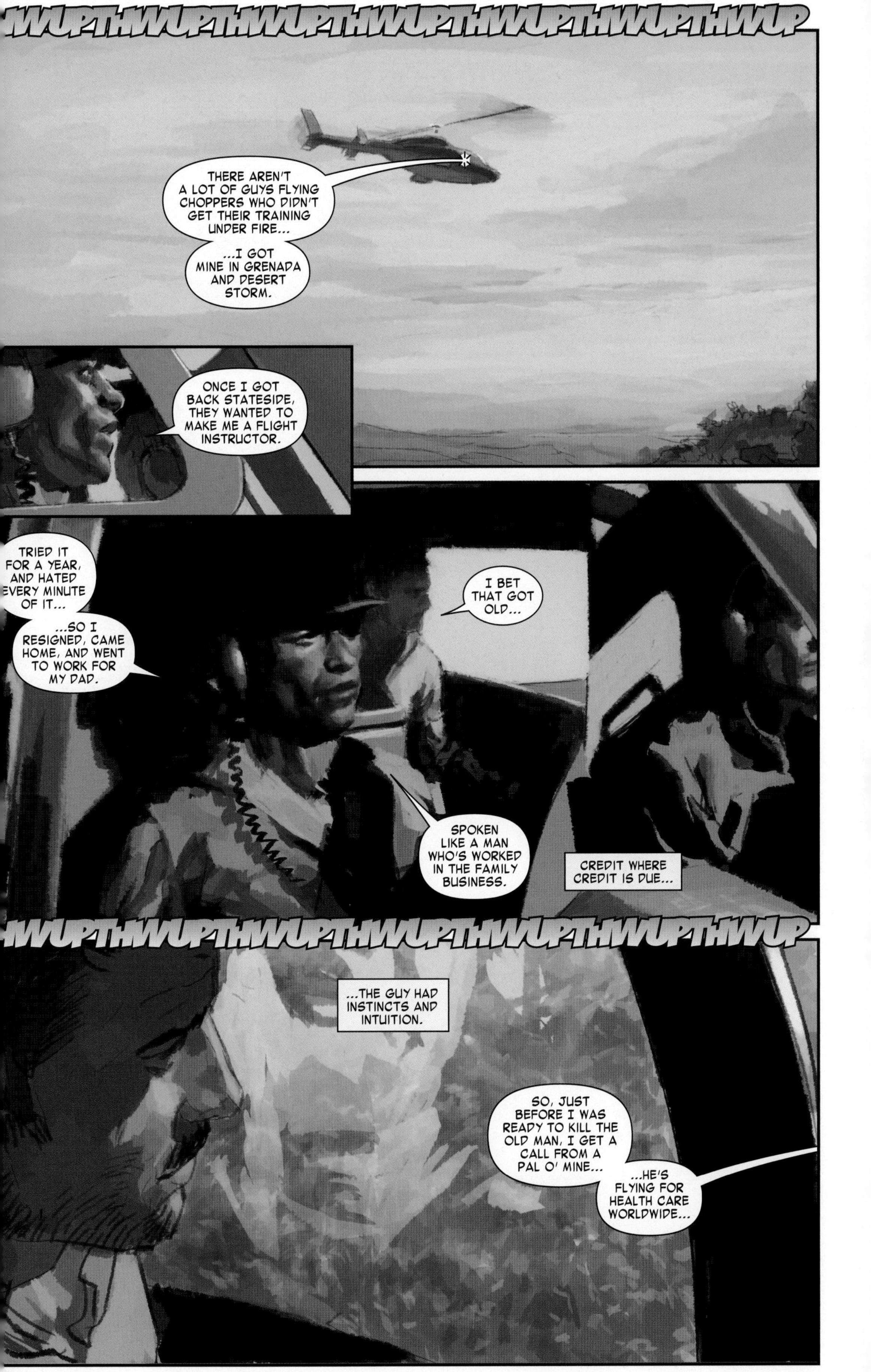
THWUPTHWUPTHWUPTHWUPTHWUPTHWUPTHWUP
THERE AREN'T A LOT OF GUYS FLYING CHOPPERS WHO DIDN'T GET THEIR TRAINING UNDER FIRE...
...I GOT MINE IN GRENADA AND DESERT STORM.
ONCE I GOT BACK STATESIDE, THEY WANTED TO MAKE ME A FLIGHT INSTRUCTOR.
TRIED IT FOR A YEAR, AND HATED EVERY MINUTE OF IT...
...SO I RESIGNED, CAME HOME, AND WENT TO WORK FOR MY DAD.
I BET THAT GOT OLD...
SPOKEN LIKE A MAN WHO'S WORKED IN THE FAMILY BUSINESS.
CREDIT WHERE CREDIT IS DUE...
THWUPTHWUPTHWUPTHWUPTHWUPTHWUPTHWUP
...THE GUY HAD INSTINCTS AND INTUITION.
SO, JUST BEFORE I WAS READY TO KILL THE OLD MAN, I GET A CALL FROM A PAL O' MINE...
...HE'S FLYING FOR HEALTH CARE WORLDWIDE...

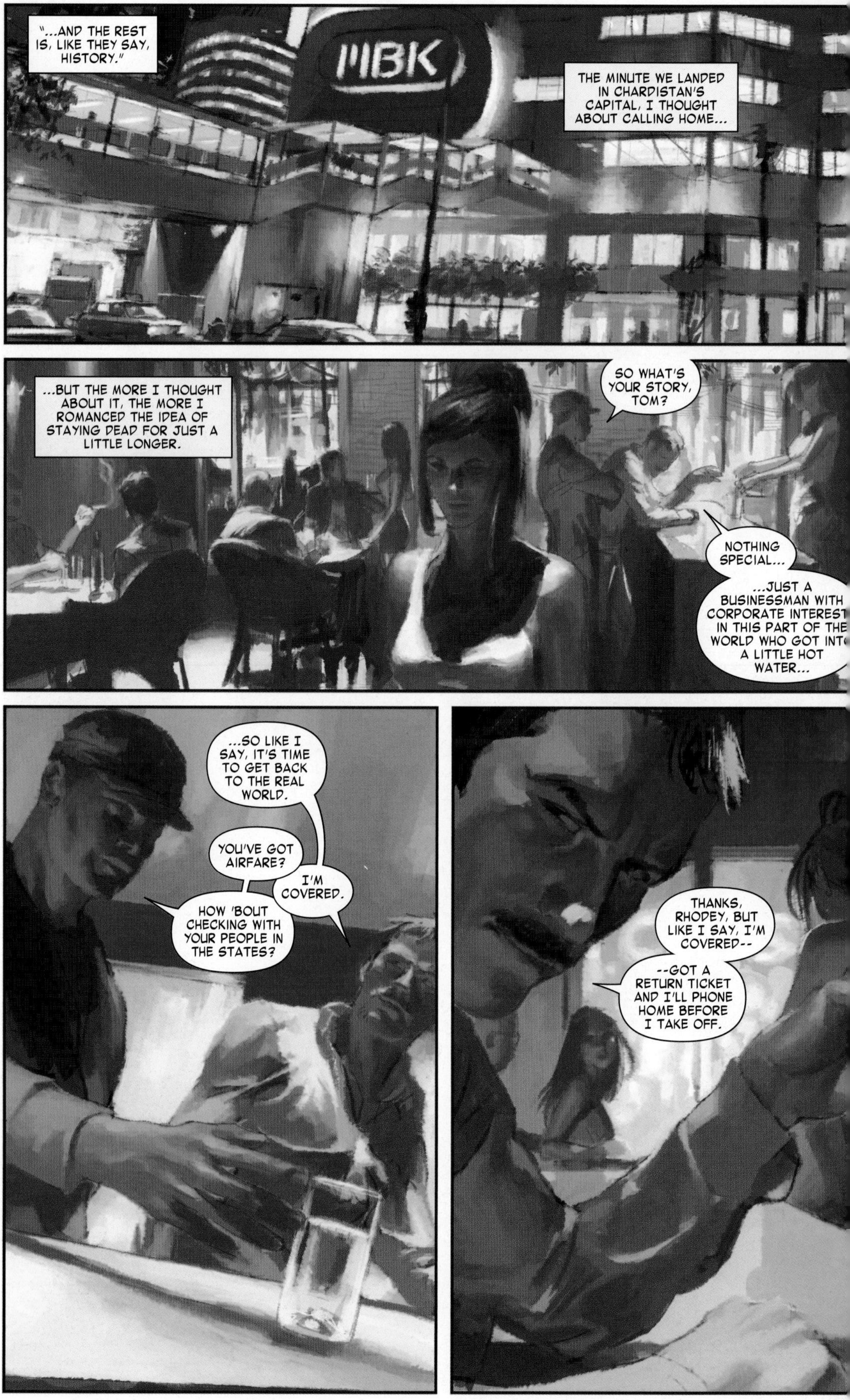
"...AND THE REST IS, LIKE THEY SAY, HISTORY."
MBK
THE MINUTE WE LANDED IN CHARDISTAN'S CAPITAL, I THOUGHT ABOUT CALLING HOME...
...BUT THE MORE I THOUGHT ABOUT IT, THE MORE I ROMANCED THE IDEA OF STAYING DEAD FOR JUST A LITTLE LONGER.
SO WHAT'S YOUR STORY, TOM?
NOTHING SPECIAL...
...JUST A BUSINESSMAN WITH CORPORATE INTEREST IN THIS PART OF THE WORLD WHO GOT INT A LITTLE HOT WATER...
...SO LIKE I SAY, IT'S TIME TO GET BACK TO THE REAL WORLD.
YOU'VE GOT AIRFARE?
I'M COVERED.
HOW 'BOUT CHECKING WITH YOUR PEOPLE IN THE STATES?
THANKS, RHODEY, BUT LIKE I SAY, I'M COVERED--
--GOT A RETURN TICKET AND I'LL PHONE HOME BEFORE I TAKE OFF.

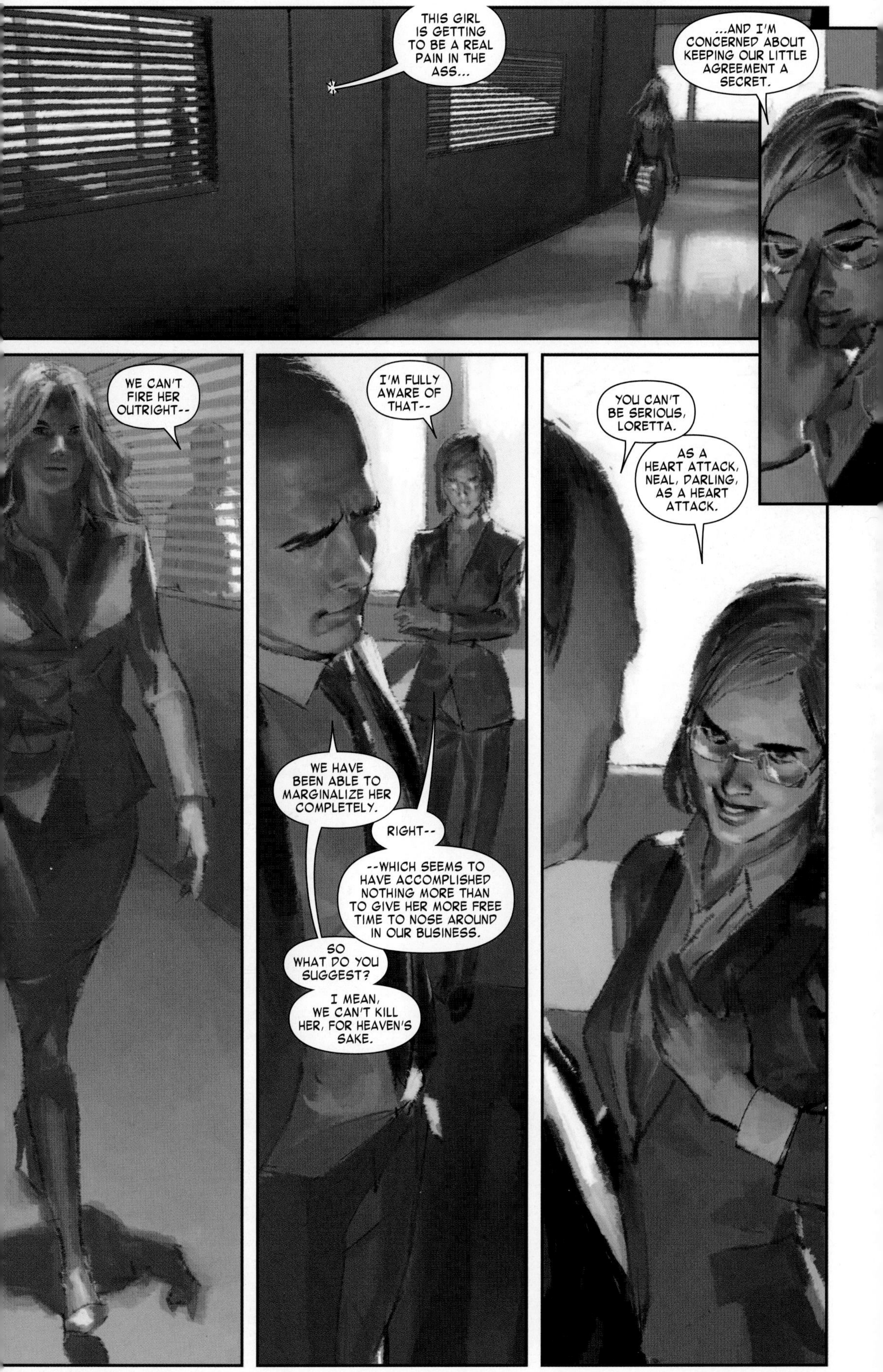
THIS GIRL IS GETTING TO BE A REAL PAIN IN THE ASS...
...AND I'M CONCERNED ABOUT KEEPING OUR LITTLE AGREEMENT A SECRET.
WE CAN'T FIRE HER OUTRIGHT--
I'M FULLY AWARE OF THAT--
WE HAVE BEEN ABLE TO MARGINALIZE HER COMPLETELY.
RIGHT--
--WHICH SEEMS TO HAVE ACCOMPLISHED NOTHING MORE THAN TO GIVE HER MORE FREE TIME TO NOSE AROUND IN OUR BUSINESS.
SO WHAT DO YOU SUGGEST?
I MEAN, WE CAN'T KILL HER, FOR HEAVEN'S SAKE.
YOU CAN'T BE SERIOUS, LORETTA.
AS A HEART ATTACK, NEAL, DARLING, AS A HEART ATTACK.

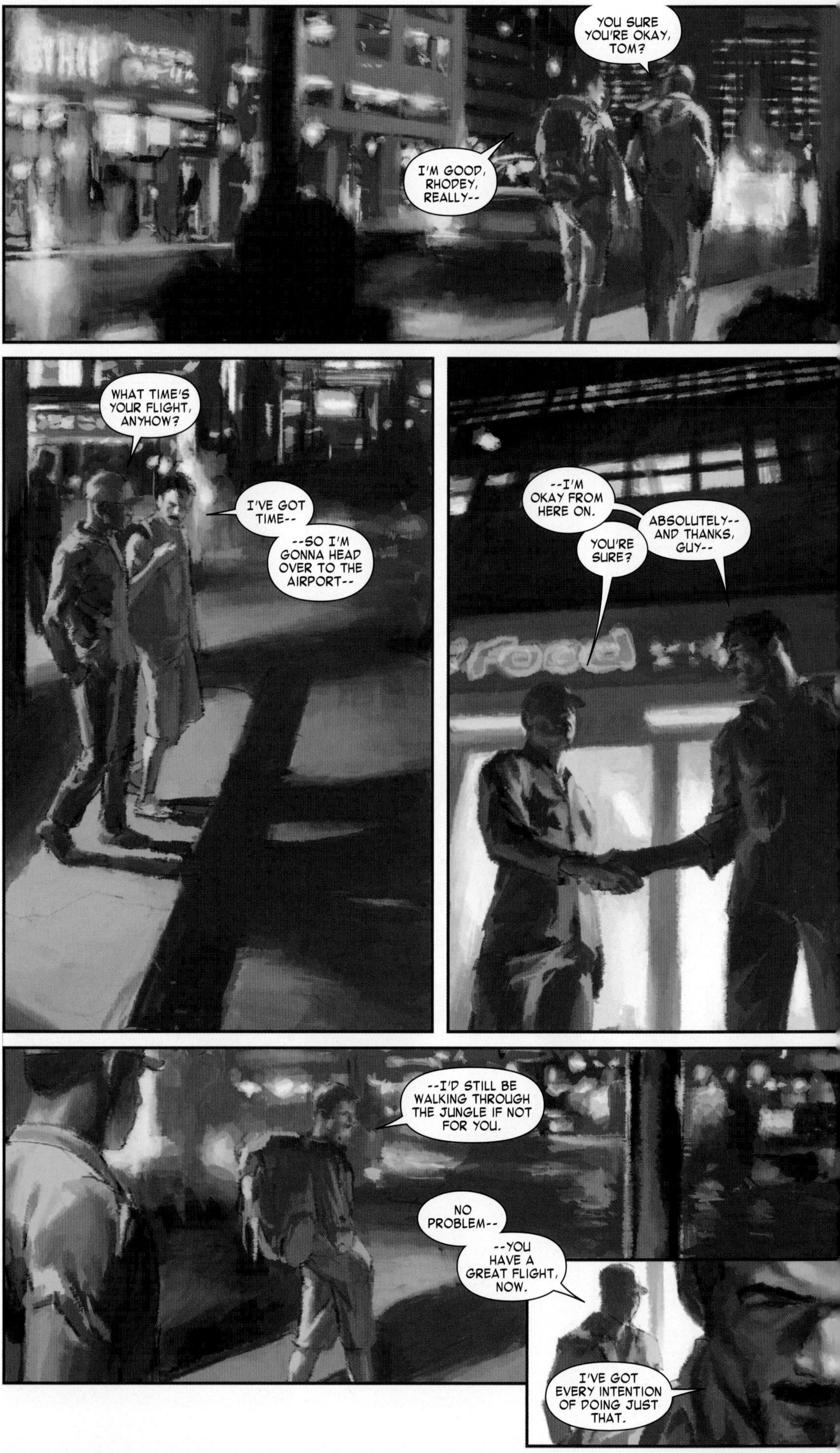
YOU SURE YOU'RE OKAY, TOM?
I'M GOOD, RHODEY, REALLY--
WHAT TIME'S YOUR FLIGHT, ANYHOW?
I'VE GOT TIME--
--SO I'M GONNA HEAD OVER TO THE AIRPORT--
--I'M OKAY FROM HERE ON.
YOU'RE SURE?
ABSOLUTELY-- AND THANKS, GUY--
--I'D STILL BE WALKING THROUGH THE JUNGLE IF NOT FOR YOU.
NO PROBLEM--
--YOU HAVE A GREAT FLIGHT, NOW.
I'VE GOT EVERY INTENTION OF DOING JUST THAT.

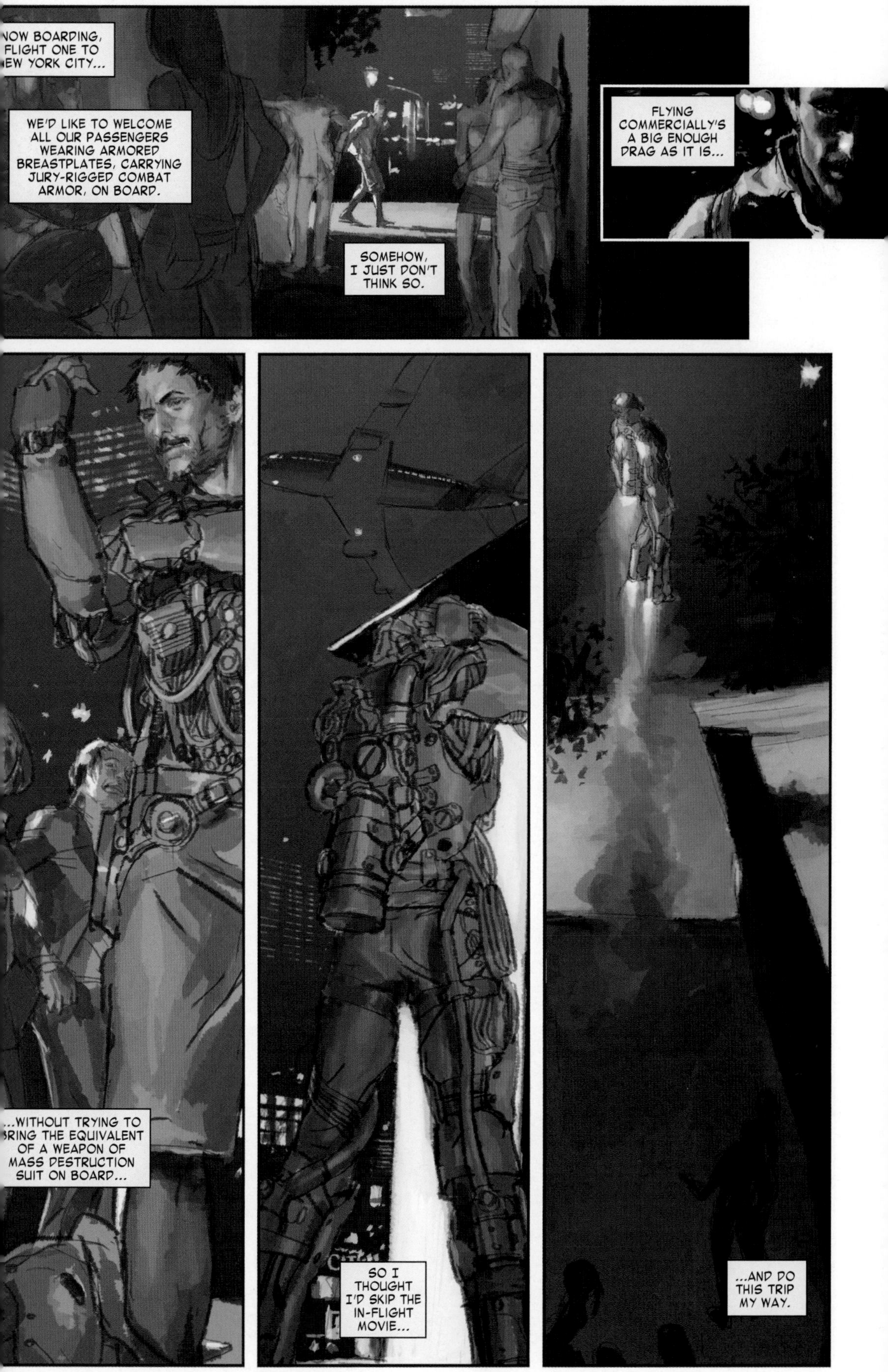
NOW BOARDING, FLIGHT ONE TO NEW YORK CITY...
WE'D LIKE TO WELCOME ALL OUR PASSENGERS WEARING ARMORED BREASTPLATES, CARRYING JURY-RIGGED COMBAT ARMOR, ON BOARD.
SOMEHOW, I JUST DON'T THINK SO.
FLYING COMMERCIALLY'S A BIG ENOUGH DRAG AS IT IS...
...WITHOUT TRYING TO BRING THE EQUIVALENT OF A WEAPON OF MASS DESTRUCTION SUIT ON BOARD...
SO I THOUGHT I'D SKIP THE IN-FLIGHT MOVIE...
...AND DO THIS TRIP MY WAY.

THIS PLACE PROBABLY GOT ITS START AS A REFUELING STOP...

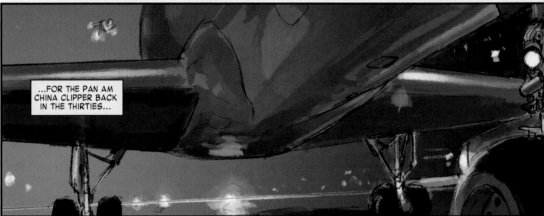

...FOR THE PAN AM CHINA CLIPPER BACK IN THE THIRTIES...

...AND THEN WAS NATIONALIZED DURING THE SECOND WORLD WAR FOR MILITARY USE...

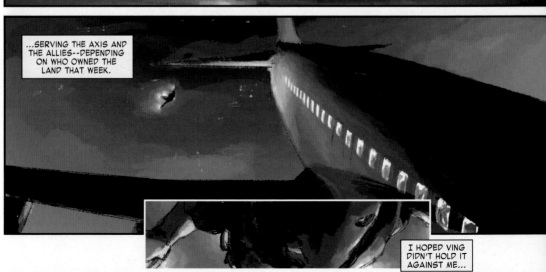

...SERVING THE AXIS AND THE ALLIES--DEPENDING ON WHO OWNED THE LAND THAT WEEK.

I HOPED VING DIDN'T HOLD IT AGAINST ME...

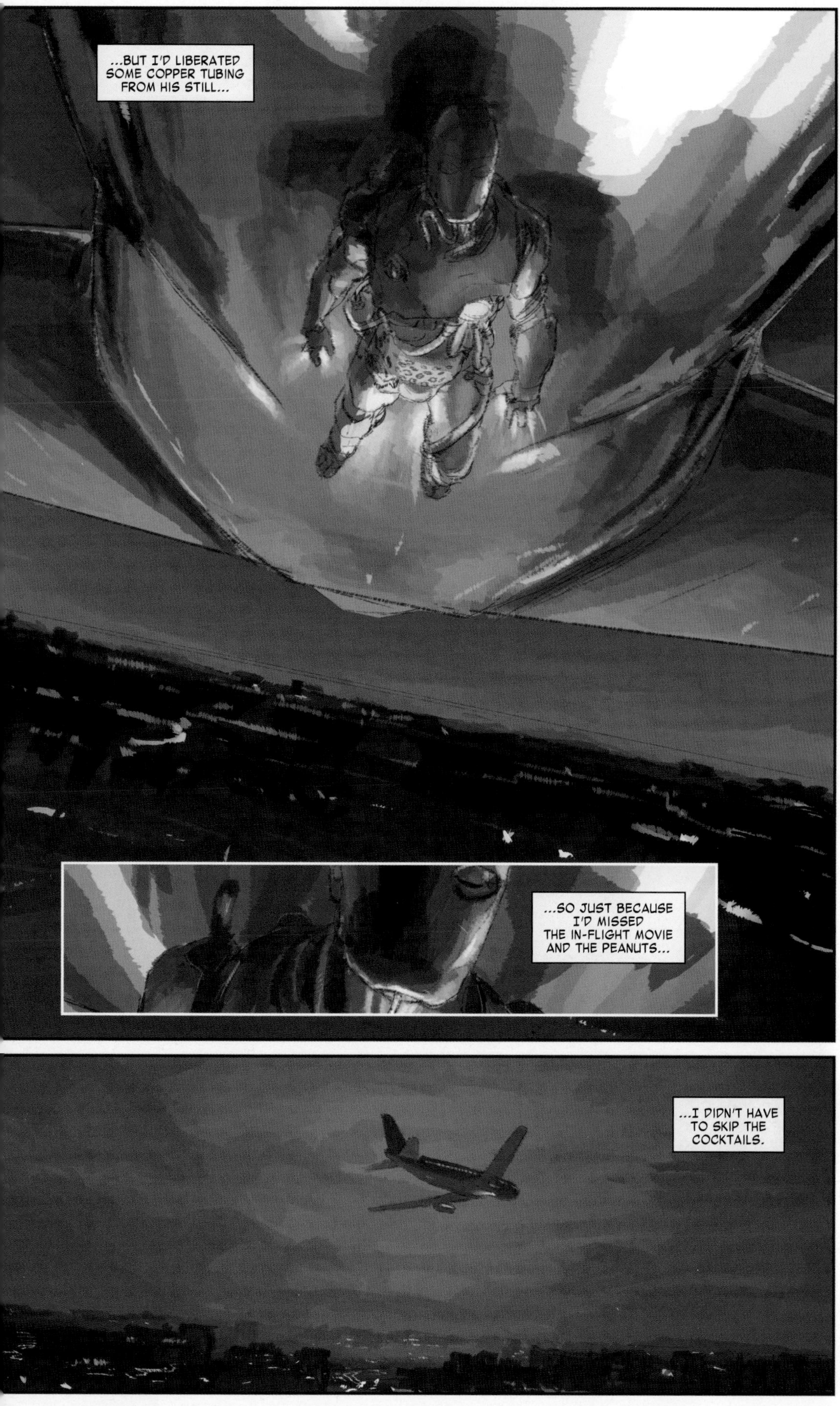
...BUT I'D LIBERATED SOME COPPER TUBING FROM HIS STILL...
...SO JUST BECAUSE I'D MISSED THE IN-FLIGHT MOVIE AND THE PEANUTS...
...I DIDN'T HAVE TO SKIP THE COCKTAILS.

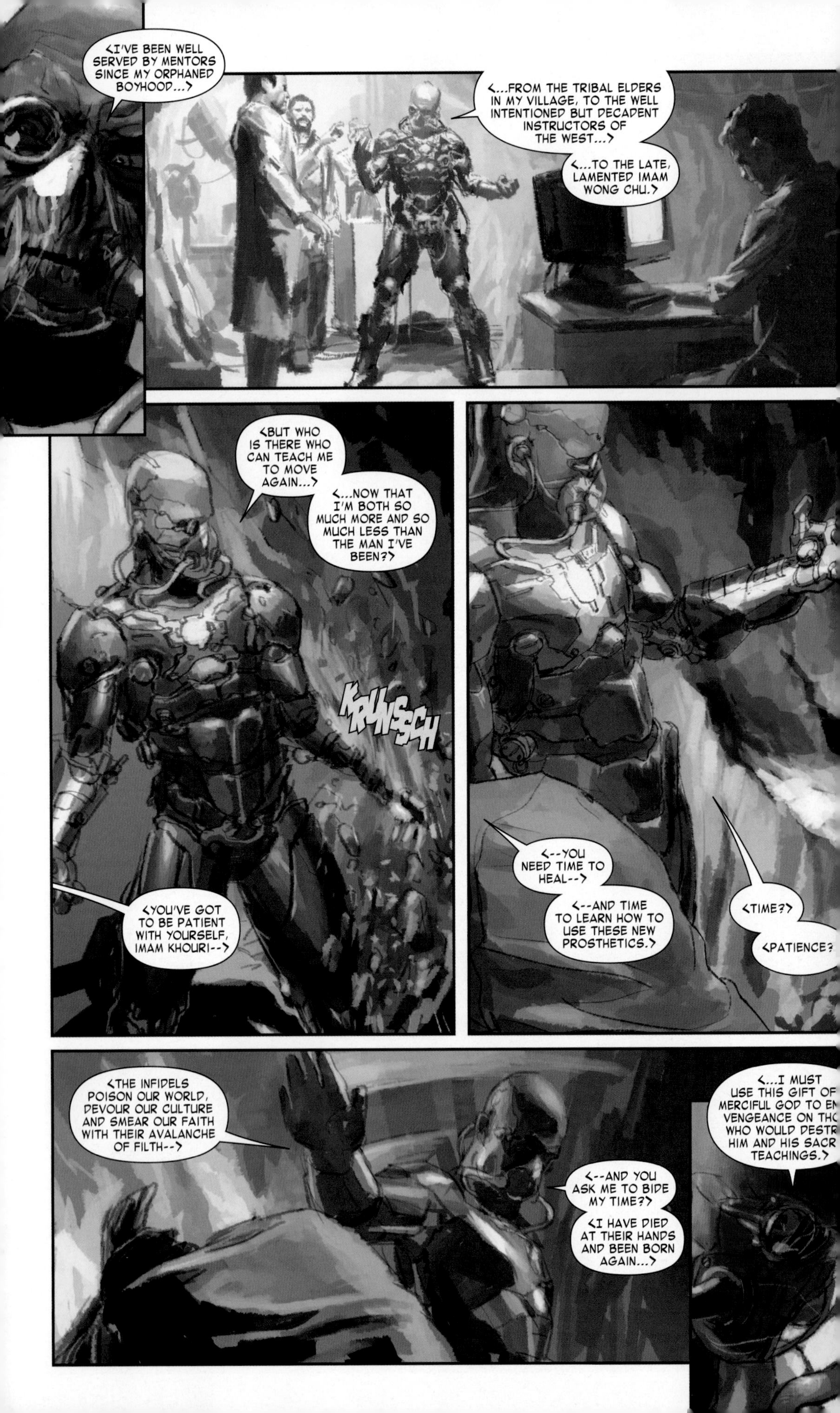

<I'VE BEEN WELL SERVED BY MENTORS SINCE MY ORPHANED BOYHOOD...>
<...FROM THE TRIBAL ELDERS IN MY VILLAGE, TO THE WELL INTENTIONED BUT DECADENT INSTRUCTORS OF THE WEST...>
<...TO THE LATE, LAMENTED IMAM WONG CHU.>
<BUT WHO IS THERE WHO CAN TEACH ME TO MOVE AGAIN...>
<...NOW THAT I'M BOTH SO MUCH MORE AND SO MUCH LESS THAN THE MAN I'VE BEEN?>
KRUNSCH
<YOU'VE GOT TO BE PATIENT WITH YOURSELF, IMAM KHOURI-->
<--YOU NEED TIME TO HEAL-->
<--AND TIME TO LEARN HOW TO USE THESE NEW PROSTHETICS.>
<TIME?>
<PATIENCE?
<THE INFIDELS POISON OUR WORLD, DEVOUR OUR CULTURE AND SMEAR OUR FAITH WITH THEIR AVALANCHE OF FILTH-->
<--AND YOU ASK ME TO BIDE MY TIME?>
<I HAVE DIED AT THEIR HANDS AND BEEN BORN AGAIN...>
<...I MUST USE THIS GIFT OF MERCIFUL GOD TO EN VENGEANCE ON THO WHO WOULD DESTR HIM AND HIS SACR TEACHINGS.>

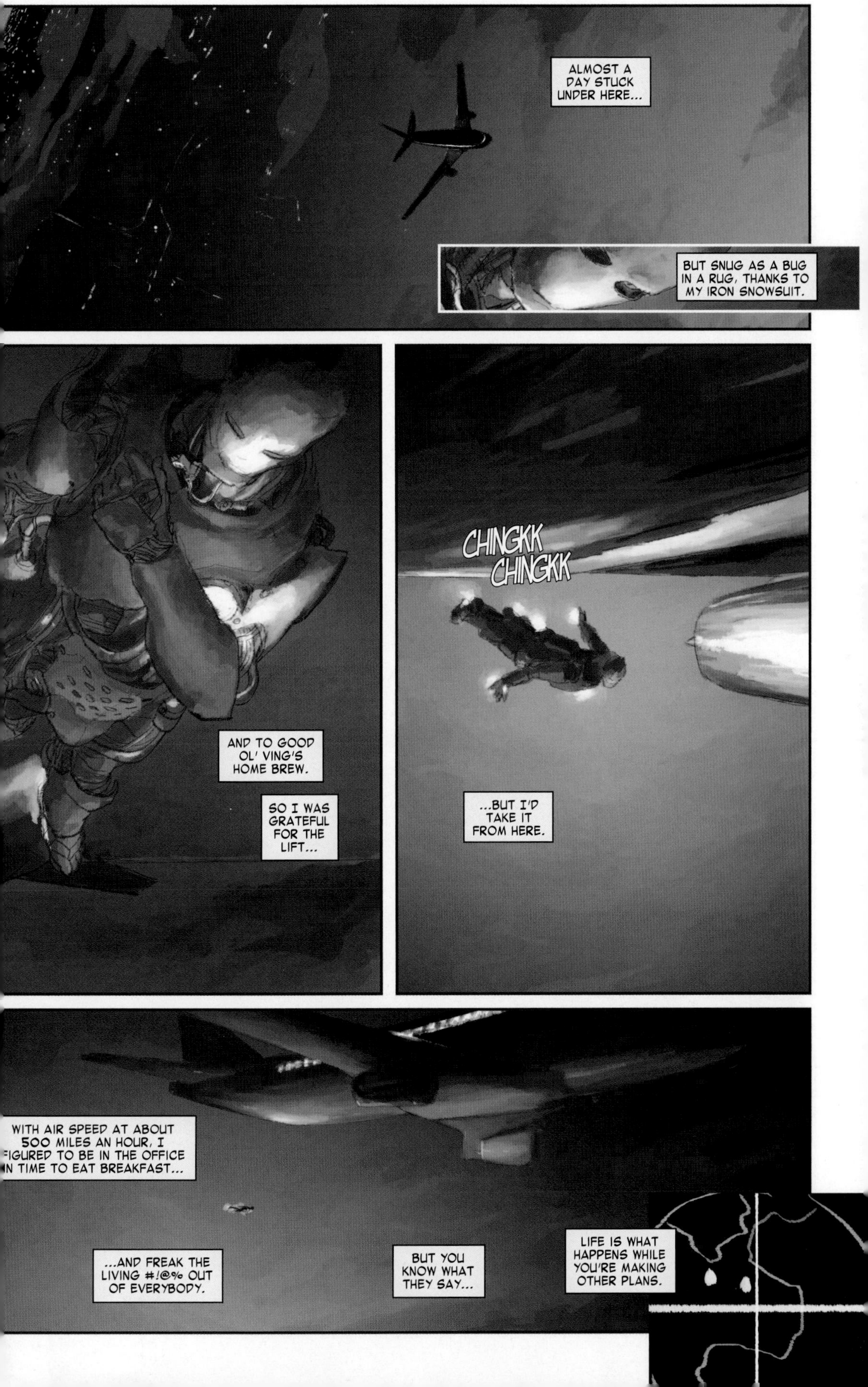
ALMOST A DAY STUCK UNDER HERE...
BUT SNUG AS A BUG IN A RUG, THANKS TO MY IRON SNOWSUIT.
AND TO GOOD OL' VING'S HOME BREW.
SO I WAS GRATEFUL FOR THE LIFT...
CHINGKK
CHINGKK
...BUT I'D TAKE IT FROM HERE.
WITH AIR SPEED AT ABOUT 500 MILES AN HOUR, I FIGURED TO BE IN THE OFFICE IN TIME TO EAT BREAKFAST...
...AND FREAK THE LIVING #!@% OUT OF EVERYBODY.
BUT YOU KNOW WHAT THEY SAY...
LIFE IS WHAT HAPPENS WHILE YOU'RE MAKING OTHER PLANS.

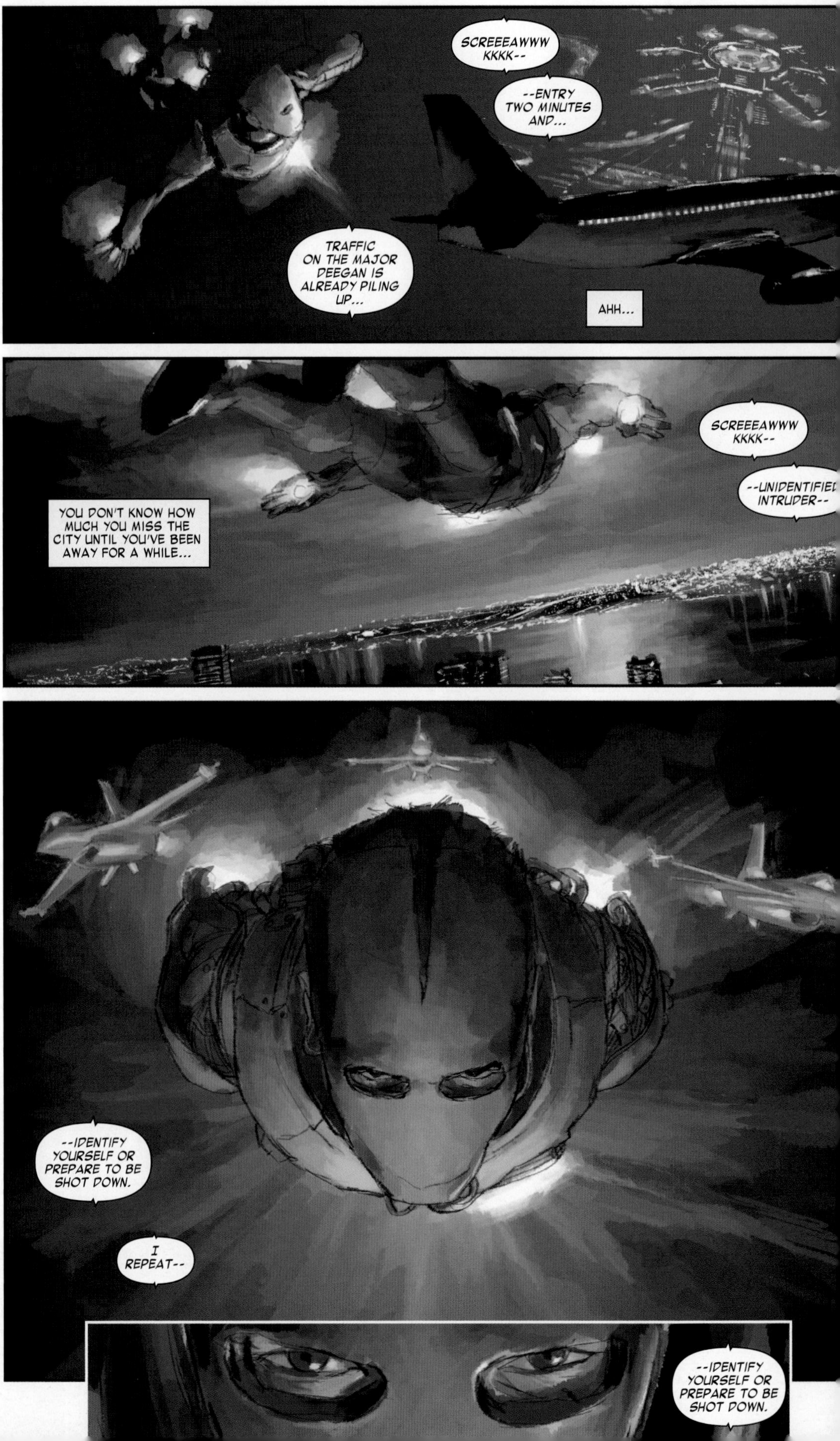

SCREEEAWWW KKKK--
--ENTRY TWO MINUTES AND...
TRAFFIC ON THE MAJOR DEEGAN IS ALREADY PILING UP...
AHH...
YOU DON'T KNOW HOW MUCH YOU MISS THE CITY UNTIL YOU'VE BEEN AWAY FOR A WHILE...
SCREEEAWWW KKKK--
--UNIDENTIFIED INTRUDER--
--IDENTIFY YOURSELF OR PREPARE TO BE SHOT DOWN.
I REPEAT--
--IDENTIFY YOURSELF OR PREPARE TO BE SHOT DOWN.

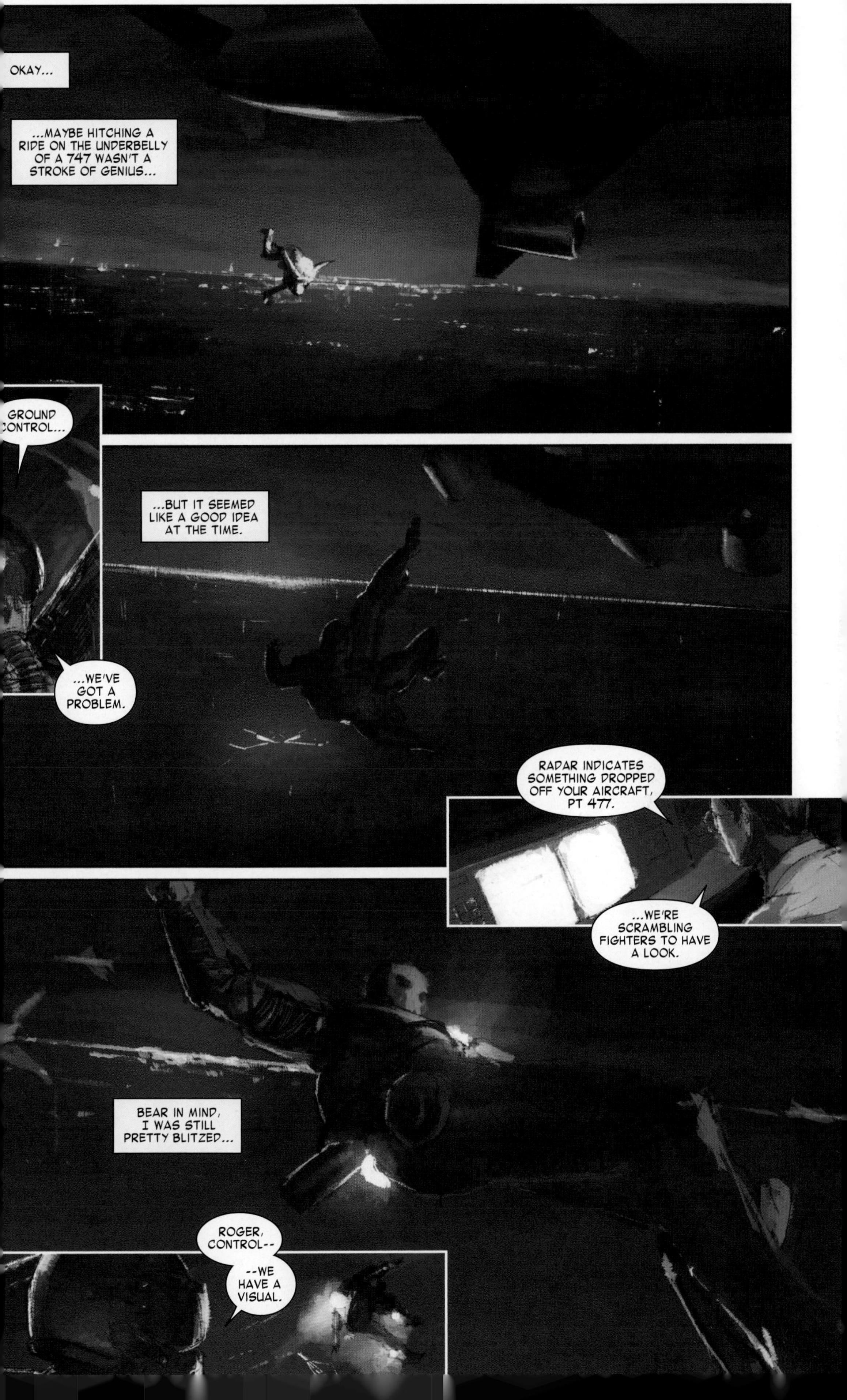

OKAY...
...MAYBE HITCHING A RIDE ON THE UNDERBELLY OF A 747 WASN'T A STROKE OF GENIUS...
GROUND CONTROL...
...BUT IT SEEMED LIKE A GOOD IDEA AT THE TIME.
...WE'VE GOT A PROBLEM.
RADAR INDICATES SOMETHING DROPPED OFF YOUR AIRCRAFT, PT 477.
...WE'RE SCRAMBLING FIGHTERS TO HAVE A LOOK.
BEAR IN MIND, I WAS STILL PRETTY BLITZED...
ROGER, CONTROL--
--WE HAVE A VISUAL.

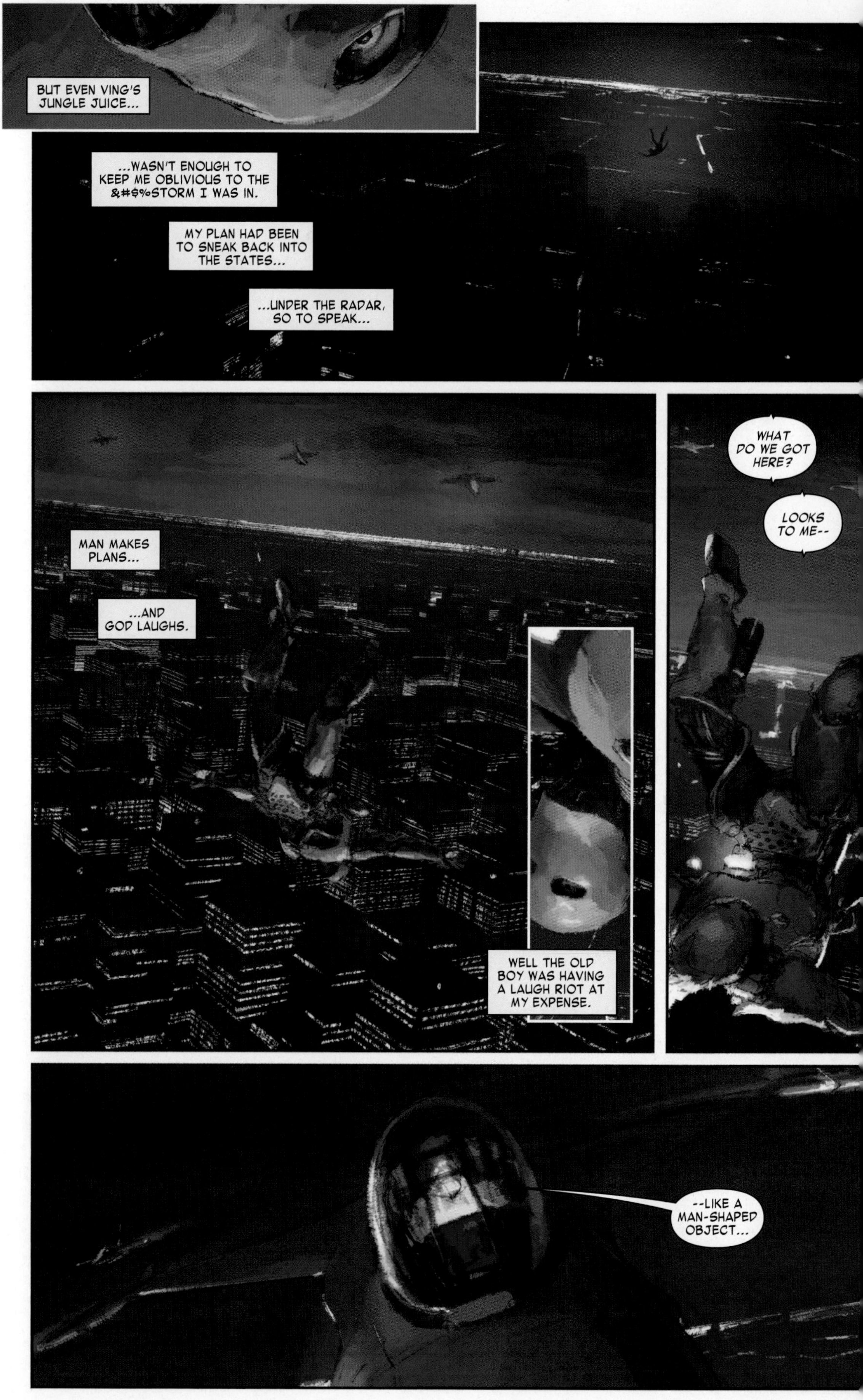
BUT EVEN VING'S JUNGLE JUICE...
...WASN'T ENOUGH TO KEEP ME OBLIVIOUS TO THE &#$%STORM I WAS IN.
MY PLAN HAD BEEN TO SNEAK BACK INTO THE STATES...
...UNDER THE RADAR, SO TO SPEAK...
MAN MAKES PLANS...
...AND GOD LAUGHS.
WELL THE OLD BOY WAS HAVING A LAUGH RIOT AT MY EXPENSE.
WHAT DO WE GOT HERE?
LOOKS TO ME--
--LIKE A MAN-SHAPED OBJECT...

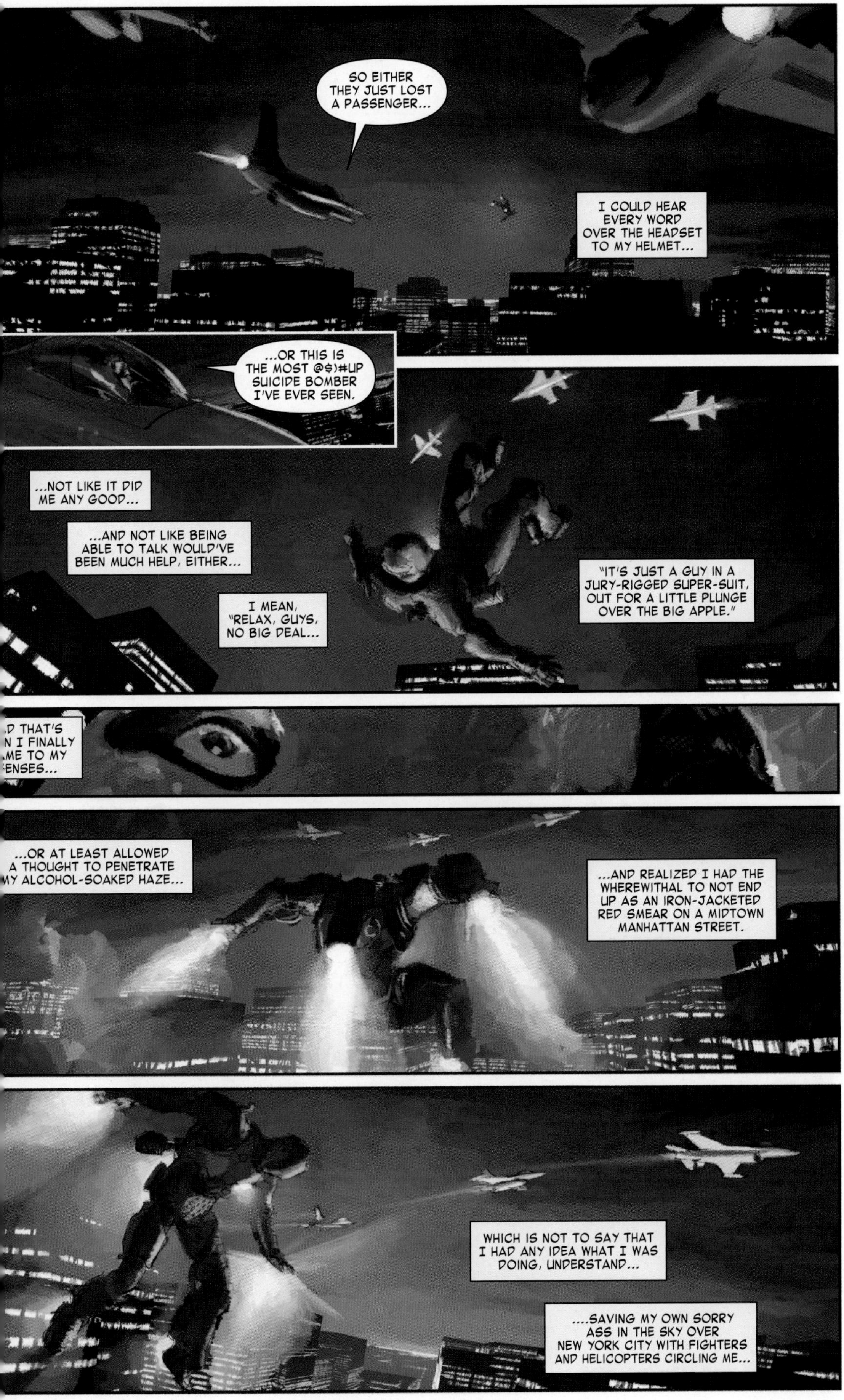
SO EITHER THEY JUST LOST A PASSENGER...
I COULD HEAR EVERY WORD OVER THE HEADSET TO MY HELMET...
...OR THIS IS THE MOST @$)#UP SUICIDE BOMBER I'VE EVER SEEN.
...NOT LIKE IT DID ME ANY GOOD...
...AND NOT LIKE BEING ABLE TO TALK WOULD'VE BEEN MUCH HELP, EITHER...
I MEAN, "RELAX, GUYS, NO BIG DEAL...
"IT'S JUST A GUY IN A JURY-RIGGED SUPER-SUIT, OUT FOR A LITTLE PLUNGE OVER THE BIG APPLE."
...OR AT LEAST ALLOWED A THOUGHT TO PENETRATE MY ALCOHOL-SOAKED HAZE...
...AND REALIZED I HAD THE WHEREWITHAL TO NOT END UP AS AN IRON-JACKETED RED SMEAR ON A MIDTOWN MANHATTAN STREET.
WHICH IS NOT TO SAY THAT I HAD ANY IDEA WHAT I WAS DOING, UNDERSTAND...
....SAVING MY OWN SORRY ASS IN THE SKY OVER NEW YORK CITY WITH FIGHTERS AND HELICOPTERS CIRCLING ME...

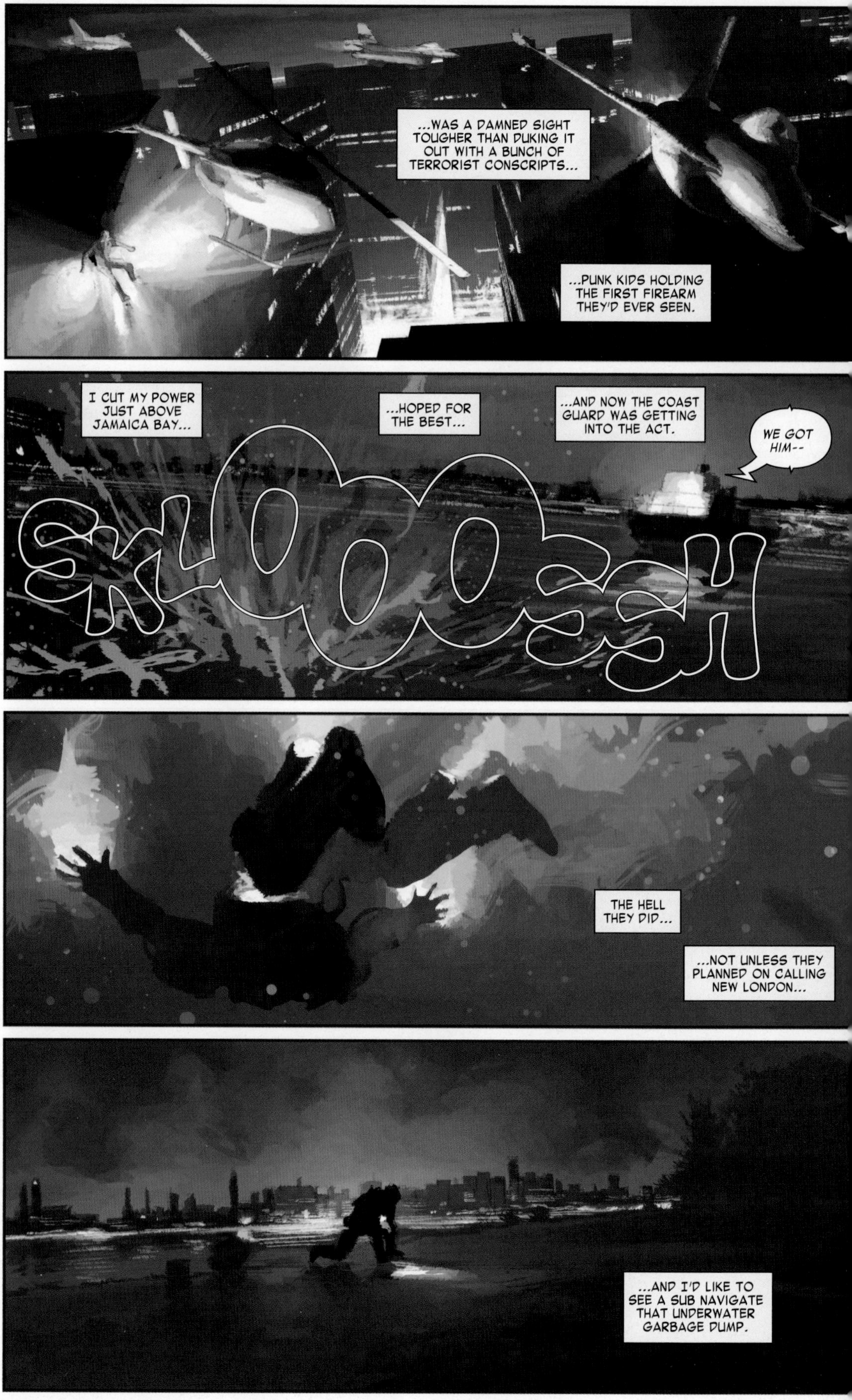
...WAS A DAMNED SIGHT TOUGHER THAN DUKING IT OUT WITH A BUNCH OF TERRORIST CONSCRIPTS...
...PUNK KIDS HOLDING THE FIRST FIREARM THEY'D EVER SEEN.
I CUT MY POWER JUST ABOVE JAMAICA BAY...
...HOPED FOR THE BEST...
...AND NOW THE COAST GUARD WAS GETTING INTO THE ACT.
WE GOT HIM--
SKLOOOSSH
THE HELL THEY DID...
...NOT UNLESS THEY PLANNED ON CALLING NEW LONDON...
...AND I'D LIKE TO SEE A SUB NAVIGATE THAT UNDERWATER GARBAGE DUMP.

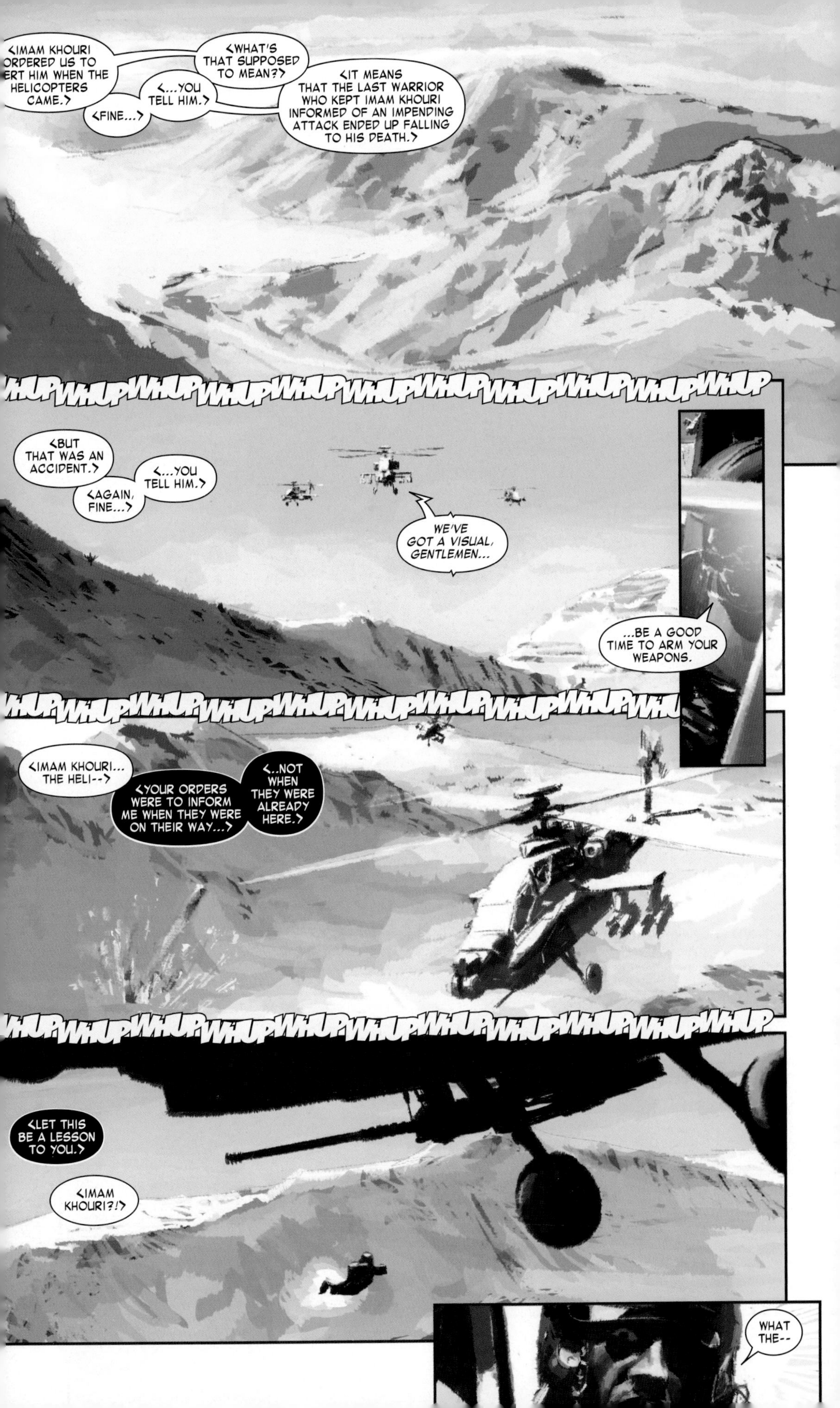

<IMAM KHOURI ORDERED US TO ERT HIM WHEN THE HELICOPTERS CAME.>
<WHAT'S THAT SUPPOSED TO MEAN?>
<...YOU TELL HIM.>
<FINE...>
<IT MEANS THAT THE LAST WARRIOR WHO KEPT IMAM KHOURI INFORMED OF AN IMPENDING ATTACK ENDED UP FALLING TO HIS DEATH.>
WHUPWHUPWHUPWHUPWHUPWHUPWHUPWHUPWHUPWHUPWHUP
<BUT THAT WAS AN ACCIDENT.>
<...YOU TELL HIM.>
<AGAIN, FINE...>
WE'VE GOT A VISUAL, GENTLEMEN...
...BE A GOOD TIME TO ARM YOUR WEAPONS.
WHUPWHUPWHUPWHUPWHUPWHUPWHUPWHUPWHUPWHU
<IMAM KHOURI... THE HELI-->
<YOUR ORDERS WERE TO INFORM ME WHEN THEY WERE ON THEIR WAY...>
<..NOT WHEN THEY WERE ALREADY HERE.>
WHUPWHUPWHUPWHUPWHUPWHUPWHUPWHUPWHUPWHUP
<LET THIS BE A LESSON TO YOU.>
<IMAM KHOURI?!>
WHAT THE--

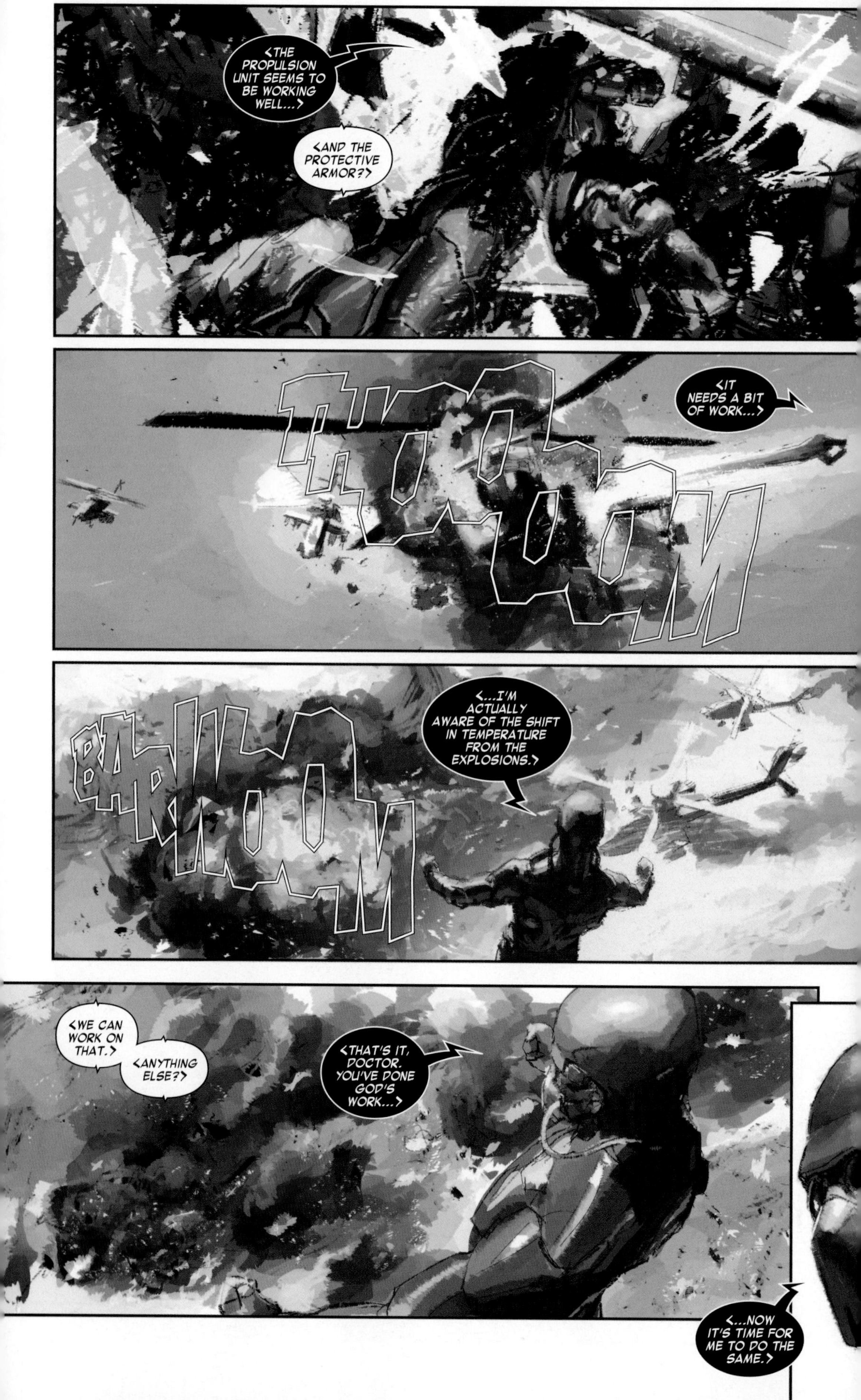

<THE PROPULSION UNIT SEEMS TO BE WORKING WELL...>
<AND THE PROTECTIVE ARMOR?>
THOOOM
<IT NEEDS A BIT OF WORK...>
BARUUOOM
<...I'M ACTUALLY AWARE OF THE SHIFT IN TEMPERATURE FROM THE EXPLOSIONS.>
<WE CAN WORK ON THAT.>
<ANYTHING ELSE?>
<THAT'S IT, DOCTOR. YOU'VE DONE GOD'S WORK...>
<...NOW IT'S TIME FOR ME TO DO THE SAME.>

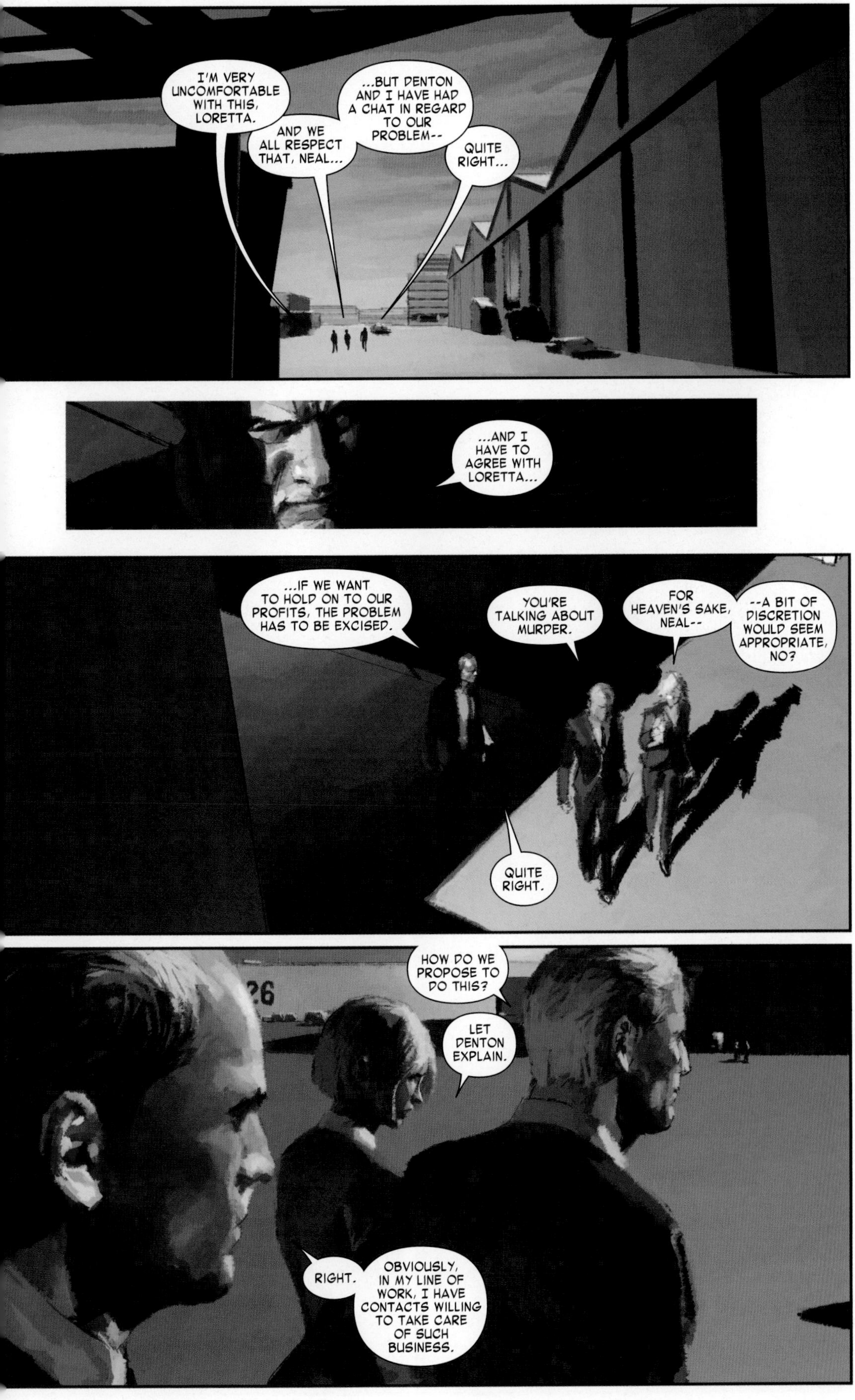
I'M VERY UNCOMFORTABLE WITH THIS, LORETTA.
AND WE ALL RESPECT THAT, NEAL...
...BUT DENTON AND I HAVE HAD A CHAT IN REGARD TO OUR PROBLEM--
QUITE RIGHT...
...AND I HAVE TO AGREE WITH LORETTA...
...IF WE WANT TO HOLD ON TO OUR PROFITS, THE PROBLEM HAS TO BE EXCISED.
QUITE RIGHT.
YOU'RE TALKING ABOUT MURDER.
FOR HEAVEN'S SAKE, NEAL--
--A BIT OF DISCRETION WOULD SEEM APPROPRIATE, NO?
26
HOW DO WE PROPOSE TO DO THIS?
LET DENTON EXPLAIN.
RIGHT.
OBVIOUSLY, IN MY LINE OF WORK, I HAVE CONTACTS WILLING TO TAKE CARE OF SUCH BUSINESS.

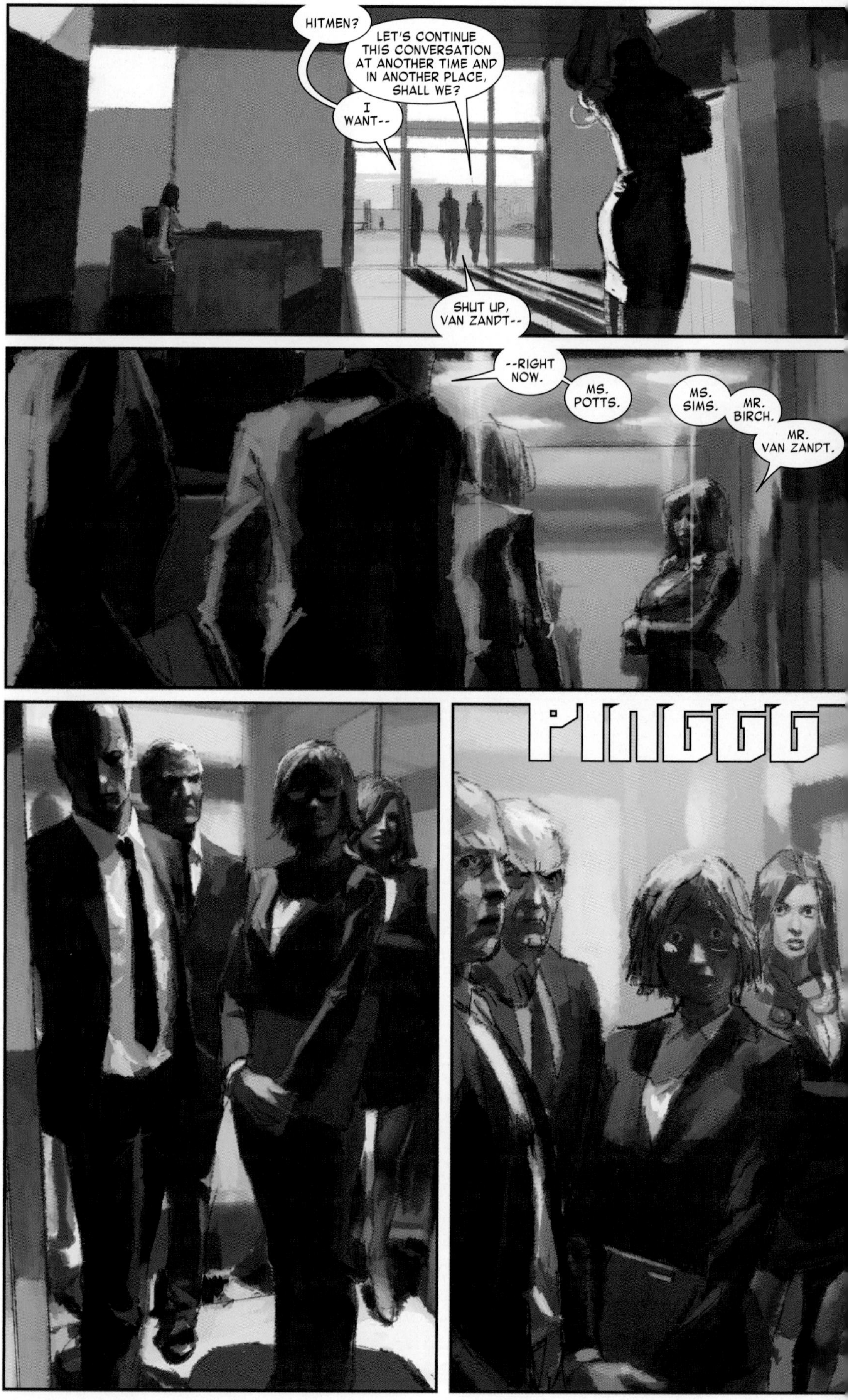
HITMEN?
I WANT--
LET'S CONTINUE THIS CONVERSATION AT ANOTHER TIME AND IN ANOTHER PLACE, SHALL WE?
SHUT UP, VAN ZANDT--
--RIGHT NOW.
MS. POTTS.
MS. SIMS.
MR. BIRCH.
MR. VAN ZANDT.
PINGGG

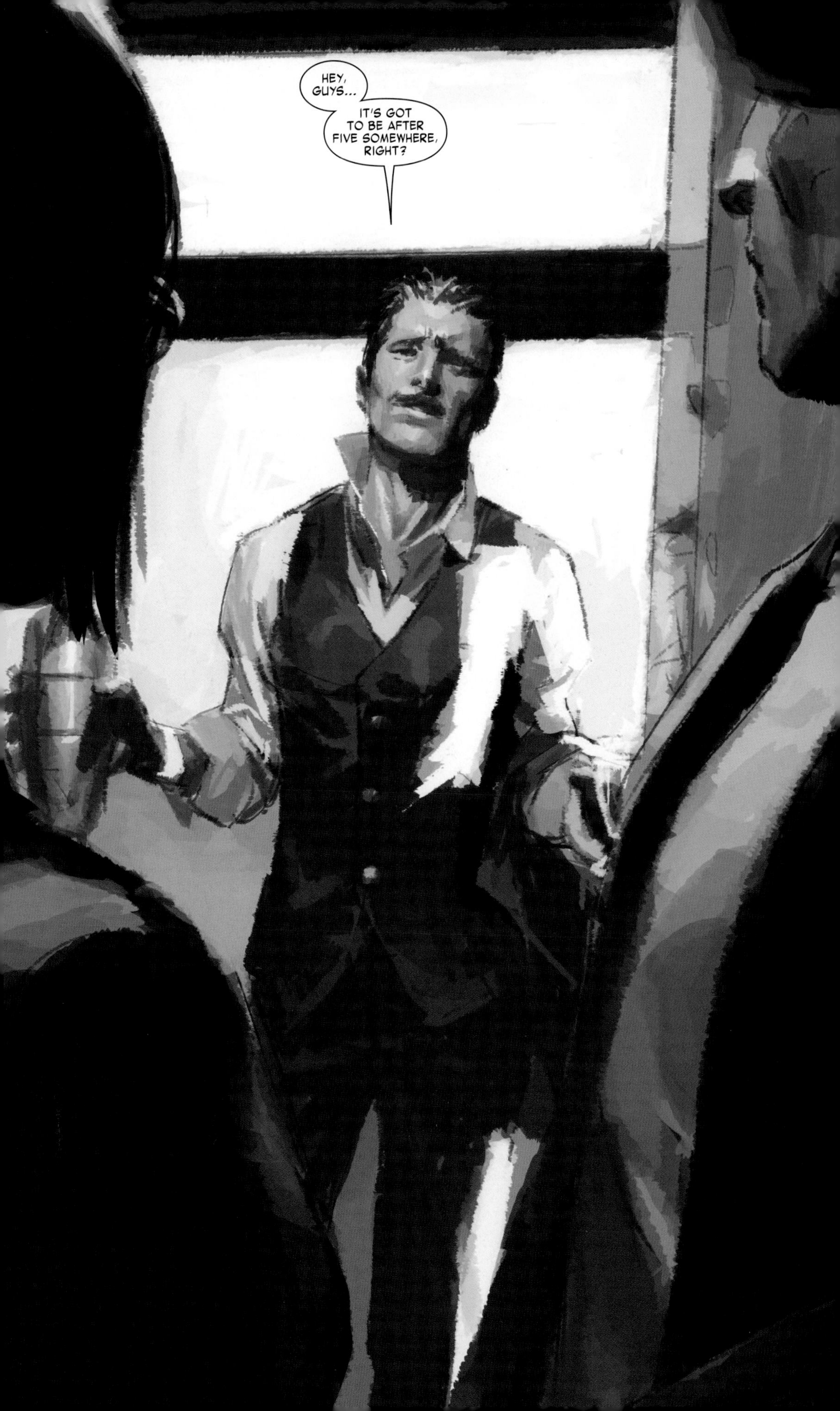
HEY, GUYS...
IT'S GOT TO BE AFTER FIVE SOMEWHERE, RIGHT?

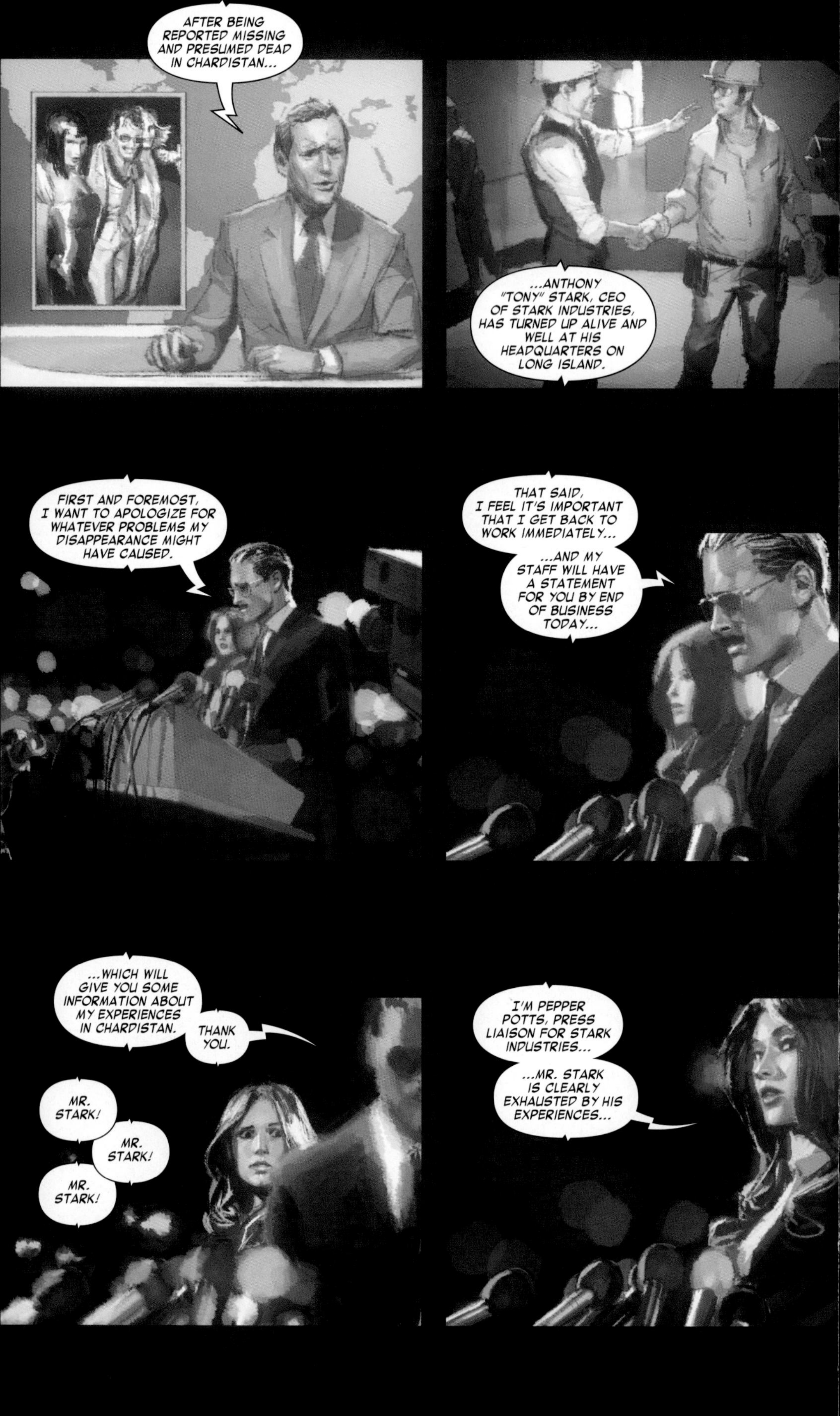
AFTER BEING REPORTED MISSING AND PRESUMED DEAD IN CHARDISTAN...
...ANTHONY "TONY" STARK, CEO OF STARK INDUSTRIES, HAS TURNED UP ALIVE AND WELL AT HIS HEADQUARTERS ON LONG ISLAND.
FIRST AND FOREMOST, I WANT TO APOLOGIZE FOR WHATEVER PROBLEMS MY DISAPPEARANCE MIGHT HAVE CAUSED.
THAT SAID, I FEEL IT'S IMPORTANT THAT I GET BACK TO WORK IMMEDIATELY...
...AND MY STAFF WILL HAVE A STATEMENT FOR YOU BY END OF BUSINESS TODAY...
...WHICH WILL GIVE YOU SOME INFORMATION ABOUT MY EXPERIENCES IN CHARDISTAN.
THANK YOU.
MR. STARK!
MR. STARK!
MR. STARK!
I'M PEPPER POTTS, PRESS LIAISON FOR STARK INDUSTRIES...
...MR. STARK IS CLEARLY EXHAUSTED BY HIS EXPERIENCES...

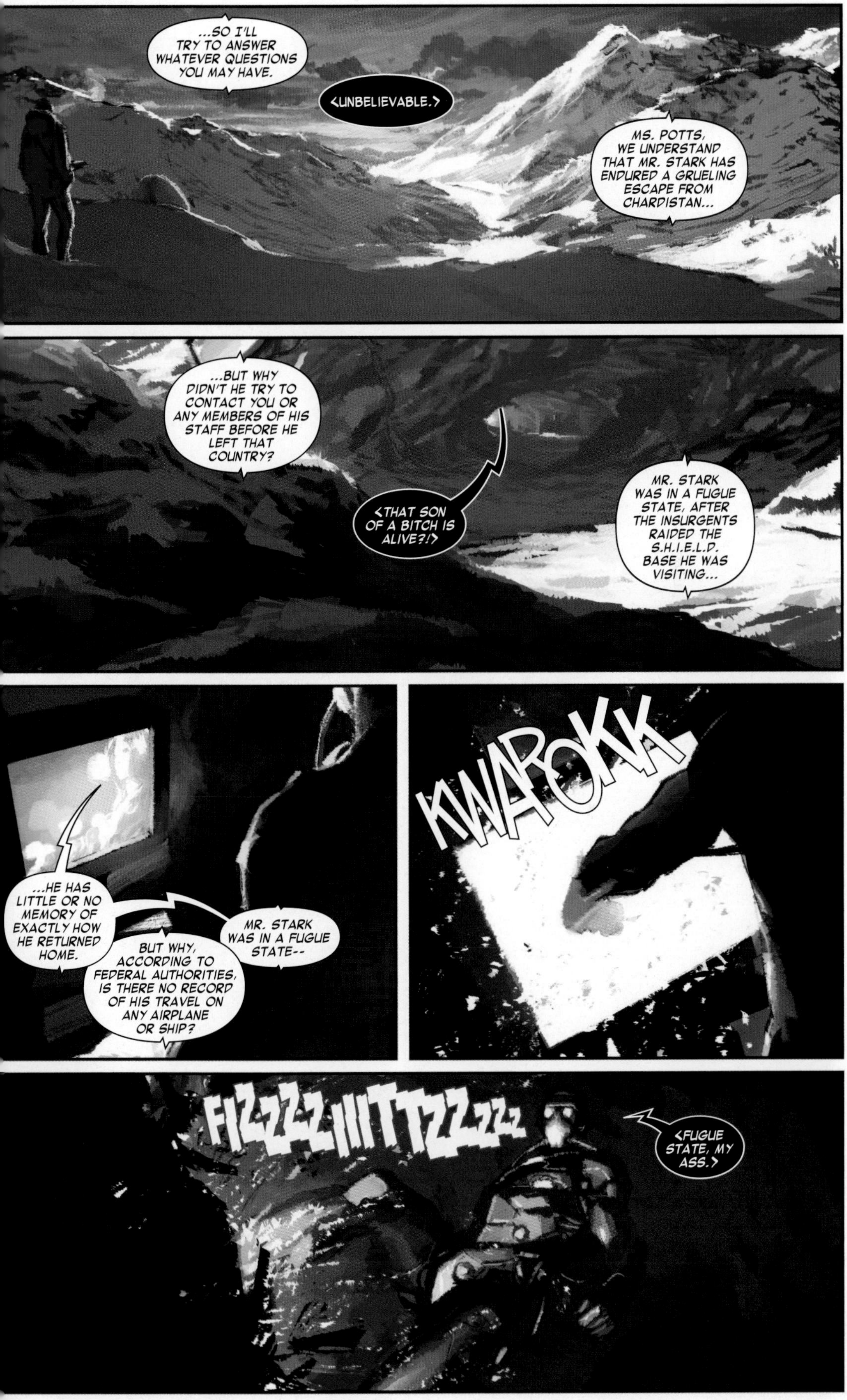
...SO I'LL TRY TO ANSWER WHATEVER QUESTIONS YOU MAY HAVE.
<UNBELIEVABLE.>
MS. POTTS, WE UNDERSTAND THAT MR. STARK HAS ENDURED A GRUELING ESCAPE FROM CHARDISTAN...
...BUT WHY DIDN'T HE TRY TO CONTACT YOU OR ANY MEMBERS OF HIS STAFF BEFORE HE LEFT THAT COUNTRY?
<THAT SON OF A BITCH IS ALIVE?!>
MR. STARK WAS IN A FUGUE STATE, AFTER THE INSURGENTS RAIDED THE S.H.I.E.L.D. BASE HE WAS VISITING...
MR. STARK WAS IN A FUGUE STATE--
...HE HAS LITTLE OR NO MEMORY OF EXACTLY HOW HE RETURNED HOME.
BUT WHY, ACCORDING TO FEDERAL AUTHORITIES, IS THERE NO RECORD OF HIS TRAVEL ON ANY AIRPLANE OR SHIP?
KWAROKK
FIZZZZZIIIITTZZZZZ
<FUGUE STATE, MY ASS.>

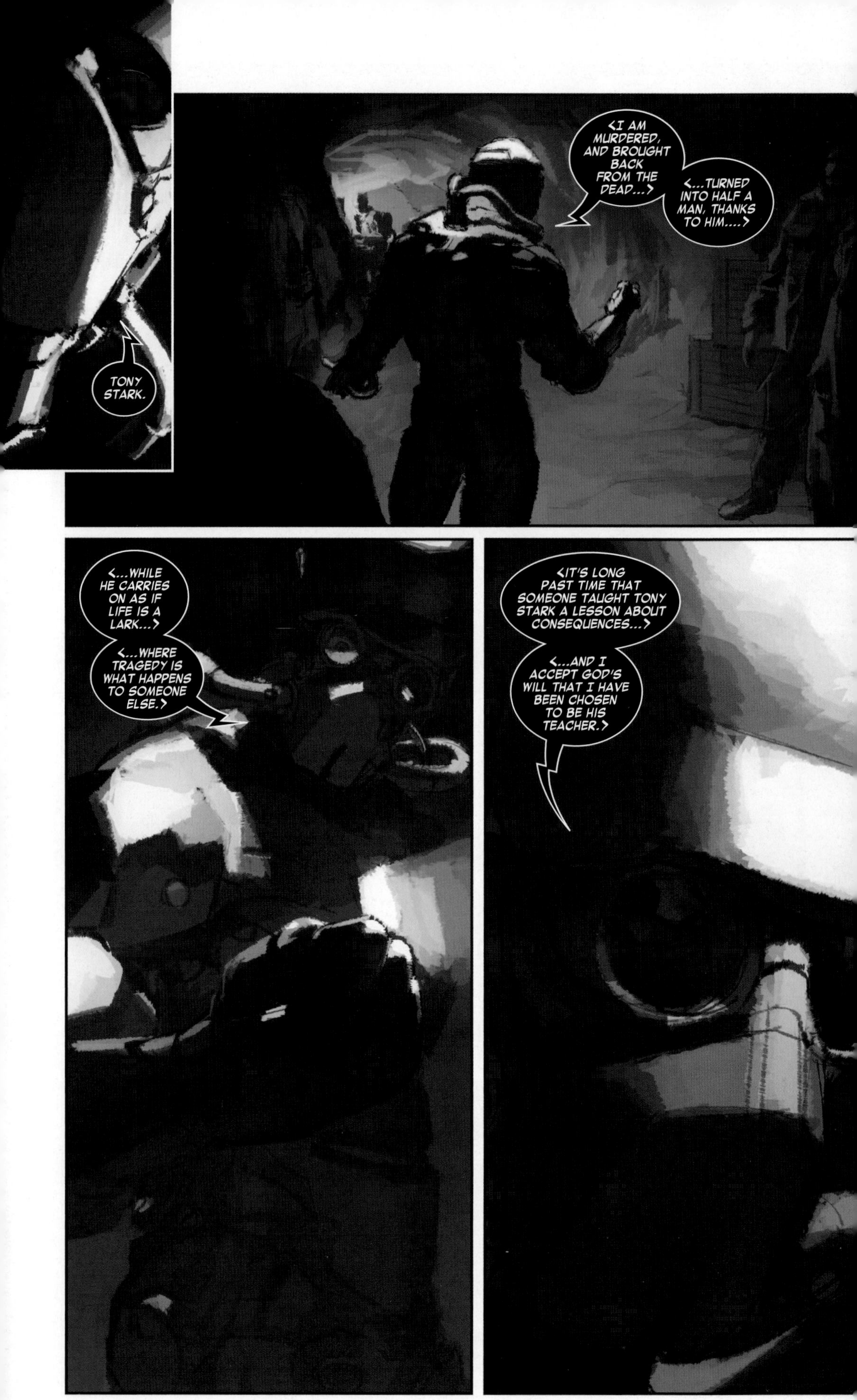
TONY STARK.
<I AM MURDERED, AND BROUGHT BACK FROM THE DEAD...>
<...TURNED INTO HALF A MAN, THANKS TO HIM....>
<...WHILE HE CARRIES ON AS IF LIFE IS A LARK...>
<...WHERE TRAGEDY IS WHAT HAPPENS TO SOMEONE ELSE.>
<IT'S LONG PAST TIME THAT SOMEONE TAUGHT TONY STARK A LESSON ABOUT CONSEQUENCES...>
<...AND I ACCEPT GOD'S WILL THAT I HAVE BEEN CHOSEN TO BE HIS TEACHER.>

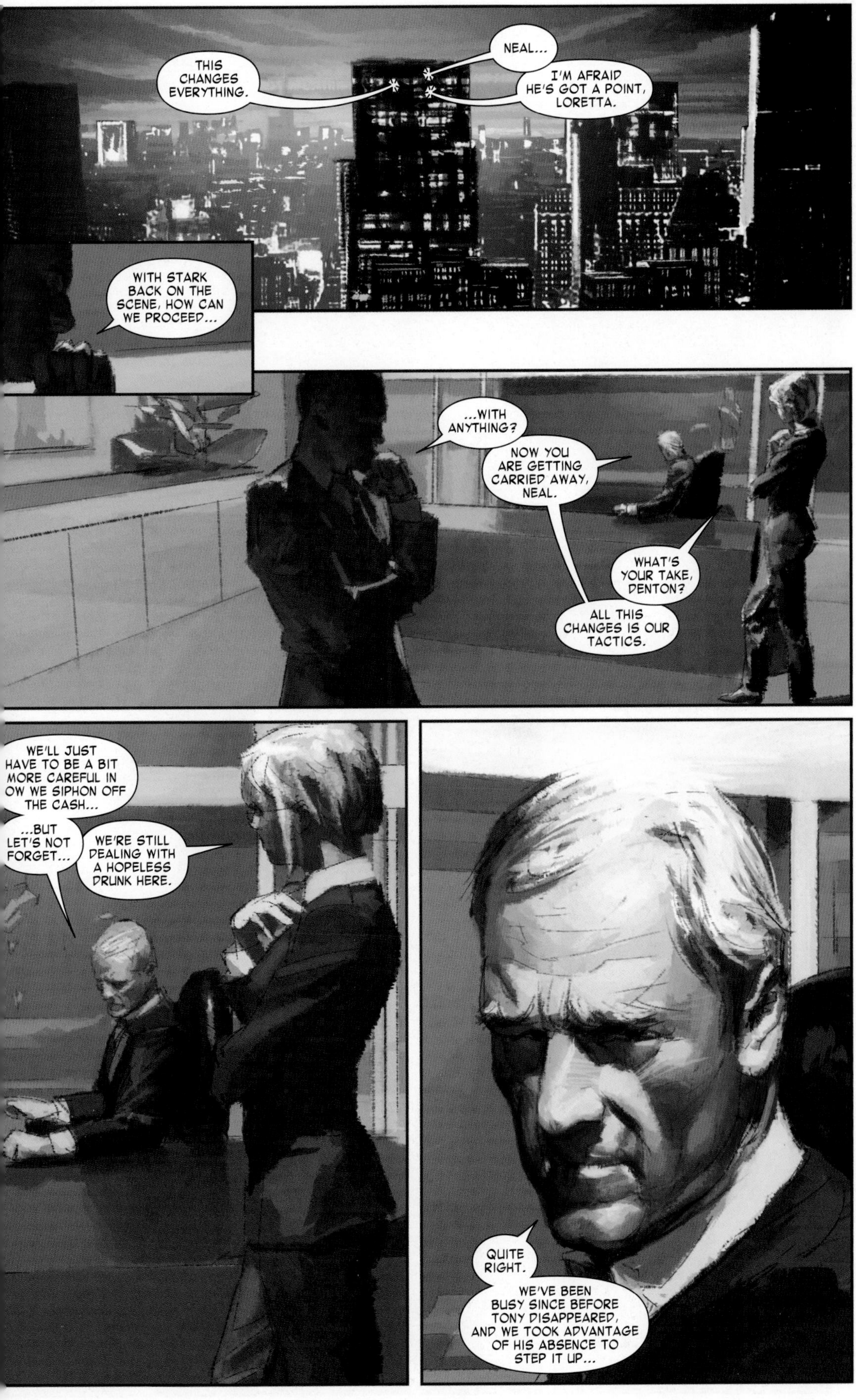
THIS CHANGES EVERYTHING.
NEAL...
I'M AFRAID HE'S GOT A POINT, LORETTA.
WITH STARK BACK ON THE SCENE, HOW CAN WE PROCEED...
...WITH ANYTHING?
NOW YOU ARE GETTING CARRIED AWAY, NEAL.
WHAT'S YOUR TAKE, DENTON?
ALL THIS CHANGES IS OUR TACTICS.
WE'LL JUST HAVE TO BE A BIT MORE CAREFUL IN OW WE SIPHON OFF THE CASH...
...BUT LET'S NOT FORGET...
WE'RE STILL DEALING WITH A HOPELESS DRUNK HERE.
QUITE RIGHT.
WE'VE BEEN BUSY SINCE BEFORE TONY DISAPPEARED, AND WE TOOK ADVANTAGE OF HIS ABSENCE TO STEP IT UP...

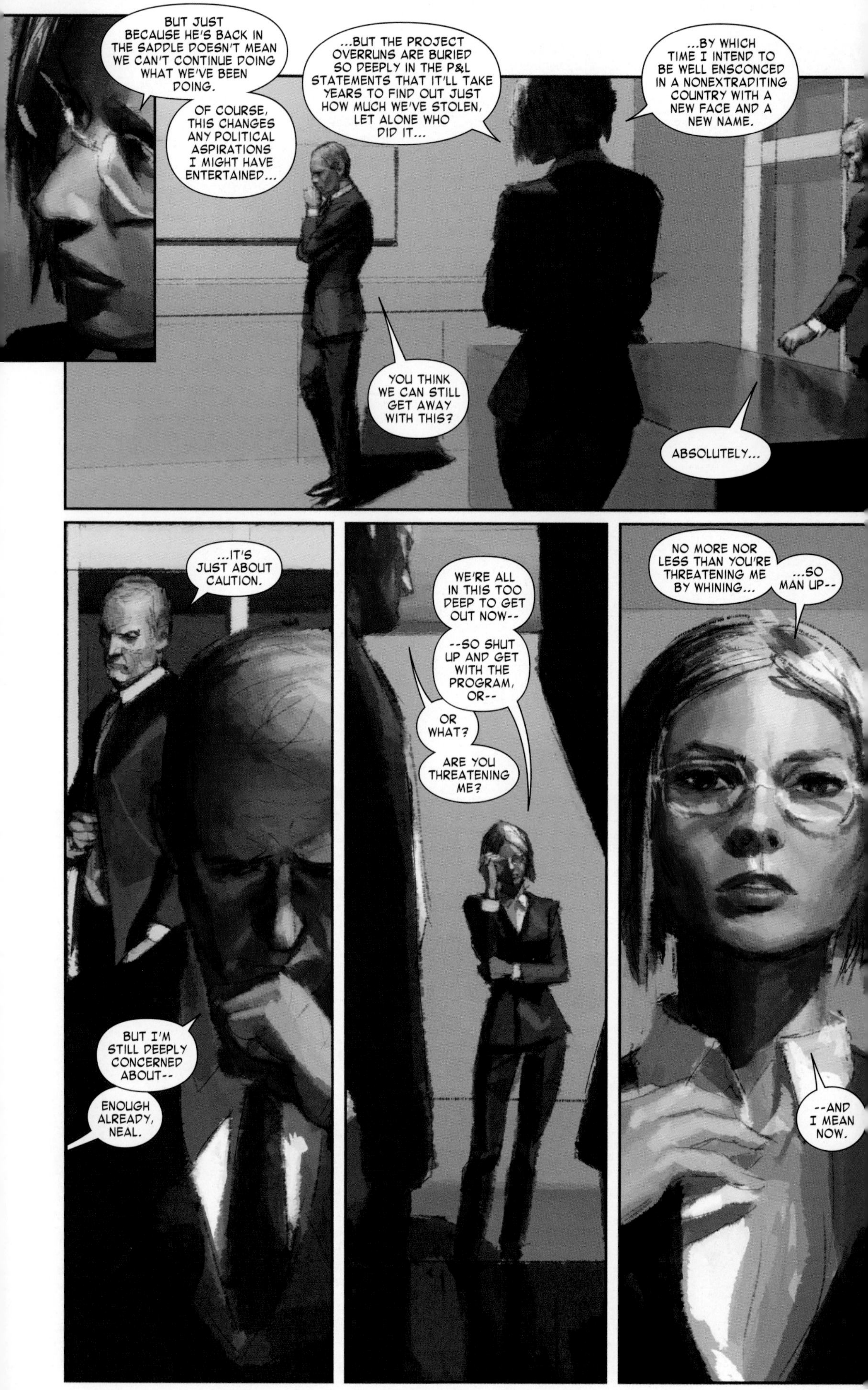

BUT JUST BECAUSE HE'S BACK IN THE SADDLE DOESN'T MEAN WE CAN'T CONTINUE DOING WHAT WE'VE BEEN DOING.
OF COURSE, THIS CHANGES ANY POLITICAL ASPIRATIONS I MIGHT HAVE ENTERTAINED...
...BUT THE PROJECT OVERRUNS ARE BURIED SO DEEPLY IN THE P&L STATEMENTS THAT IT'LL TAKE YEARS TO FIND OUT JUST HOW MUCH WE'VE STOLEN, LET ALONE WHO DID IT...
...BY WHICH TIME I INTEND TO BE WELL ENSCONCED IN A NONEXTRADITING COUNTRY WITH A NEW FACE AND A NEW NAME.
YOU THINK WE CAN STILL GET AWAY WITH THIS?
ABSOLUTELY...
...IT'S JUST ABOUT CAUTION.
BUT I'M STILL DEEPLY CONCERNED ABOUT--
ENOUGH ALREADY, NEAL.
WE'RE ALL IN THIS TOO DEEP TO GET OUT NOW--
--SO SHUT UP AND GET WITH THE PROGRAM, OR--
OR WHAT?
ARE YOU THREATENING ME?
NO MORE NOR LESS THAN YOU'RE THREATENING ME BY WHINING...
...SO MAN UP--
--AND I MEAN NOW.

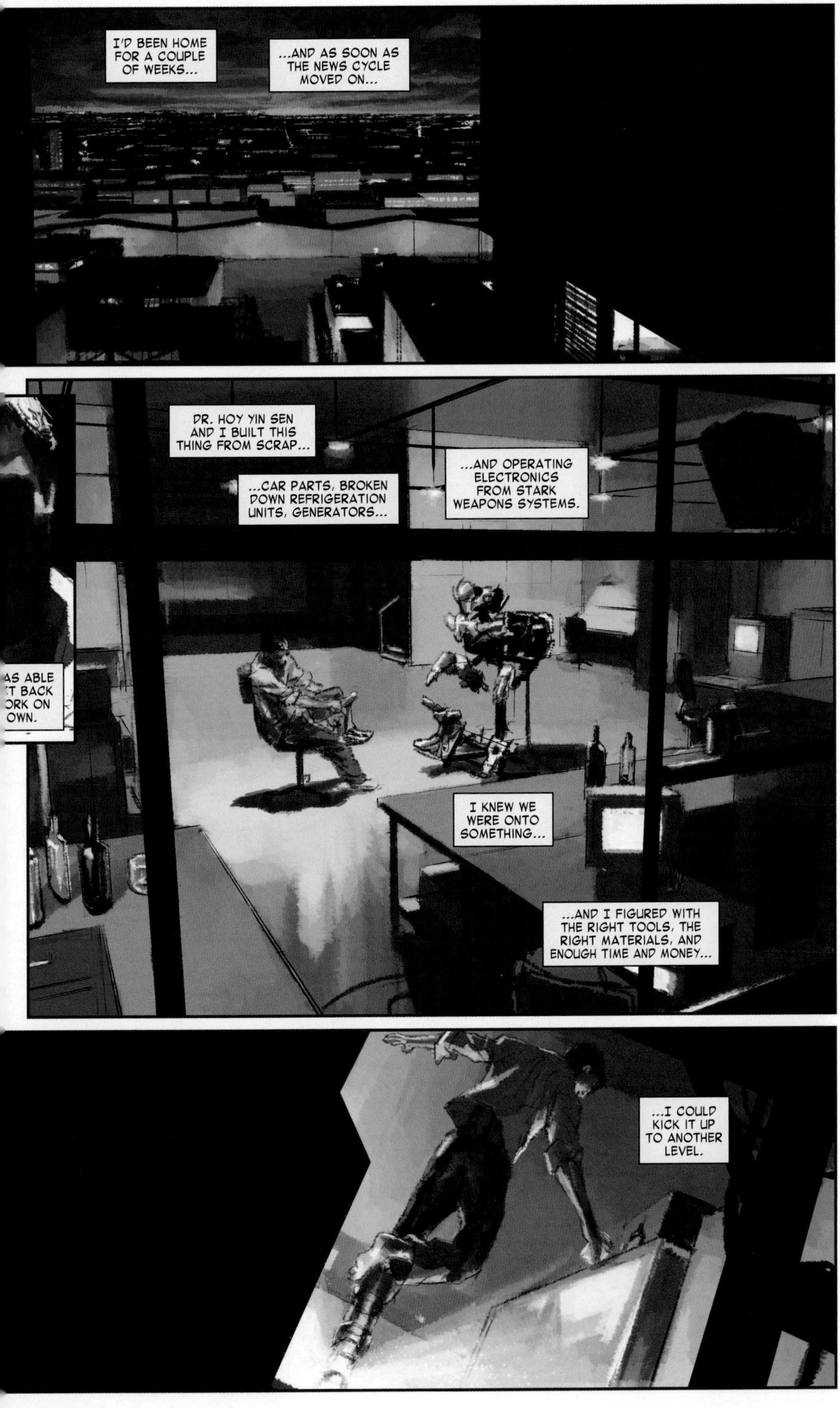
I'D BEEN HOME FOR A COUPLE OF WEEKS...
...AND AS SOON AS THE NEWS CYCLE MOVED ON...
DR. HOY YIN SEN AND I BUILT THIS THING FROM SCRAP...
...CAR PARTS, BROKEN DOWN REFRIGERATION UNITS, GENERATORS...
...AND OPERATING ELECTRONICS FROM STARK WEAPONS SYSTEMS.
I KNEW WE WERE ONTO SOMETHING...
...AND I FIGURED WITH THE RIGHT TOOLS, THE RIGHT MATERIALS, AND ENOUGH TIME AND MONEY...
...I COULD KICK IT UP TO ANOTHER LEVEL.

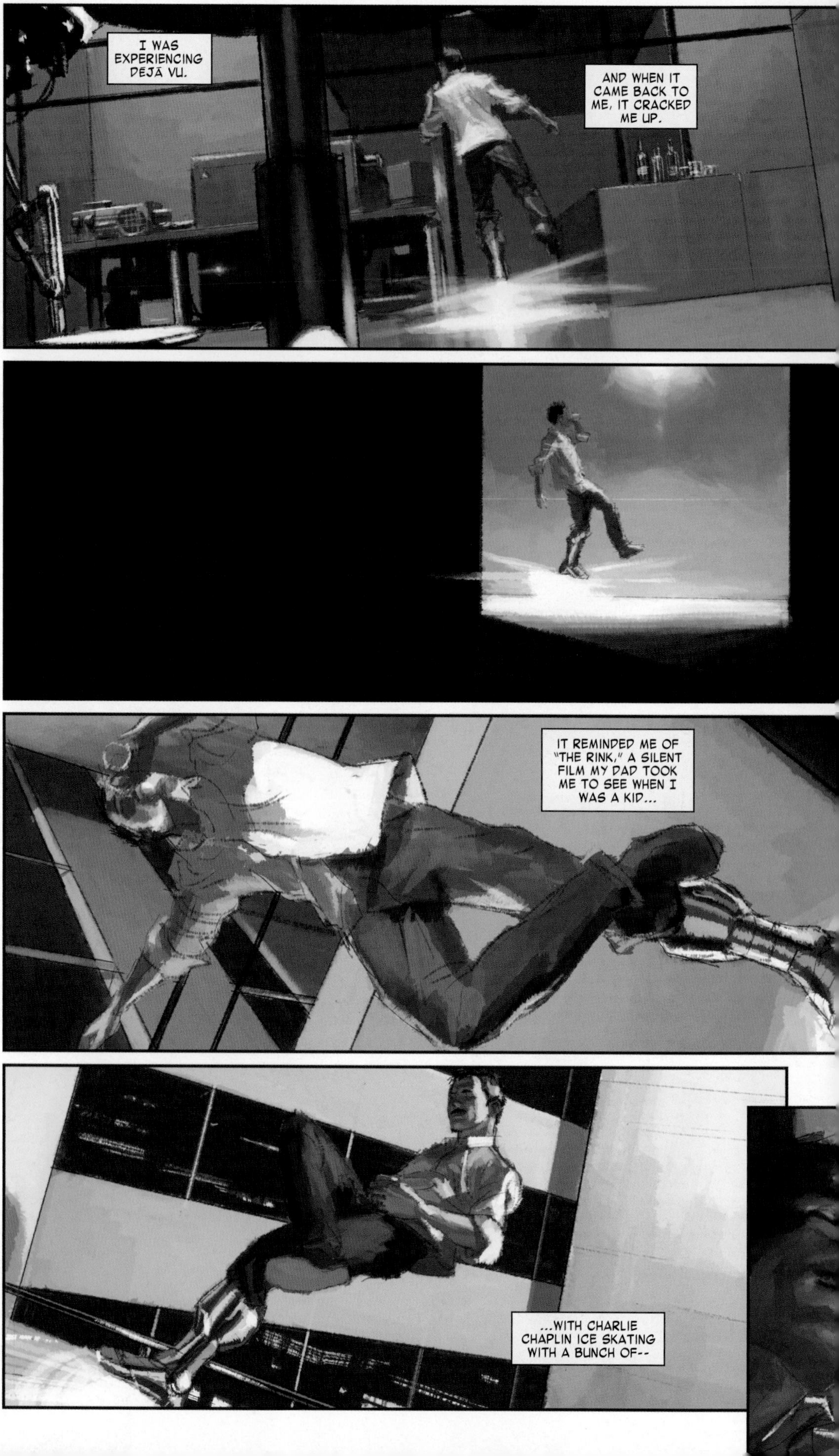
I WAS EXPERIENCING DÉJÀ VU.
AND WHEN IT CAME BACK TO ME, IT CRACKED ME UP.
IT REMINDED ME OF "THE RINK," A SILENT FILM MY DAD TOOK ME TO SEE WHEN I WAS A KID...
...WITH CHARLIE CHAPLIN ICE SKATING WITH A BUNCH OF--

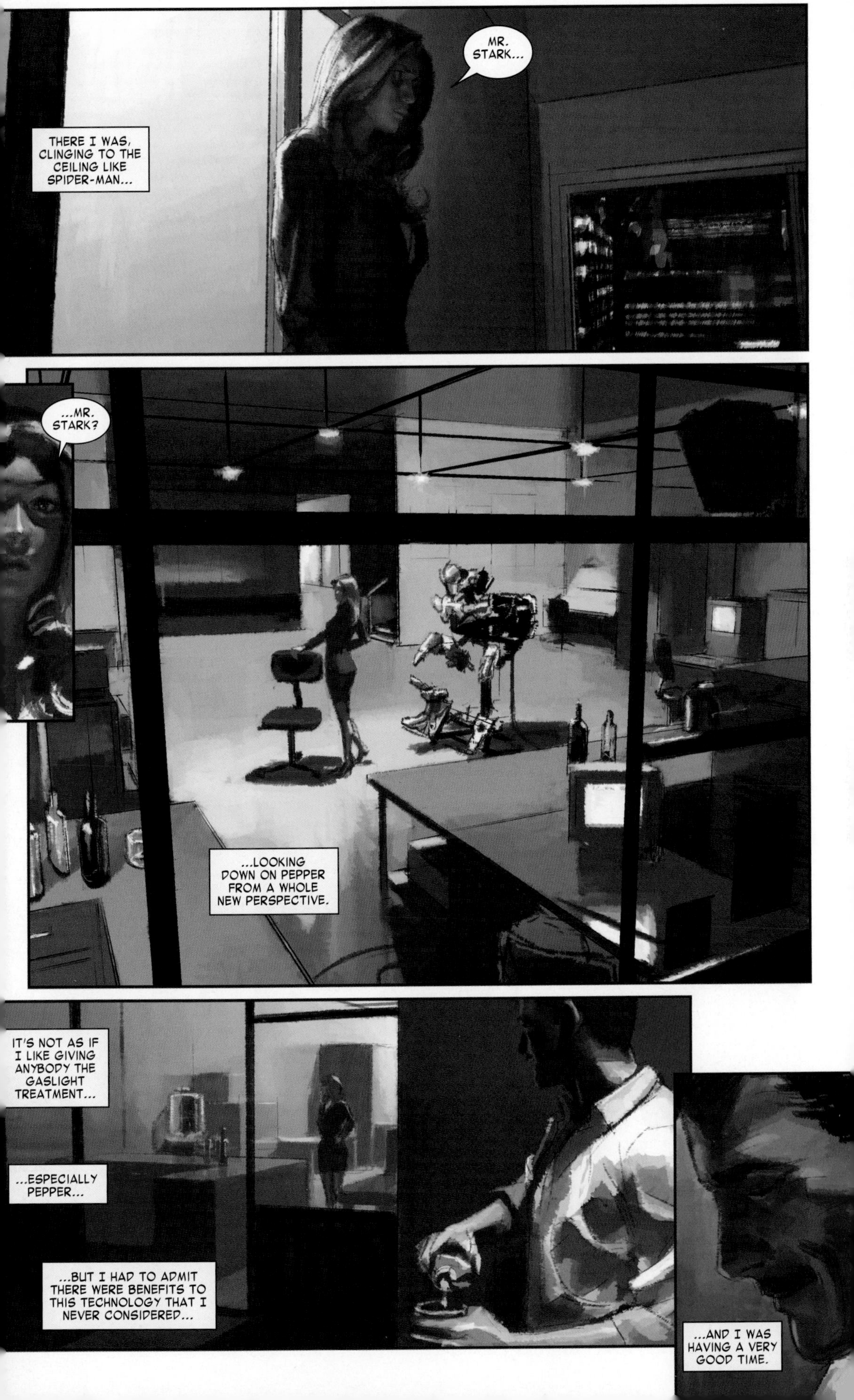
THERE I WAS, CLINGING TO THE CEILING LIKE SPIDER-MAN...
MR. STARK...
...MR. STARK?
...LOOKING DOWN ON PEPPER FROM A WHOLE NEW PERSPECTIVE.
IT'S NOT AS IF I LIKE GIVING ANYBODY THE GASLIGHT TREATMENT...
...ESPECIALLY PEPPER...
...BUT I HAD TO ADMIT THERE WERE BENEFITS TO THIS TECHNOLOGY THAT I NEVER CONSIDERED...
...AND I WAS HAVING A VERY GOOD TIME.

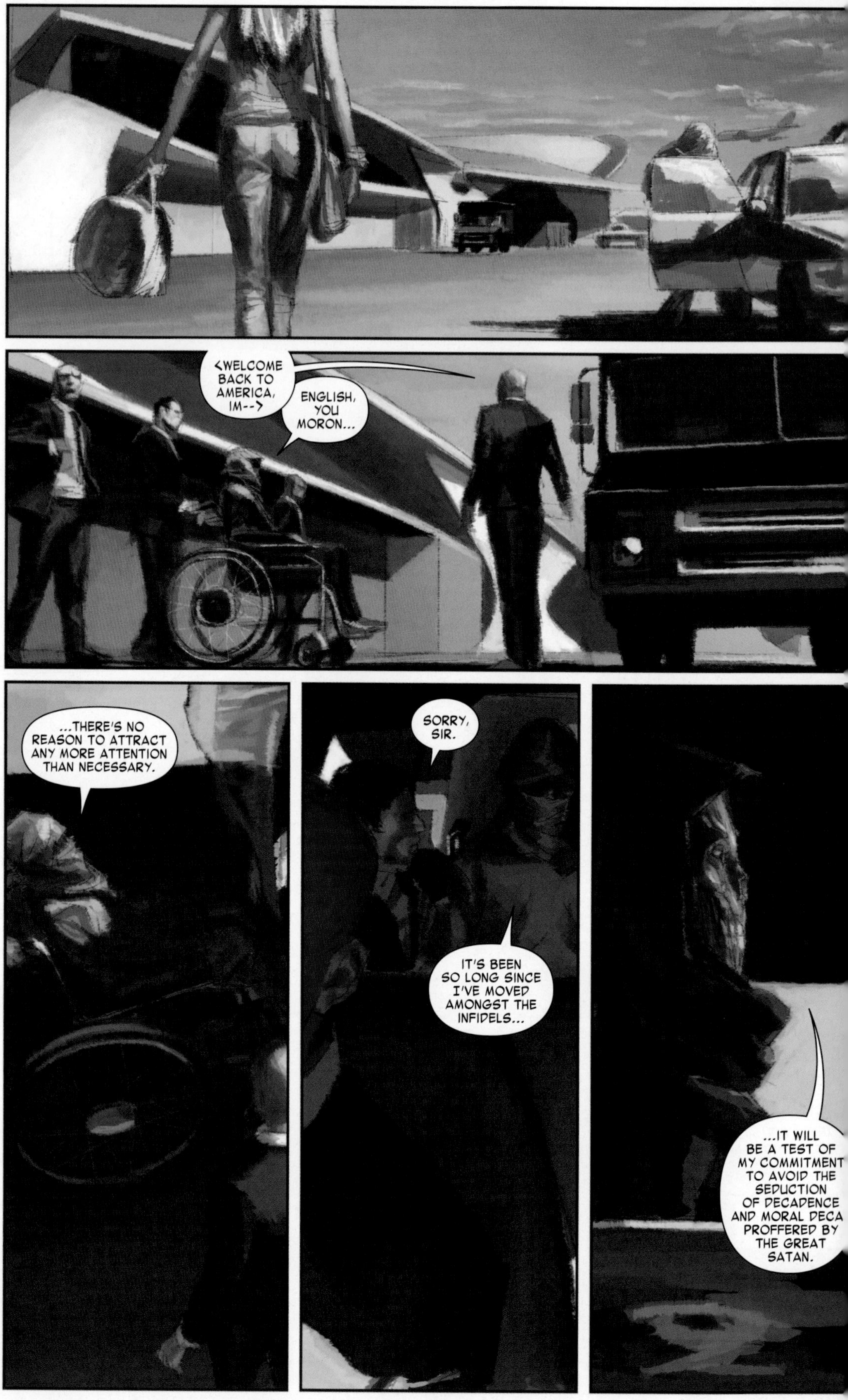

<WELCOME BACK TO AMERICA, IM-->
ENGLISH, YOU MORON...
...THERE'S NO REASON TO ATTRACT ANY MORE ATTENTION THAN NECESSARY.
SORRY, SIR.
IT'S BEEN SO LONG SINCE I'VE MOVED AMONGST THE INFIDELS...
...IT WILL BE A TEST OF MY COMMITMENT TO AVOID THE SEDUCTION OF DECADENCE AND MORAL DECA PROFFERED BY THE GREAT SATAN.

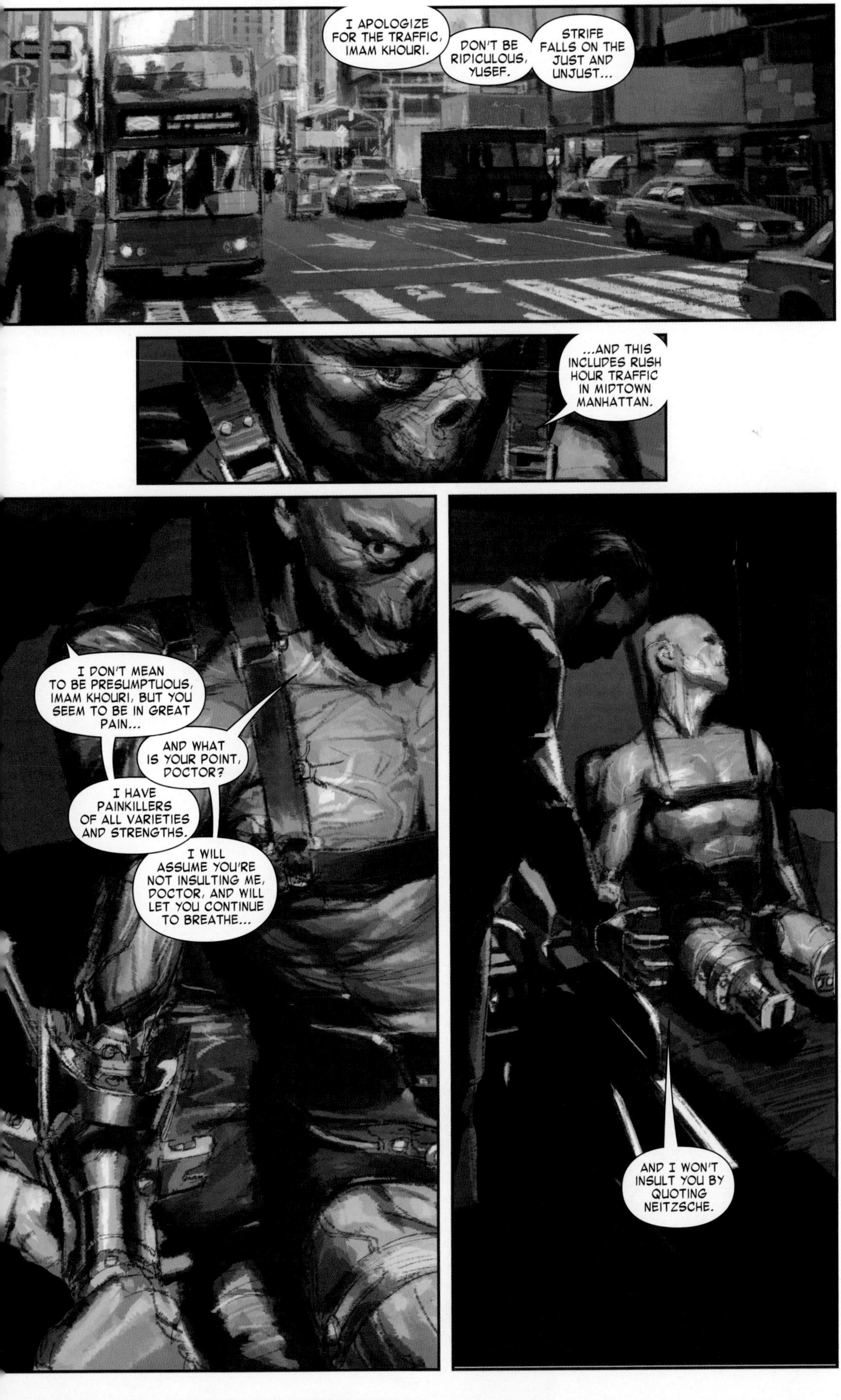
I APOLOGIZE FOR THE TRAFFIC, IMAM KHOURI.
DON'T BE RIDICULOUS, YUSEF.
STRIFE FALLS ON THE JUST AND UNJUST...
...AND THIS INCLUDES RUSH HOUR TRAFFIC IN MIDTOWN MANHATTAN.
I DON'T MEAN TO BE PRESUMPTUOUS, IMAM KHOURI, BUT YOU SEEM TO BE IN GREAT PAIN...
AND WHAT IS YOUR POINT, DOCTOR?
I HAVE PAINKILLERS OF ALL VARIETIES AND STRENGTHS.
I WILL ASSUME YOU'RE NOT INSULTING ME, DOCTOR, AND WILL LET YOU CONTINUE TO BREATHE...
AND I WON'T INSULT YOU BY QUOTING NEITZSCHE.

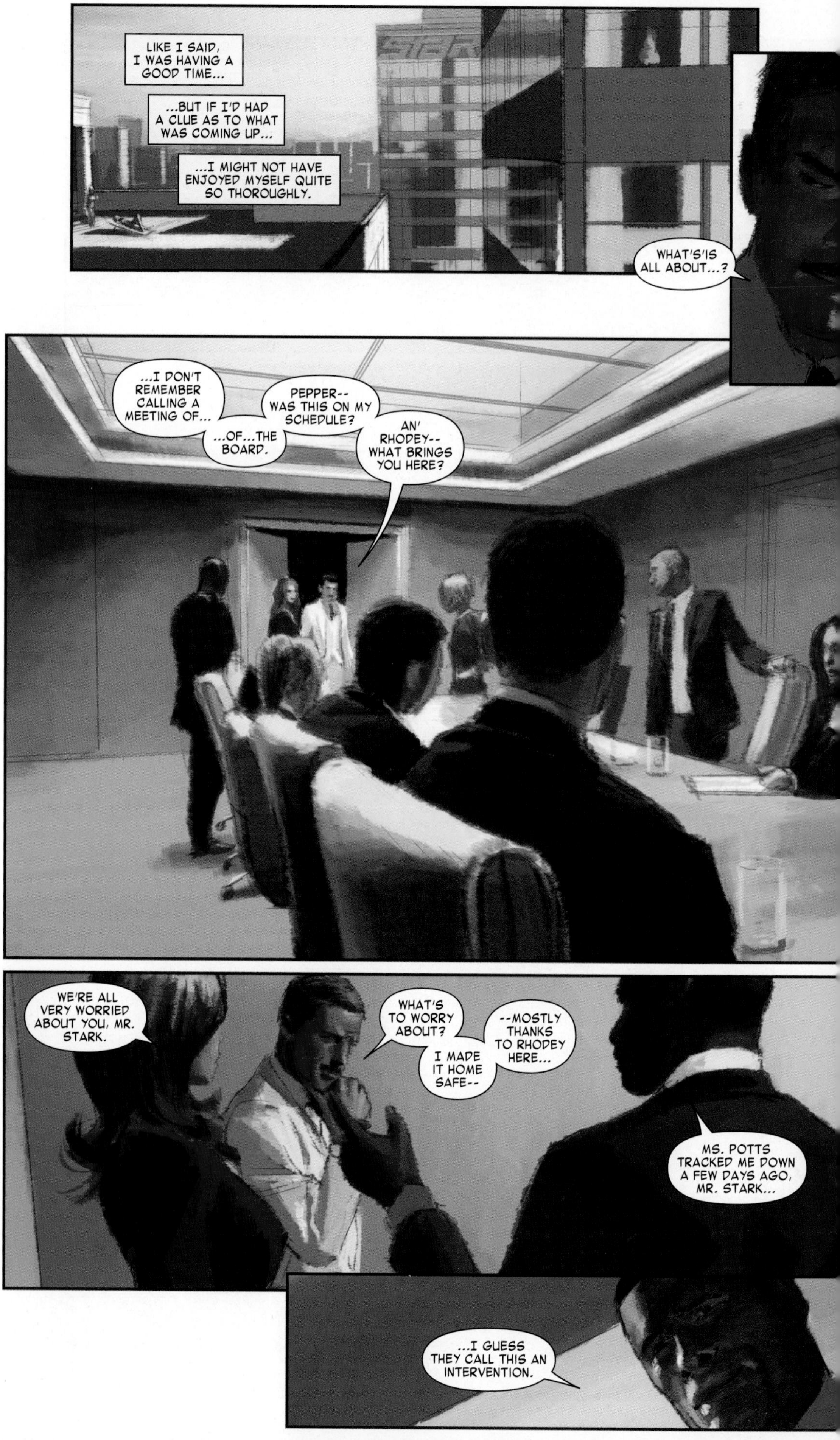

LIKE I SAID, I WAS HAVING A GOOD TIME...
...BUT IF I'D HAD A CLUE AS TO WHAT WAS COMING UP...
...I MIGHT NOT HAVE ENJOYED MYSELF QUITE SO THOROUGHLY.
WHAT'S'IS ALL ABOUT...?
...I DON'T REMEMBER CALLING A MEETING OF...
...OF...THE BOARD.
PEPPER--WAS THIS ON MY SCHEDULE?
AN' RHODEY--WHAT BRINGS YOU HERE?
WE'RE ALL VERY WORRIED ABOUT YOU, MR. STARK.
WHAT'S TO WORRY ABOUT?
I MADE IT HOME SAFE--
--MOSTLY THANKS TO RHODEY HERE...
MS. POTTS TRACKED ME DOWN A FEW DAYS AGO, MR. STARK...
...I GUESS THEY CALL THIS AN INTERVENTION.

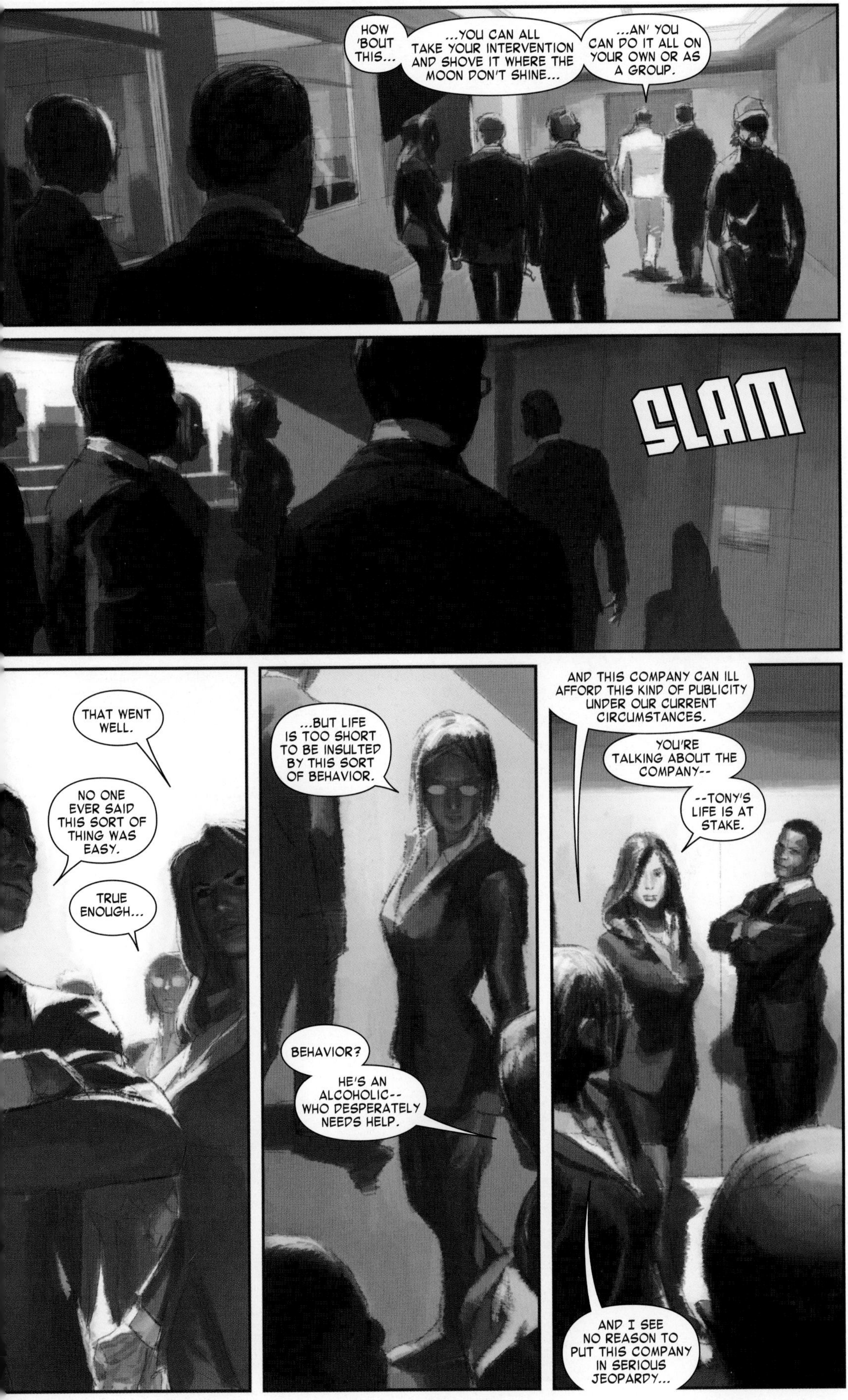
HOW 'BOUT THIS...
...YOU CAN ALL TAKE YOUR INTERVENTION AND SHOVE IT WHERE THE MOON DON'T SHINE...
...AN' YOU CAN DO IT ALL ON YOUR OWN OR AS A GROUP.
SLAM
THAT WENT WELL.
NO ONE EVER SAID THIS SORT OF THING WAS EASY.
TRUE ENOUGH...
...BUT LIFE IS TOO SHORT TO BE INSULTED BY THIS SORT OF BEHAVIOR.
BEHAVIOR?
HE'S AN ALCOHOLIC-- WHO DESPERATELY NEEDS HELP.
AND THIS COMPANY CAN ILL AFFORD THIS KIND OF PUBLICITY UNDER OUR CURRENT CIRCUMSTANCES.
YOU'RE TALKING ABOUT THE COMPANY--
--TONY'S LIFE IS AT STAKE.
AND I SEE NO REASON TO PUT THIS COMPANY IN SERIOUS JEOPARDY...

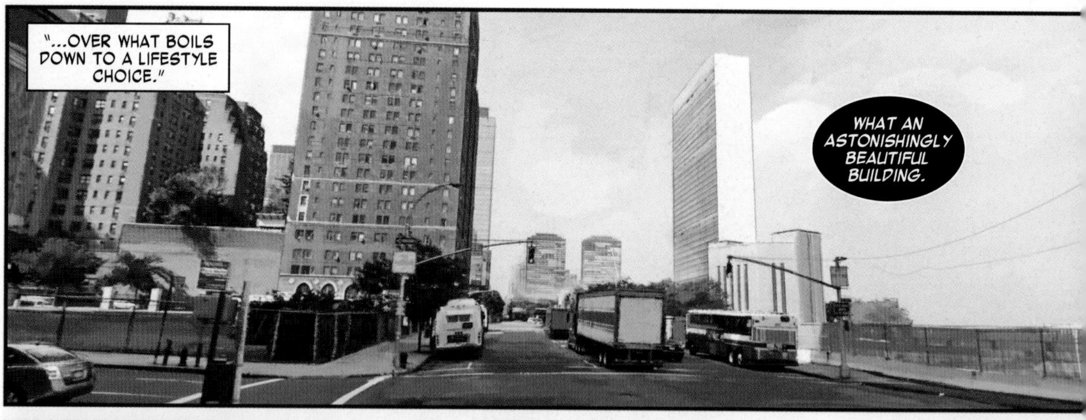
"...OVER WHAT BOILS DOWN TO A LIFESTYLE CHOICE."
WHAT AN ASTONISHINGLY BEAUTIFUL BUILDING.

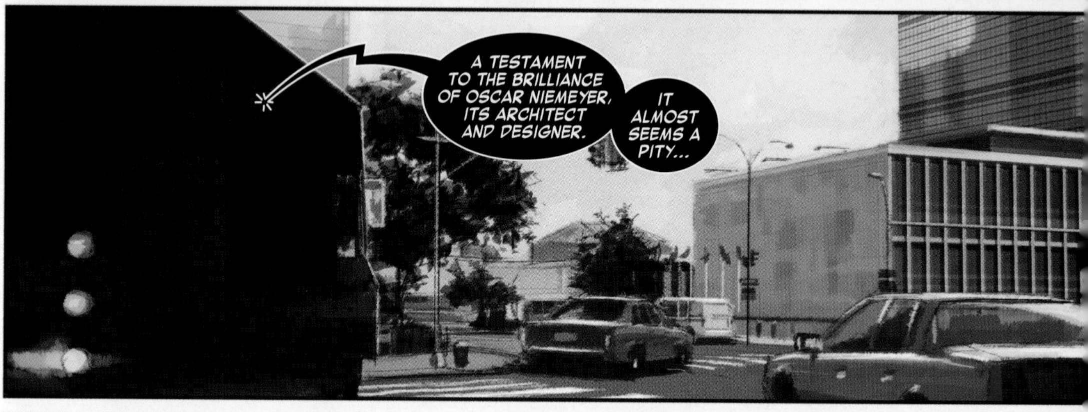
A TESTAMENT TO THE BRILLIANCE OF OSCAR NIEMEYER, ITS ARCHITECT AND DESIGNER.
IT ALMOST SEEMS A PITY...

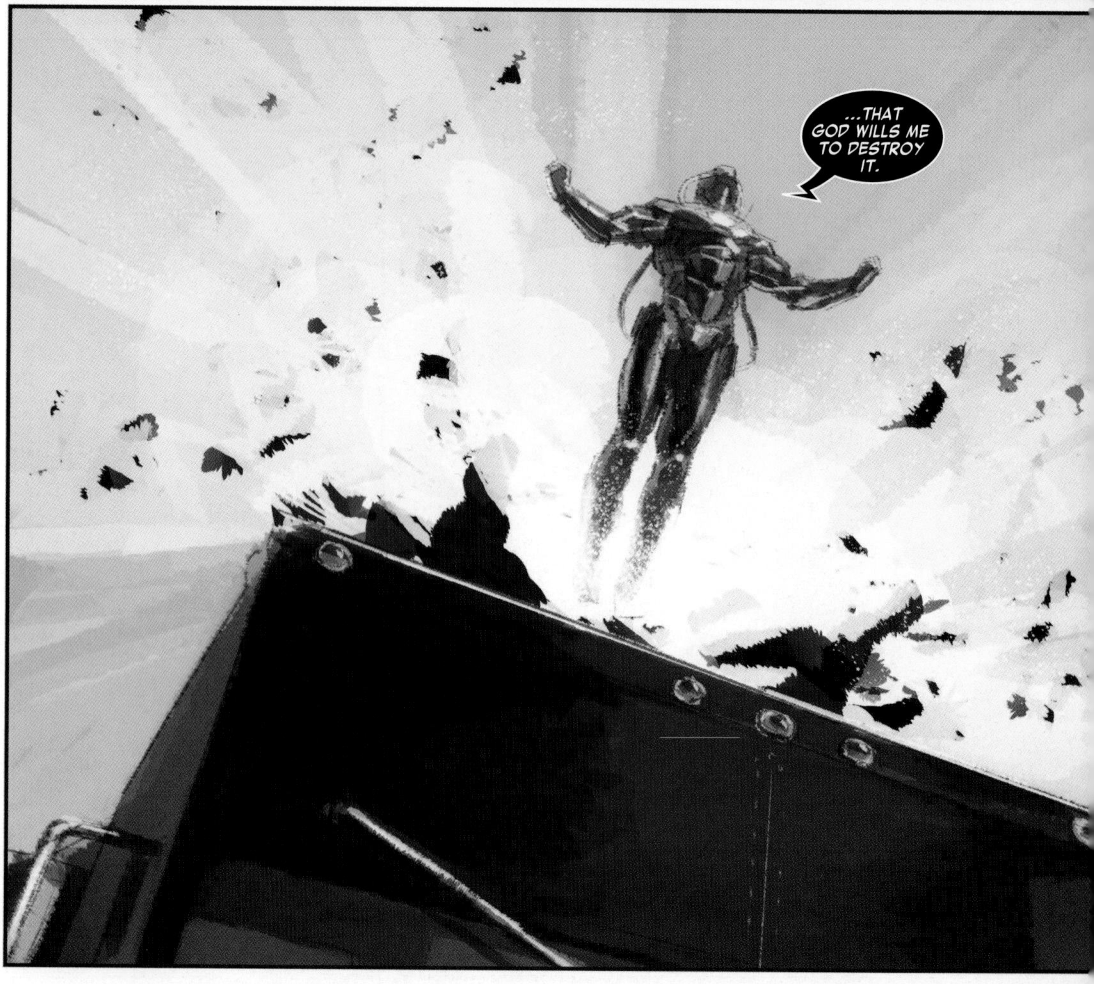
...THAT GOD WILLS ME TO DESTROY IT.

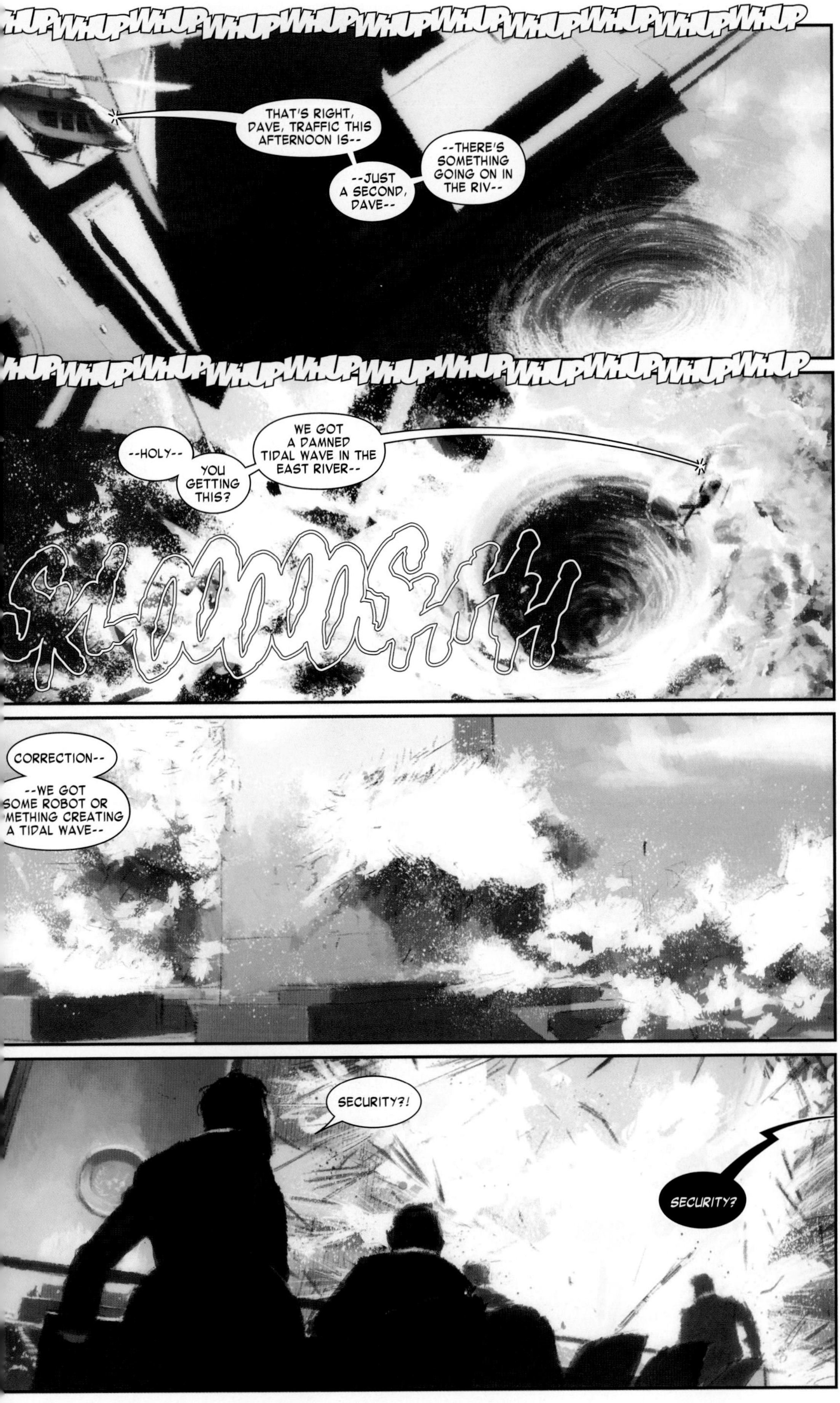
WHUPWHUPWHUPWHUPWHUPWHUPWHUPWHUPWHUPWHUPWHUP
THAT'S RIGHT, DAVE, TRAFFIC THIS AFTERNOON IS--
--JUST A SECOND, DAVE--
--THERE'S SOMETHING GOING ON IN THE RIV--
WHUPWHUPWHUPWHUPWHUPWHUPWHUPWHUPWHUPWHUPWHUP
--HOLY--
YOU GETTING THIS?
WE GOT A DAMNED TIDAL WAVE IN THE EAST RIVER--
SPLOOOOSHHH
CORRECTION--
--WE GOT SOME ROBOT OR METHING CREATING A TIDAL WAVE--
SECURITY?!
SECURITY?

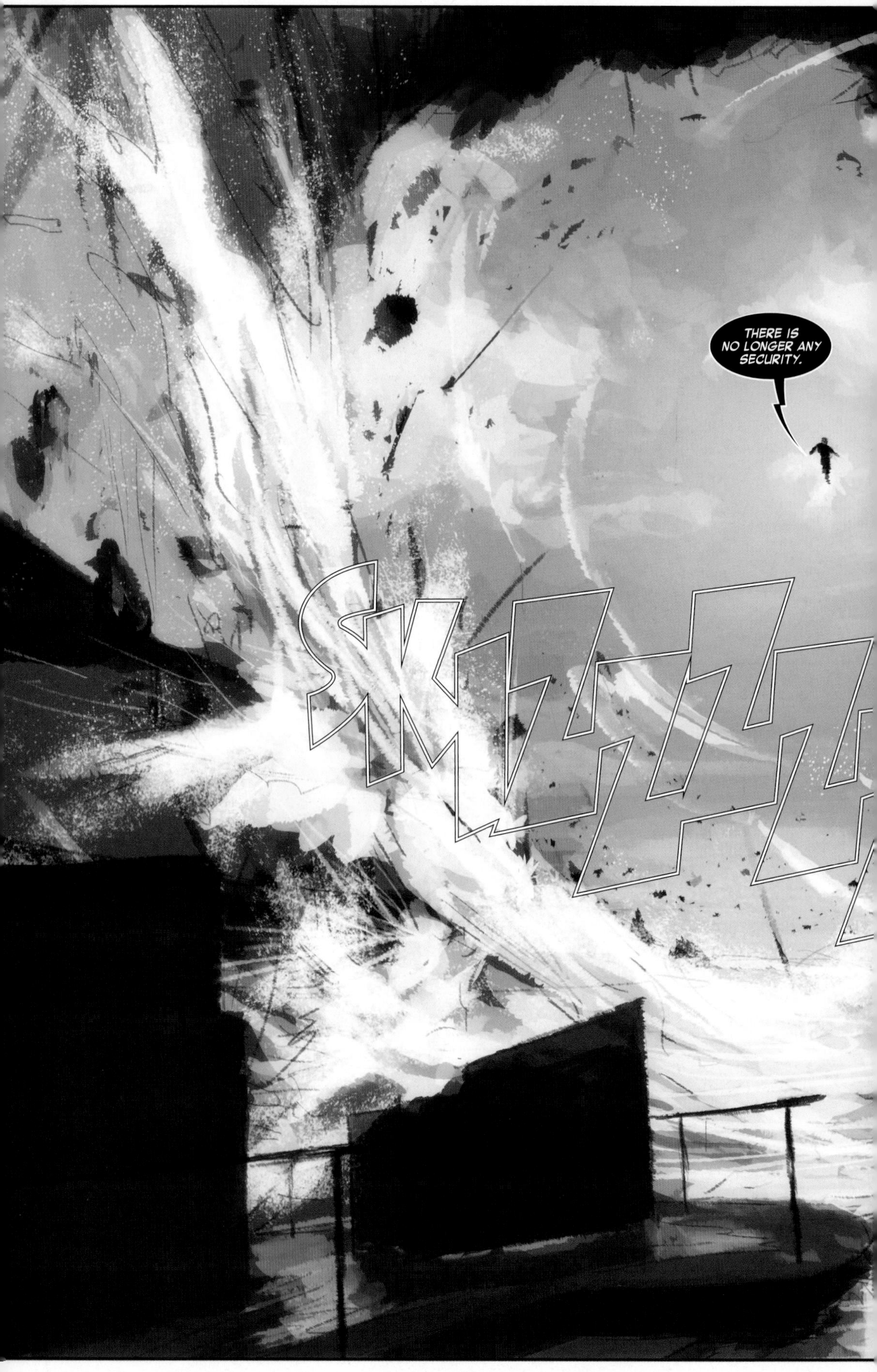
THERE IS NO LONGER ANY SECURITY.
SKZZZZZ

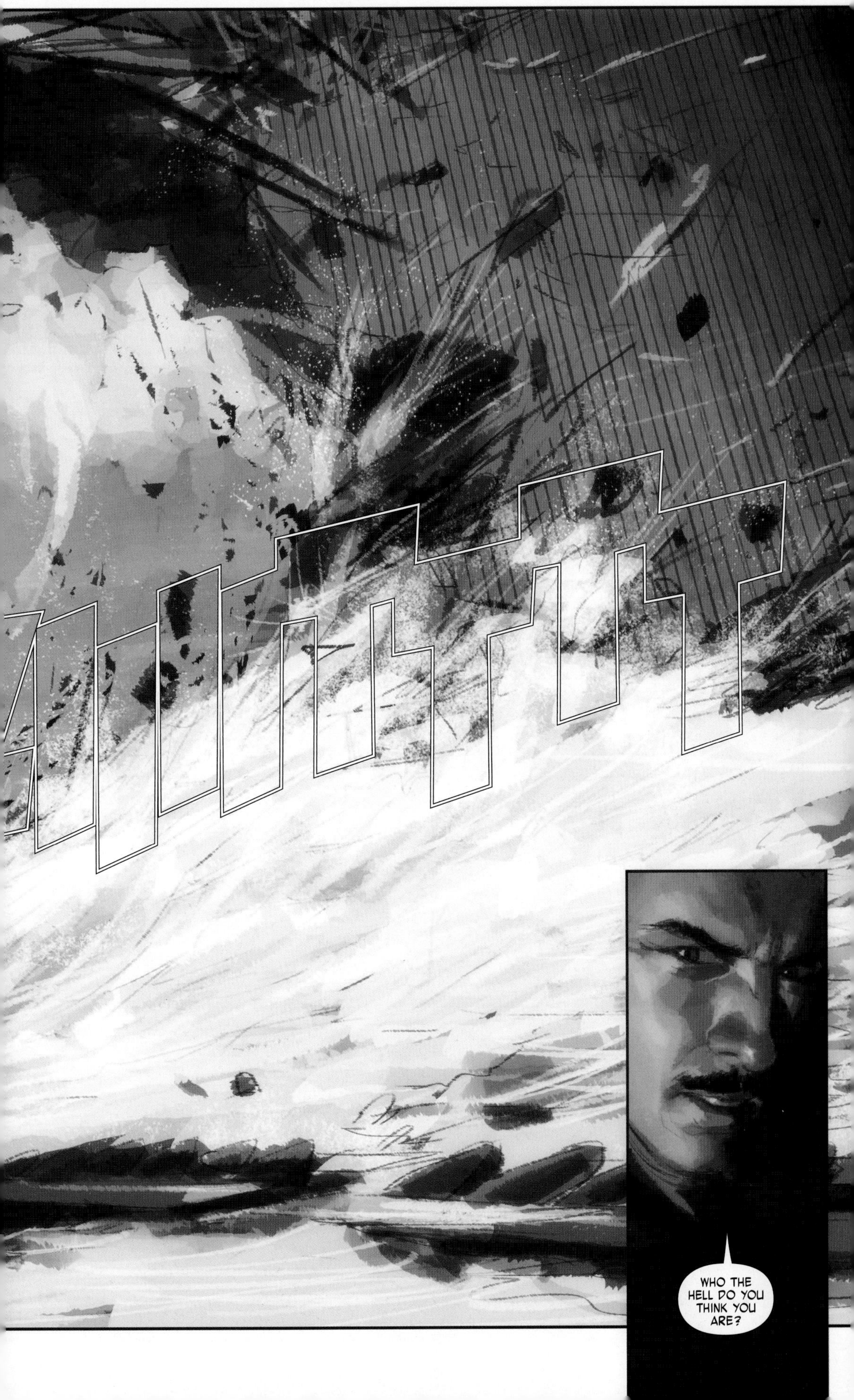
WHO THE HELL DO YOU THINK YOU ARE?

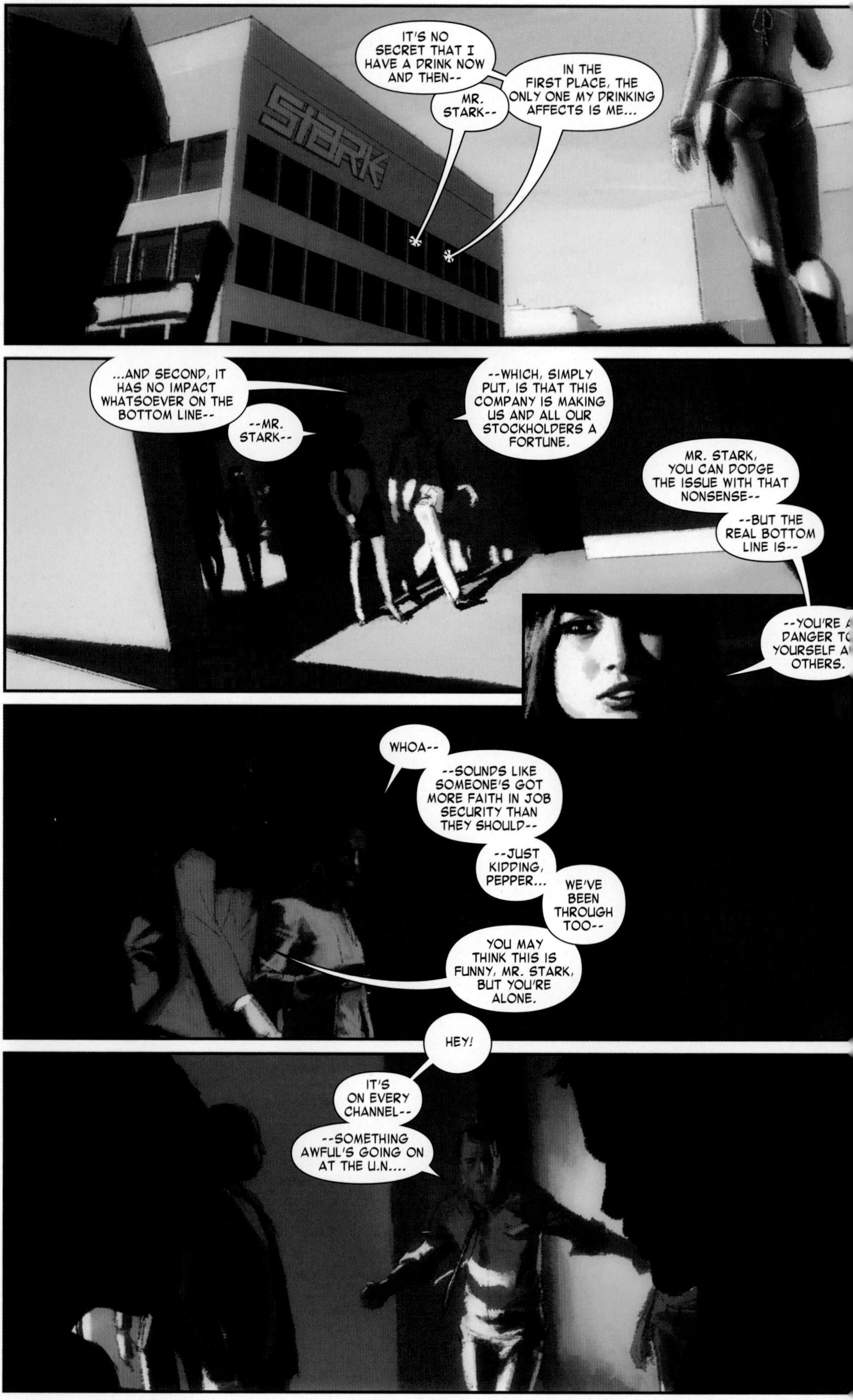
IT'S NO SECRET THAT I HAVE A DRINK NOW AND THEN--
MR. STARK--
IN THE FIRST PLACE, THE ONLY ONE MY DRINKING AFFECTS IS ME...
...AND SECOND, IT HAS NO IMPACT WHATSOEVER ON THE BOTTOM LINE--
--MR. STARK--
--WHICH, SIMPLY PUT, IS THAT THIS COMPANY IS MAKING US AND ALL OUR STOCKHOLDERS A FORTUNE.
MR. STARK, YOU CAN DODGE THE ISSUE WITH THAT NONSENSE--
--BUT THE REAL BOTTOM LINE IS--
WHOA--
--SOUNDS LIKE SOMEONE'S GOT MORE FAITH IN JOB SECURITY THAN THEY SHOULD--
--JUST KIDDING, PEPPER...
WE'VE BEEN THROUGH TOO--
YOU MAY THINK THIS IS FUNNY, MR. STARK, BUT YOU'RE ALONE.
HEY!
IT'S ON EVERY CHANNEL--
--SOMETHING AWFUL'S GOING ON AT THE U.N....

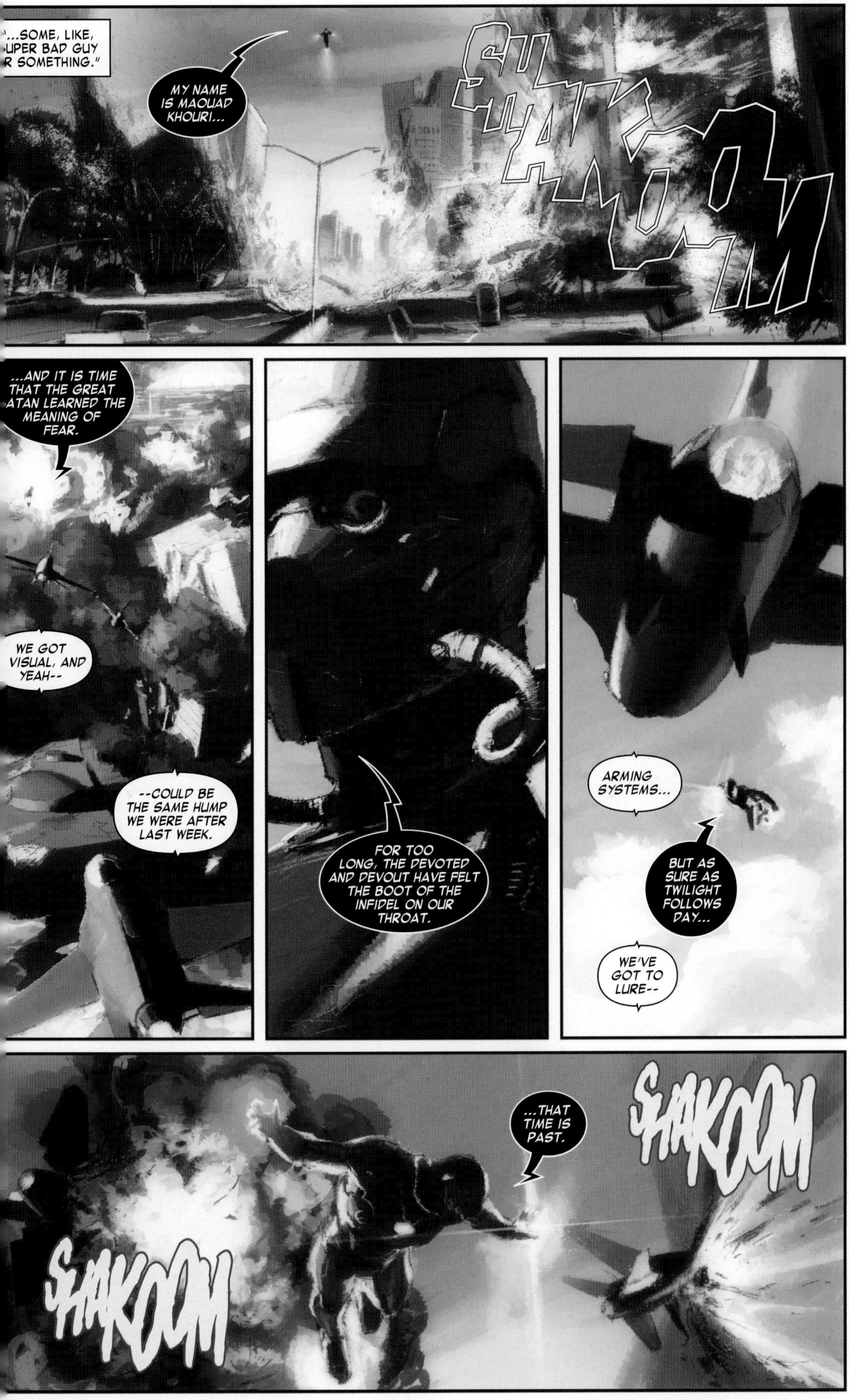
"...SOME, LIKE,
SUPER BAD GUY
OR SOMETHING."
MY NAME IS MAOUAD KHOURI...
SHAKOOM
...AND IT IS TIME THAT THE GREAT SATAN LEARNED THE MEANING OF FEAR.
WE GOT VISUAL, AND YEAH--
--COULD BE THE SAME HUMP WE WERE AFTER LAST WEEK.
FOR TOO LONG, THE DEVOTED AND DEVOUT HAVE FELT THE BOOT OF THE INFIDEL ON OUR THROAT.
ARMING SYSTEMS...
BUT AS SURE AS TWILIGHT FOLLOWS DAY...
WE'VE GOT TO LURE--
...THAT TIME IS PAST.
SHAKOOM
SHAKOOM

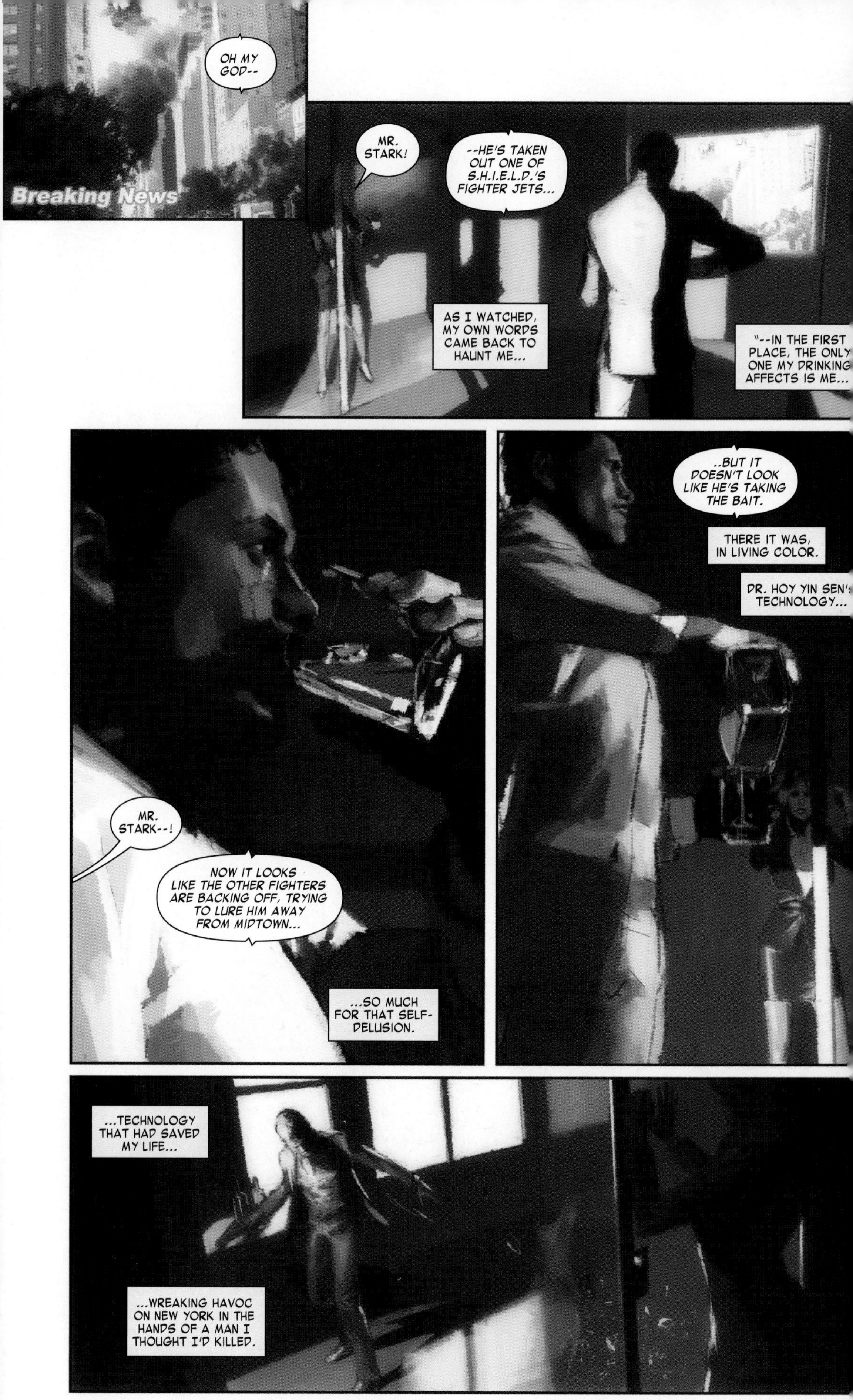

Breaking News
OH MY GOD--
MR. STARK!
--HE'S TAKEN OUT ONE OF S.H.I.E.L.D.'S FIGHTER JETS...
AS I WATCHED, MY OWN WORDS CAME BACK TO HAUNT ME...
"--IN THE FIRST PLACE, THE ONLY ONE MY DRINKING AFFECTS IS ME...
MR. STARK--!
NOW IT LOOKS LIKE THE OTHER FIGHTERS ARE BACKING OFF, TRYING TO LURE HIM AWAY FROM MIDTOWN...
...SO MUCH FOR THAT SELF-DELUSION.
..BUT IT DOESN'T LOOK LIKE HE'S TAKING THE BAIT.
THERE IT WAS, IN LIVING COLOR.
DR. HOY YIN SEN'S TECHNOLOGY...
...TECHNOLOGY THAT HAD SAVED MY LIFE...
...WREAKING HAVOC ON NEW YORK IN THE HANDS OF A MAN I THOUGHT I'D KILLED.

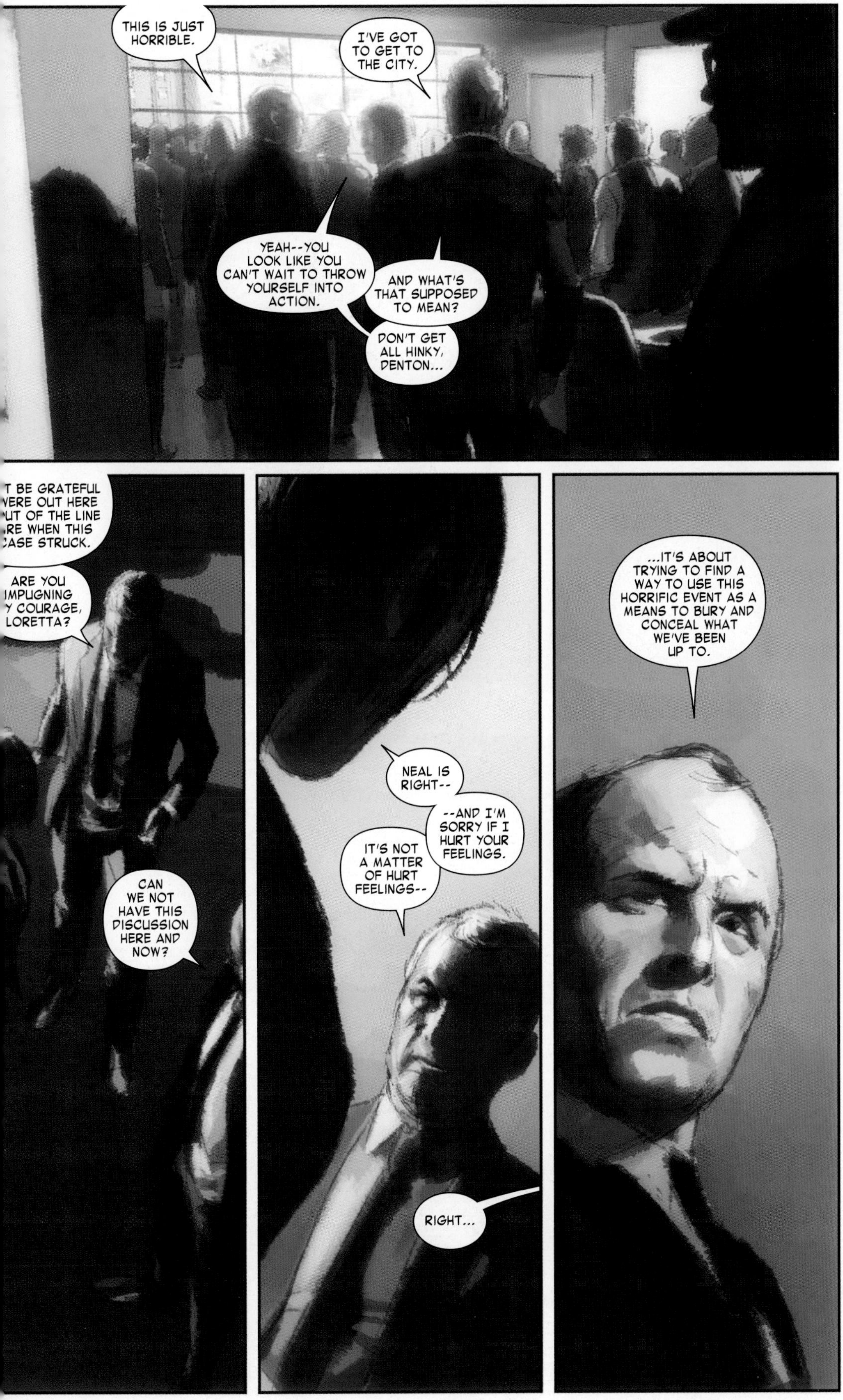
THIS IS JUST HORRIBLE.
I'VE GOT TO GET TO THE CITY.
YEAH--YOU LOOK LIKE YOU CAN'T WAIT TO THROW YOURSELF INTO ACTION.
AND WHAT'S THAT SUPPOSED TO MEAN?
DON'T GET ALL HINKY, DENTON...
T BE GRATEFUL VERE OUT HERE UT OF THE LINE RE WHEN THIS CASE STRUCK.
ARE YOU IMPUGNING Y COURAGE, LORETTA?
CAN WE NOT HAVE THIS DISCUSSION HERE AND NOW?
NEAL IS RIGHT--
--AND I'M SORRY IF I HURT YOUR FEELINGS.
IT'S NOT A MATTER OF HURT FEELINGS--
...IT'S ABOUT TRYING TO FIND A WAY TO USE THIS HORRIFIC EVENT AS A MEANS TO BURY AND CONCEAL WHAT WE'VE BEEN UP TO.
RIGHT...

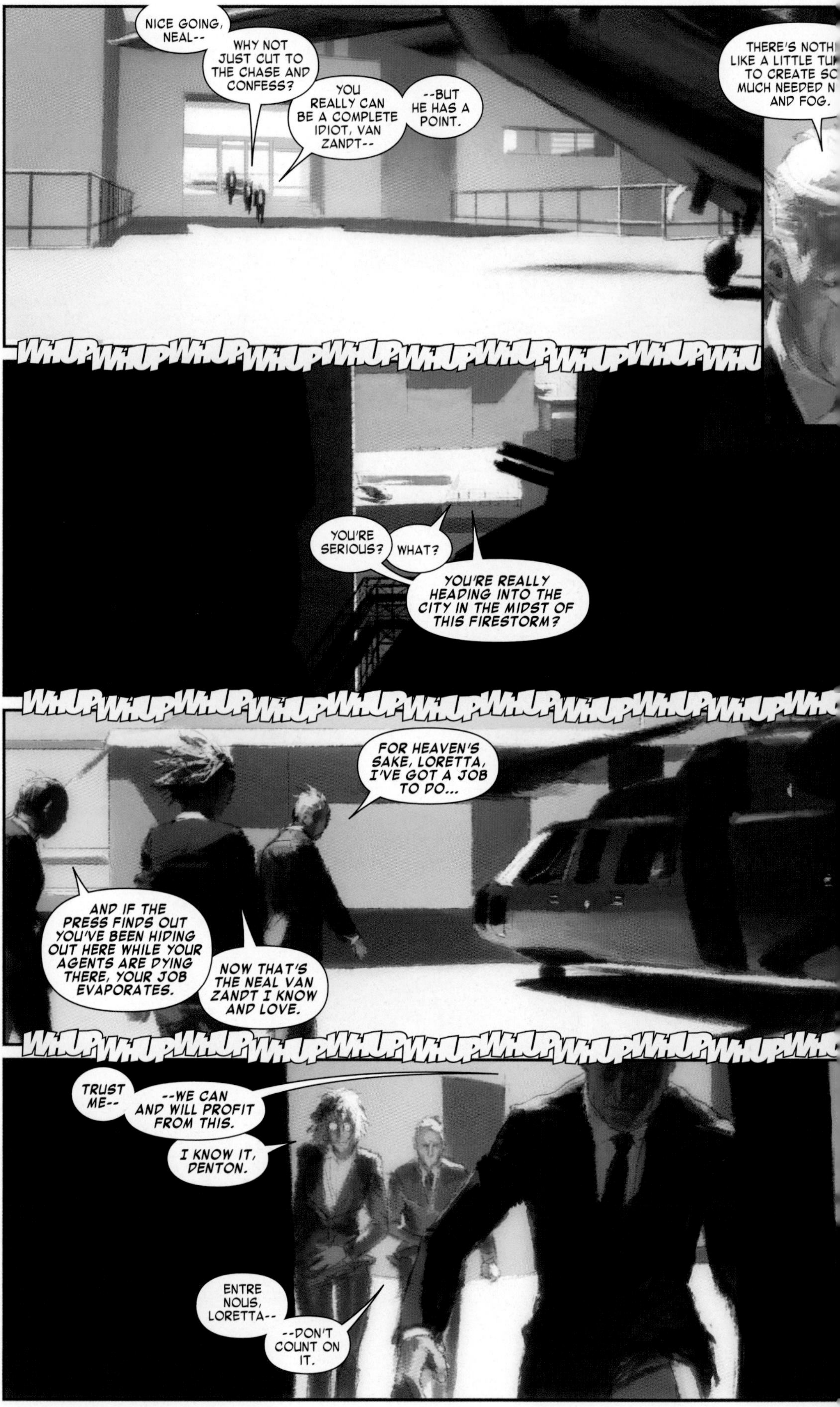
NICE GOING, NEAL--
WHY NOT JUST CUT TO THE CHASE AND CONFESS?
YOU REALLY CAN BE A COMPLETE IDIOT, VAN ZANDT--
--BUT HE HAS A POINT.
THERE'S NOTH LIKE A LITTLE TU TO CREATE SC MUCH NEEDED N AND FOG.
WHUPWHUPWHUPWHUPWHUPWHUPWHUPWHUPWHUPWHU
YOU'RE SERIOUS?
WHAT?
YOU'RE REALLY HEADING INTO THE CITY IN THE MIDST OF THIS FIRESTORM?
WHUPWHUPWHUPWHUPWHUPWHUPWHUPWHUPWHUPWHUPWHU
FOR HEAVEN'S SAKE, LORETTA, I'VE GOT A JOB TO DO...
AND IF THE PRESS FINDS OUT YOU'VE BEEN HIDING OUT HERE WHILE YOUR AGENTS ARE DYING THERE, YOUR JOB EVAPORATES.
NOW THAT'S THE NEAL VAN ZANDT I KNOW AND LOVE.
WHUPWHUPWHUPWHUPWHUPWHUPWHUPWHUPWHUPWHU
TRUST ME--
--WE CAN AND WILL PROFIT FROM THIS.
I KNOW IT, DENTON.
ENTRE NOUS, LORETTA--
--DON'T COUNT ON IT.

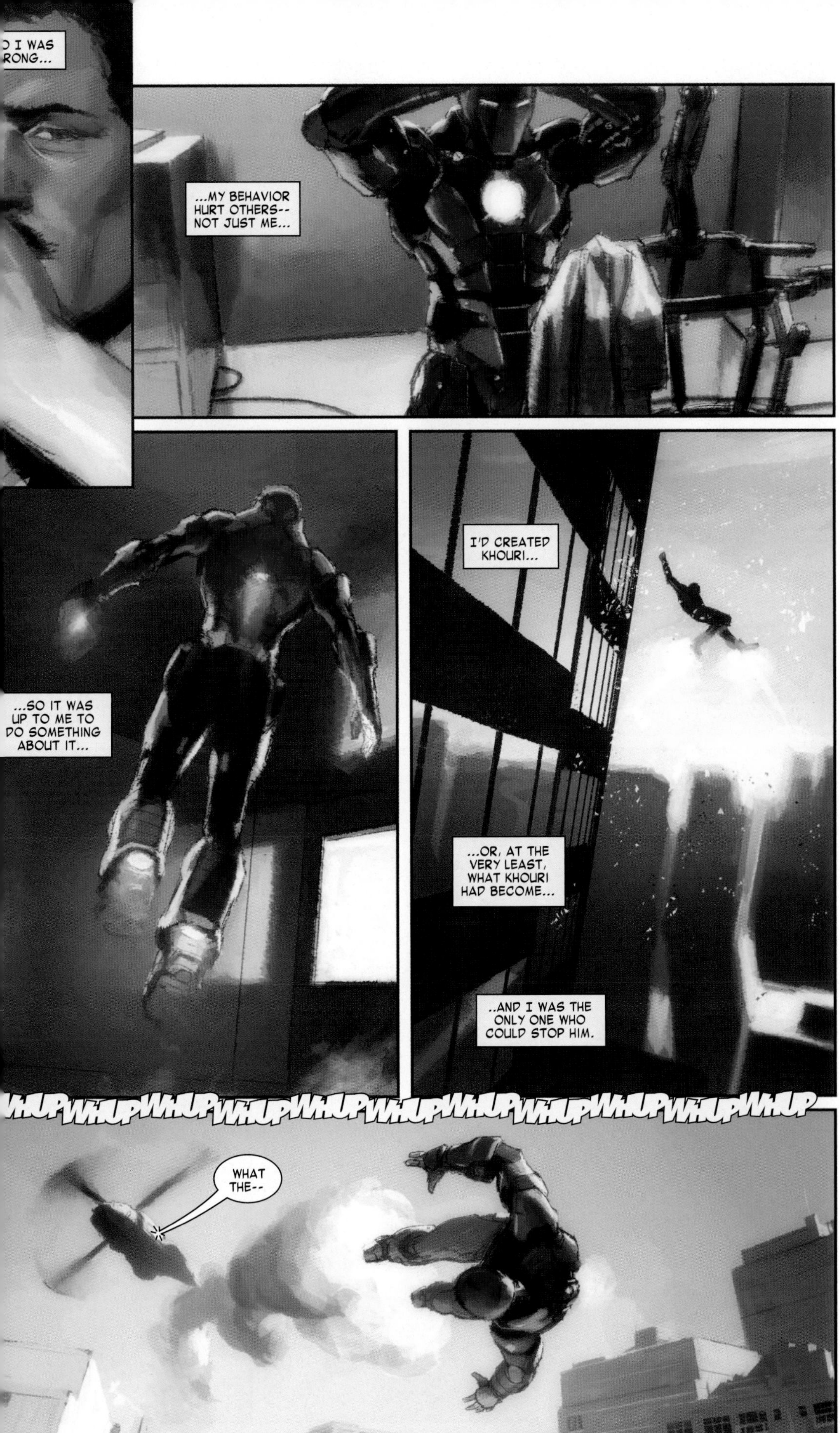

O I WAS
RONG...
...MY BEHAVIOR HURT OTHERS-- NOT JUST ME...
...SO IT WAS UP TO ME TO DO SOMETHING ABOUT IT...
I'D CREATED KHOURI...
...OR, AT THE VERY LEAST, WHAT KHOURI HAD BECOME...
..AND I WAS THE ONLY ONE WHO COULD STOP HIM.
WHUPWHUPWHUPWHUPWHUPWHUPWHUPWHUPWHUPWHUPWHUP
WHAT THE--

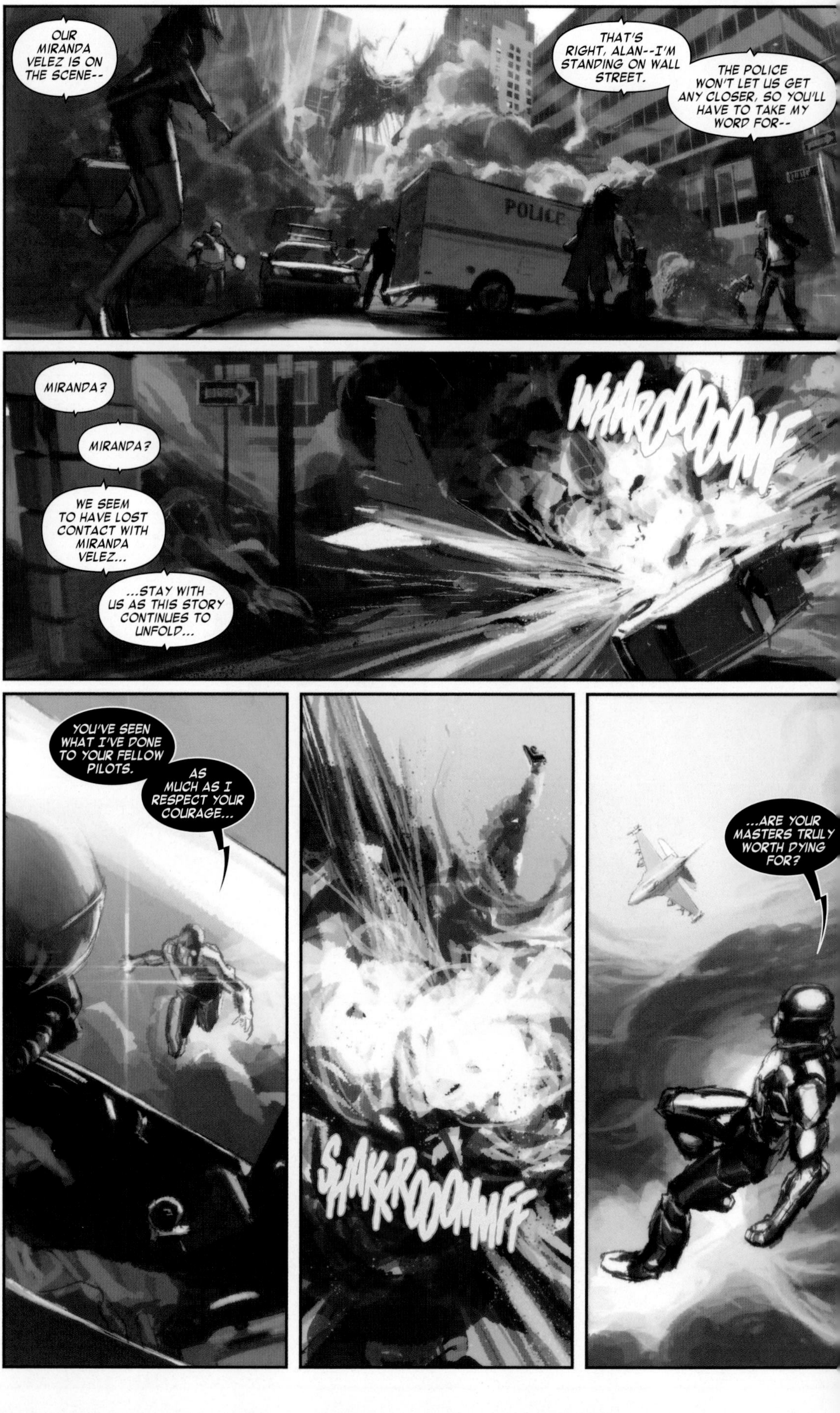
OUR MIRANDA VELEZ IS ON THE SCENE--
THAT'S RIGHT, ALAN--I'M STANDING ON WALL STREET.
THE POLICE WON'T LET US GET ANY CLOSER, SO YOU'LL HAVE TO TAKE MY WORD FOR--
POLICE
MIRANDA?
MIRANDA?
WE SEEM TO HAVE LOST CONTACT WITH MIRANDA VELEZ...
...STAY WITH US AS THIS STORY CONTINUES TO UNFOLD...
WHAROOOOMF
YOU'VE SEEN WHAT I'VE DONE TO YOUR FELLOW PILOTS.
AS MUCH AS I RESPECT YOUR COURAGE...
SHAKKROOOMMFF
...ARE YOUR MASTERS TRULY WORTH DYING FOR?

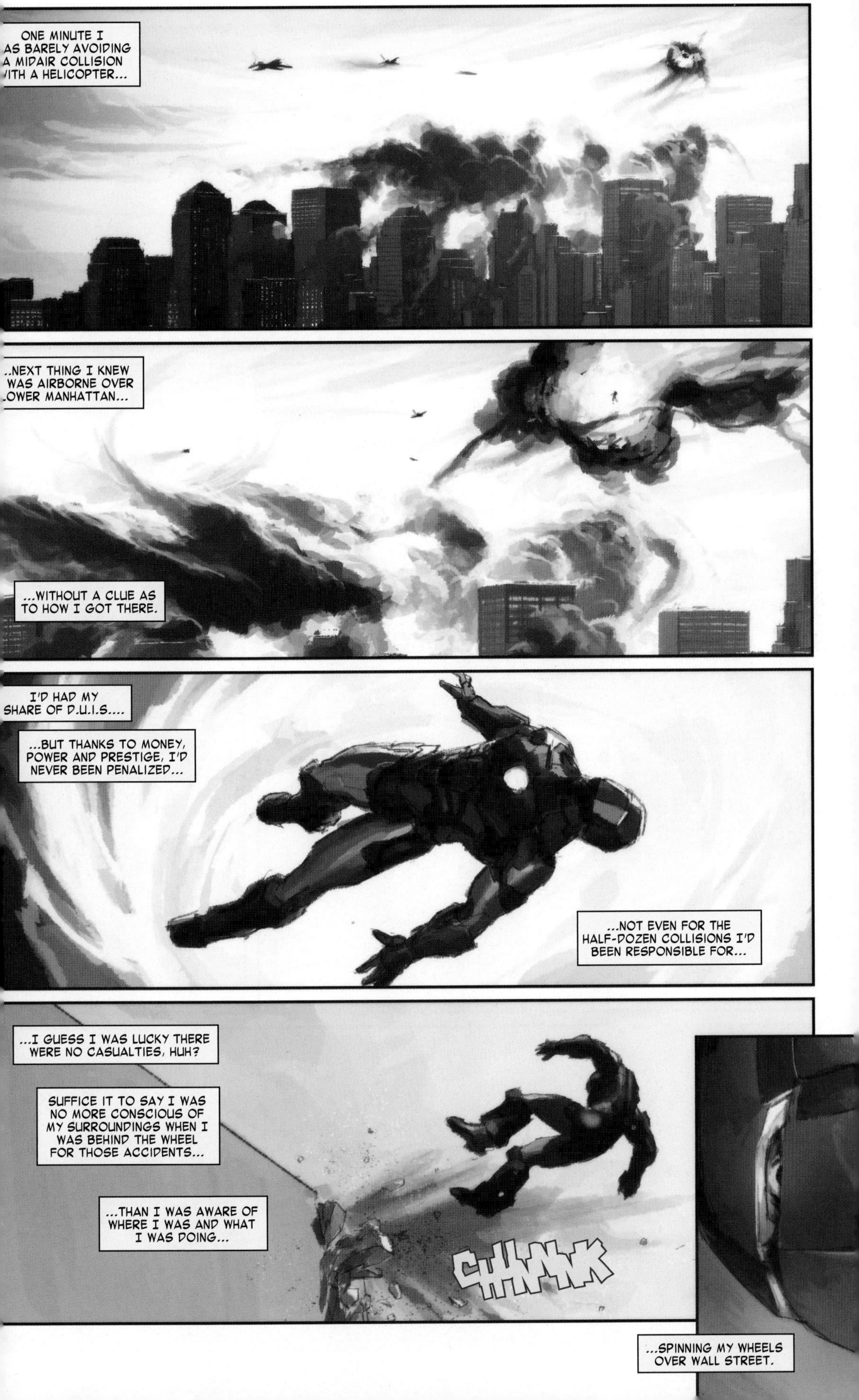
ONE MINUTE I
AS BARELY AVOIDING
A MIDAIR COLLISION
ITH A HELICOPTER...
..NEXT THING I KNEW
WAS AIRBORNE OVER
OWER MANHATTAN...
...WITHOUT A CLUE AS
TO HOW I GOT THERE.
I'D HAD MY
SHARE OF D.U.I.S....
...BUT THANKS TO MONEY,
POWER AND PRESTIGE, I'D
NEVER BEEN PENALIZED...
...NOT EVEN FOR THE
HALF-DOZEN COLLISIONS I'D
BEEN RESPONSIBLE FOR...
...I GUESS I WAS LUCKY THERE
WERE NO CASUALTIES, HUH?
SUFFICE IT TO SAY I WAS
NO MORE CONSCIOUS OF
MY SURROUNDINGS WHEN I
WAS BEHIND THE WHEEL
FOR THOSE ACCIDENTS...
...THAN I WAS AWARE OF
WHERE I WAS AND WHAT
I WAS DOING...
CHUNNNK
...SPINNING MY WHEELS
OVER WALL STREET.

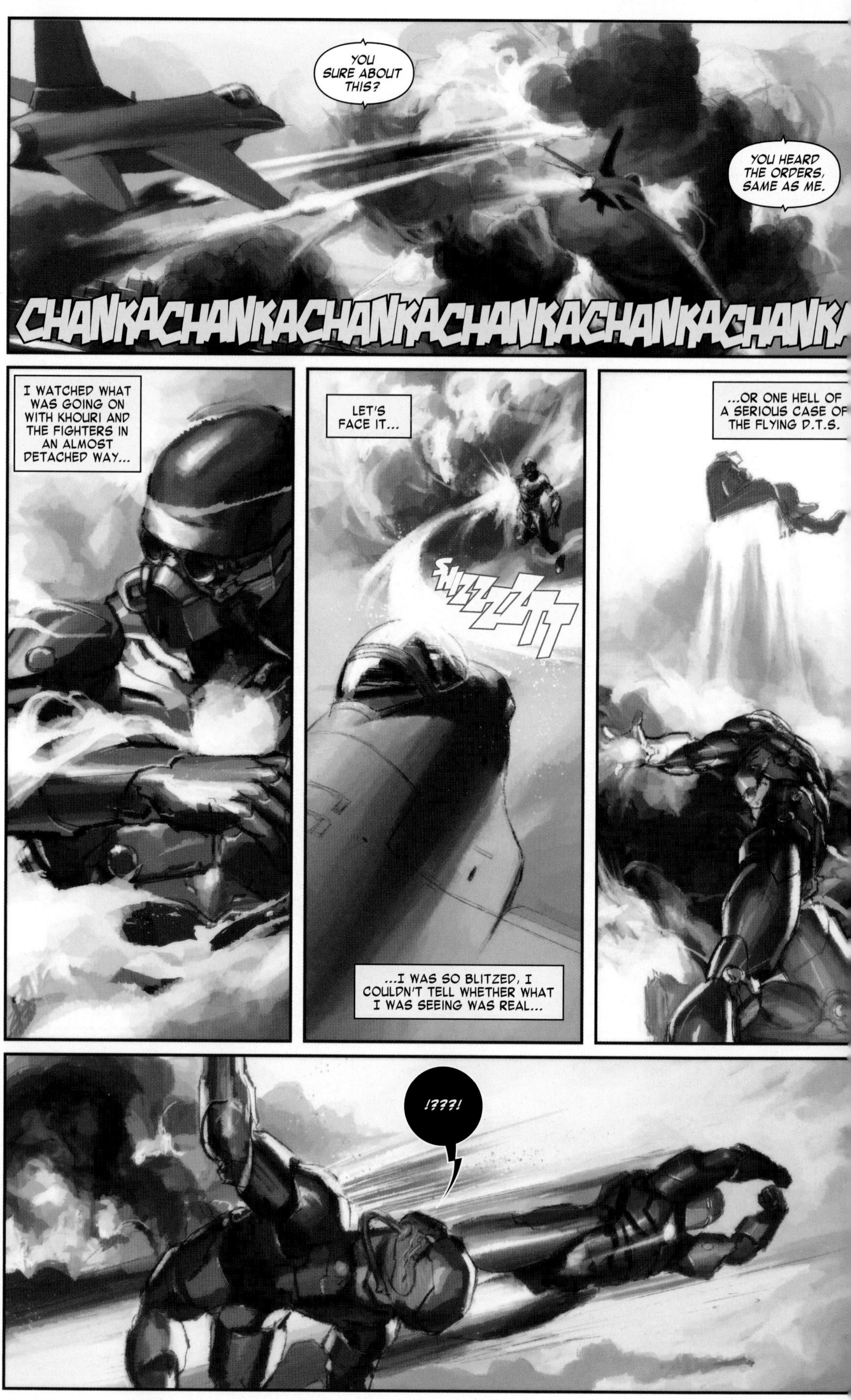
YOU SURE ABOUT THIS?
YOU HEARD THE ORDERS, SAME AS ME.
CHANKACHANKACHANKACHANKACHANKACHANK
I WATCHED WHAT WAS GOING ON WITH KHOURI AND THE FIGHTERS IN AN ALMOST DETACHED WAY...
LET'S FACE IT...
SHIZZZAT
...I WAS SO BLITZED, I COULDN'T TELL WHETHER WHAT I WAS SEEING WAS REAL...
...OR ONE HELL OF A SERIOUS CASE OF THE FLYING D.T.S.
!???!

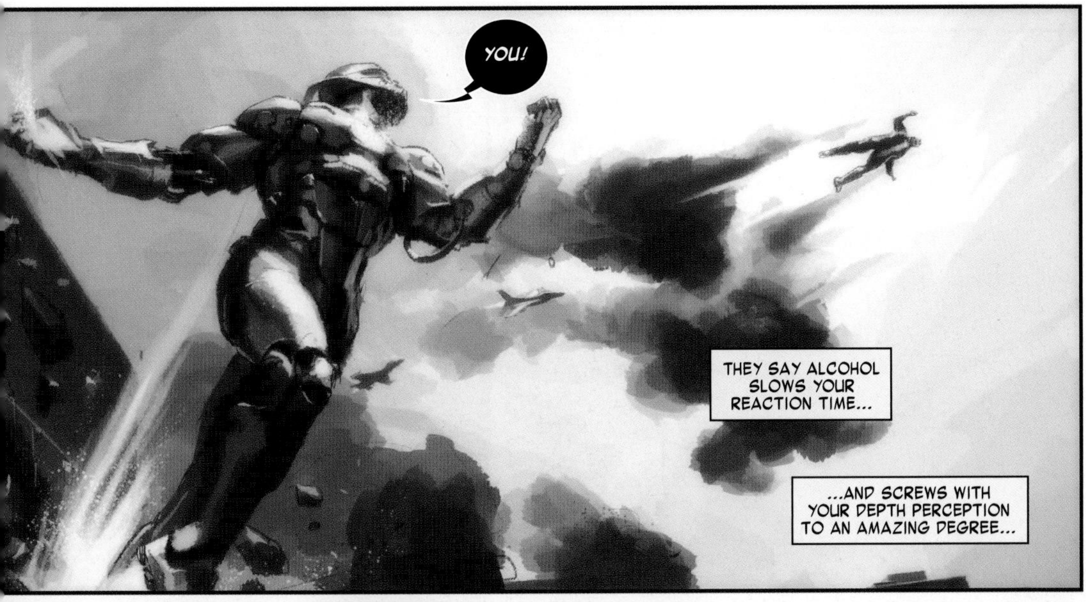
YOU!
THEY SAY ALCOHOL SLOWS YOUR REACTION TIME...
...AND SCREWS WITH YOUR DEPTH PERCEPTION TO AN AMAZING DEGREE...

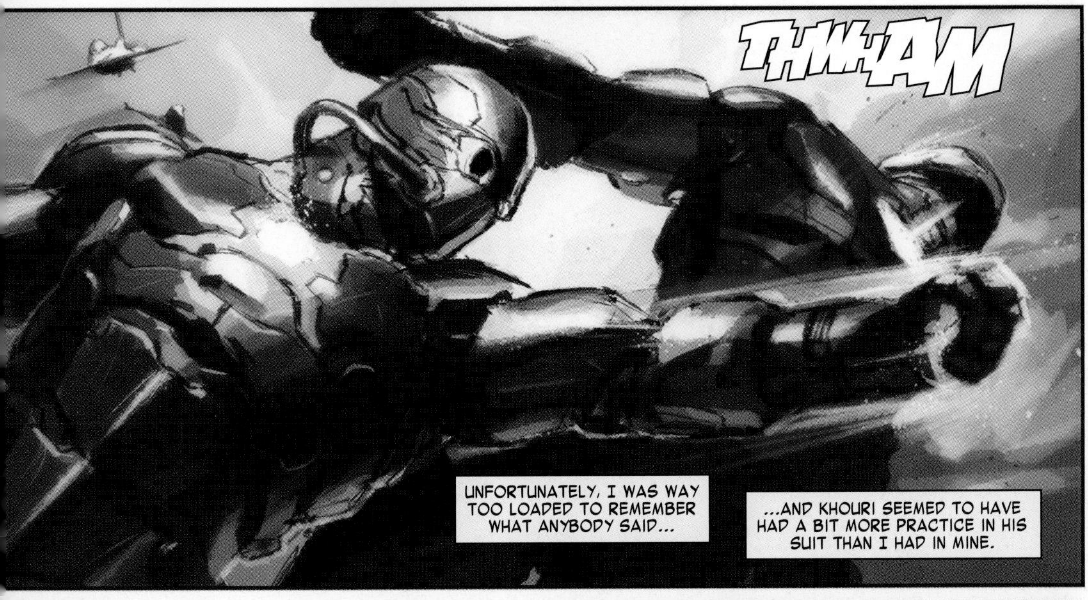
THWHAM
UNFORTUNATELY, I WAS WAY TOO LOADED TO REMEMBER WHAT ANYBODY SAID...
...AND KHOURI SEEMED TO HAVE HAD A BIT MORE PRACTICE IN HIS SUIT THAN I HAD IN MINE.

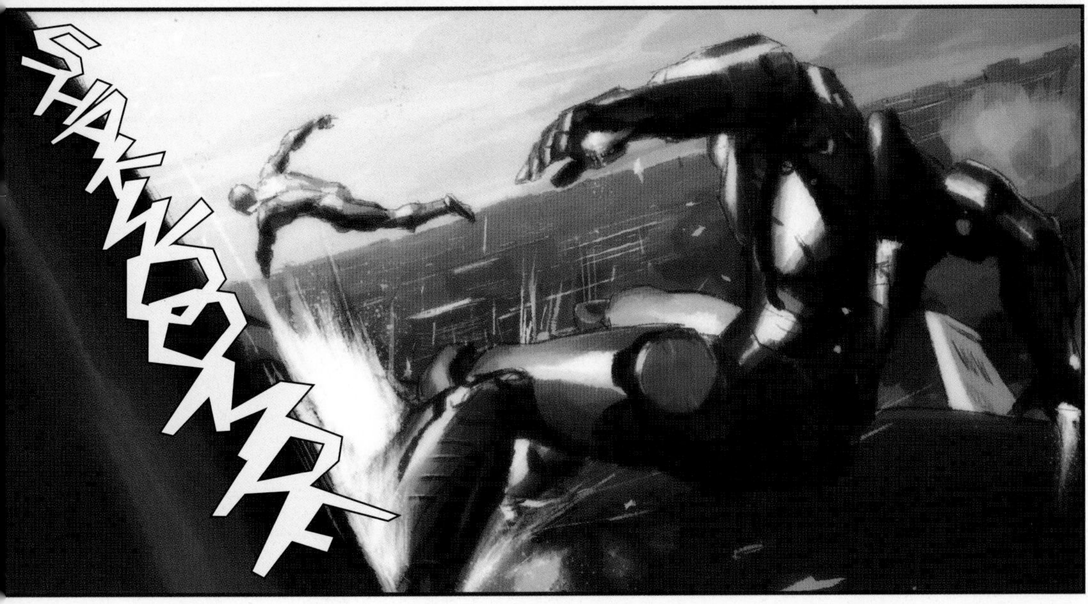
SHAKWOOMPF

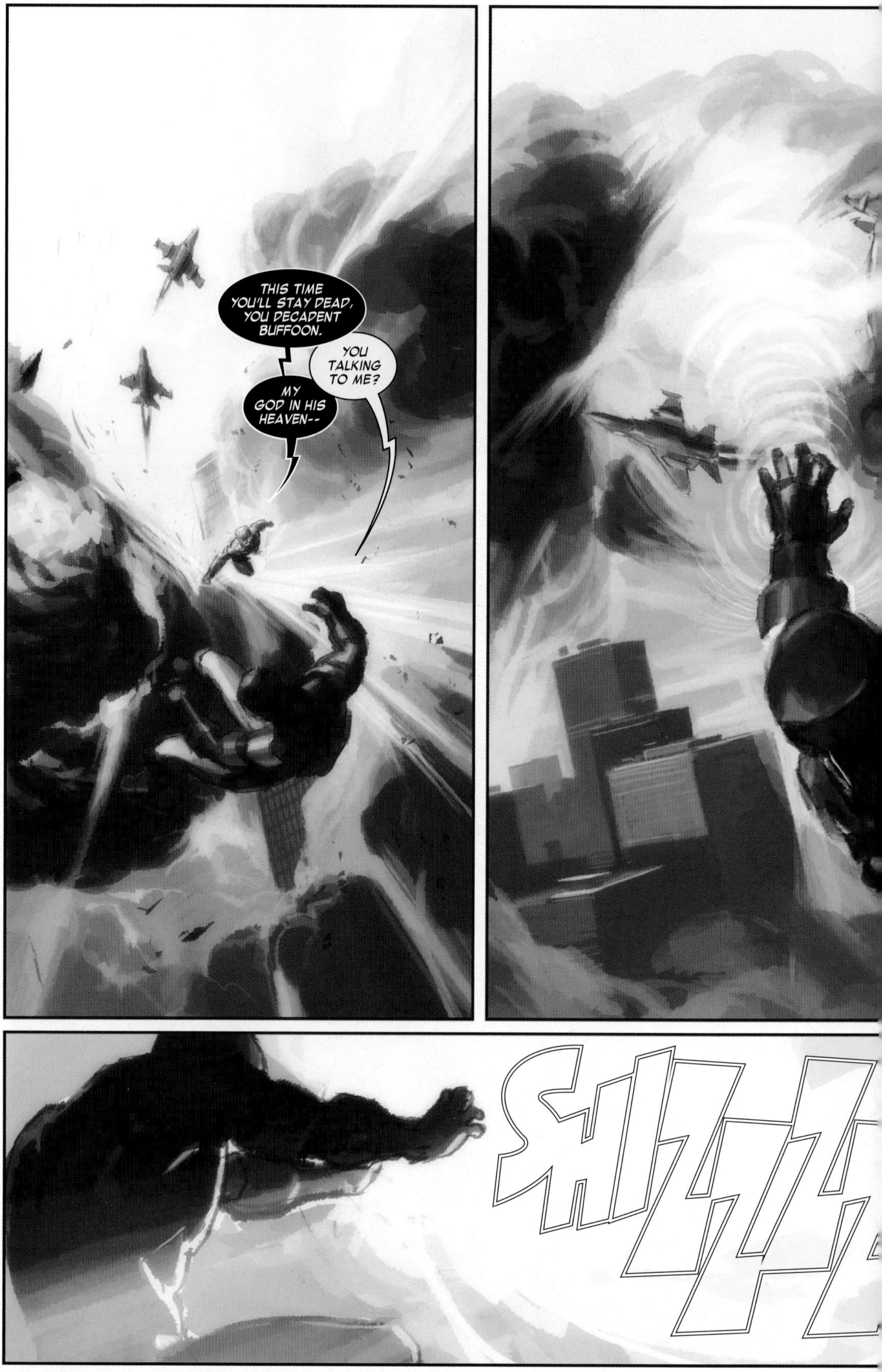
THIS TIME YOU'LL STAY DEAD, YOU DECADENT BUFFOON.
YOU TALKING TO ME?
MY GOD IN HIS HEAVEN--
SHZZZZ

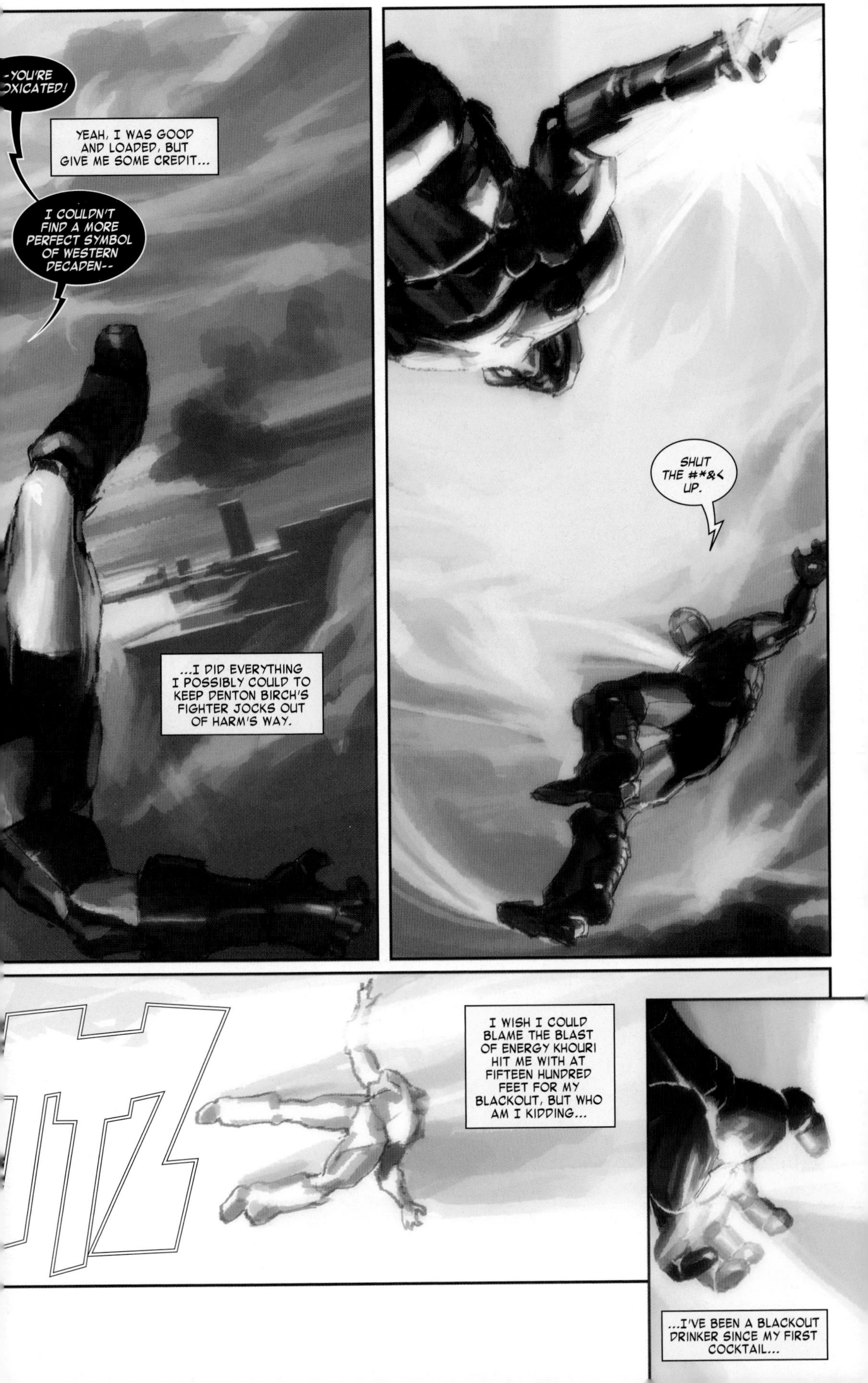

-YOU'RE
OXICATED!
YEAH, I WAS GOOD AND LOADED, BUT GIVE ME SOME CREDIT...
I COULDN'T FIND A MORE PERFECT SYMBOL OF WESTERN DECADEN--
...I DID EVERYTHING I POSSIBLY COULD TO KEEP DENTON BIRCH'S FIGHTER JOCKS OUT OF HARM'S WAY.
SHUT THE #*< UP.
I WISH I COULD BLAME THE BLAST OF ENERGY KHOURI HIT ME WITH AT FIFTEEN HUNDRED FEET FOR MY BLACKOUT, BUT WHO AM I KIDDING...
...I'VE BEEN A BLACKOUT DRINKER SINCE MY FIRST COCKTAIL...

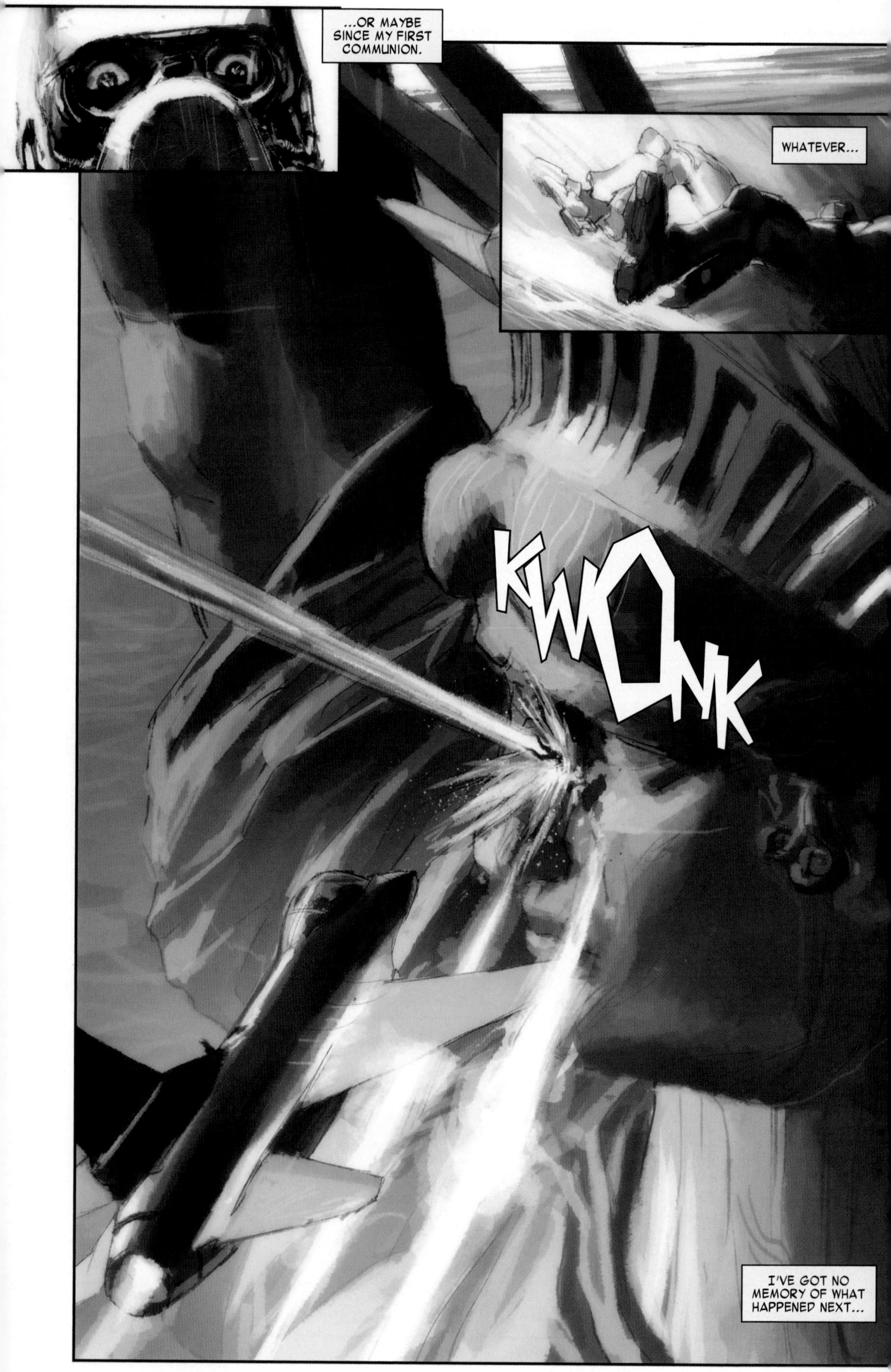
...OR MAYBE SINCE MY FIRST COMMUNION.
WHATEVER...
KWONK
I'VE GOT NO MEMORY OF WHAT HAPPENED NEXT...

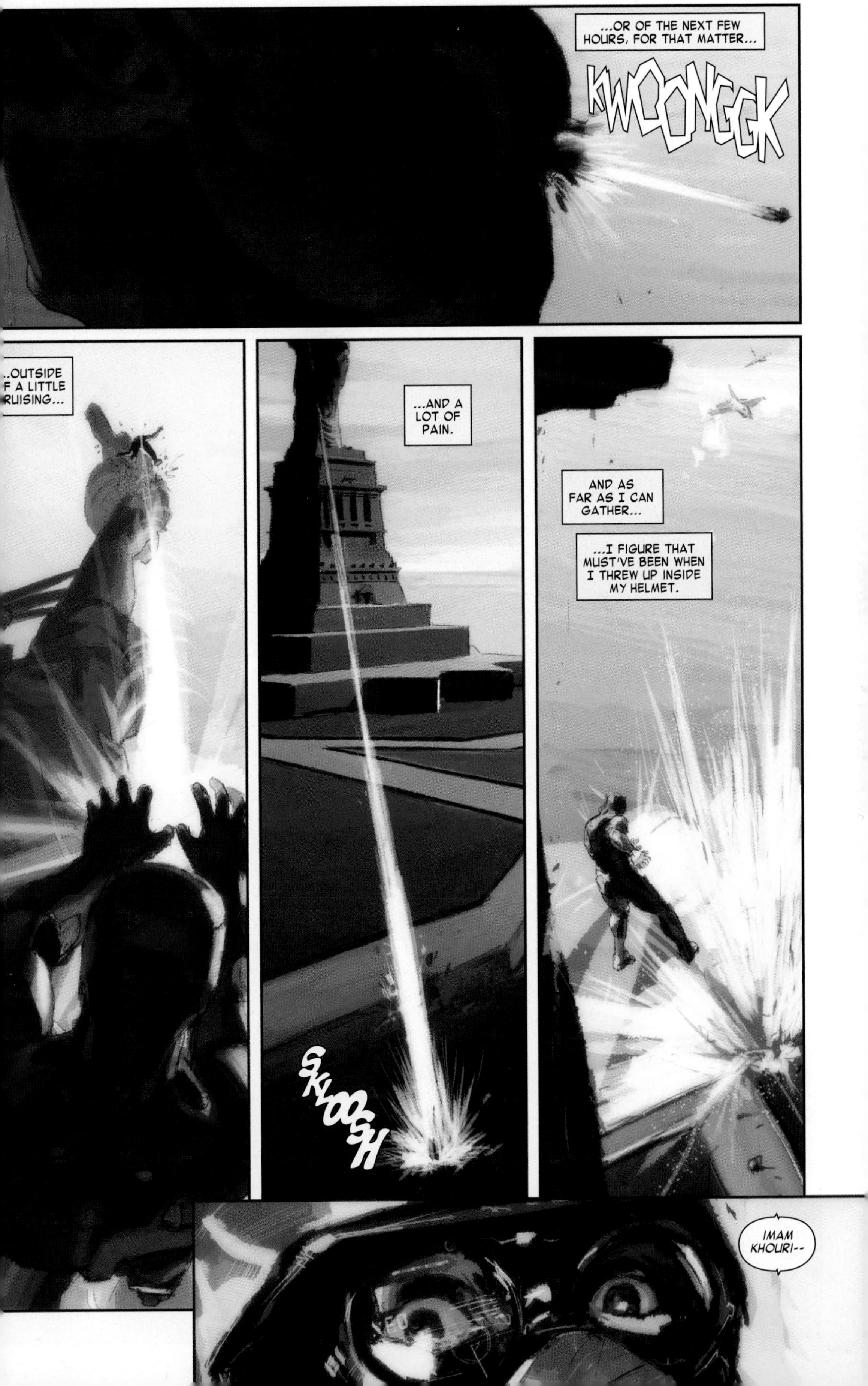

...OR OF THE NEXT FEW HOURS, FOR THAT MATTER...
KWOONGGK
..OUTSIDE
F A LITTLE
RUISING...
...AND A LOT OF PAIN.
SKLOOSH
AND AS FAR AS I CAN GATHER...
...I FIGURE THAT MUST'VE BEEN WHEN I THREW UP INSIDE MY HELMET.
IMAM KHOURI--

--OUR SENSORS INDICATE YOU'RE ABOUT TO HIT A DANGEROUS LOW POWER THRESHOLD.

I GUES THAT'S H KHOURI DISAPPEAR

YES, I SEE...

...AND DOCTOR...

...OFF MY RADAR...

...AND EVERYBODY ELSE'S, TOO.

...ALLOW ME TO APOLOGIZE.

FOR WHAT, IMAM?

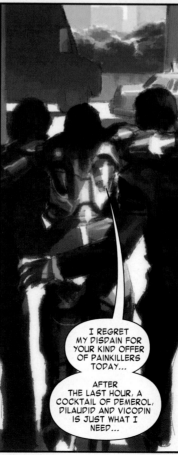

I REGRET MY DISDAIN FOR YOUR KIND OFFER OF PAINKILLERS TODAY...

AFTER THE LAST HOUR, A COCKTAIL OF DEMEROL, DILAUDID AND VICODIN IS JUST WHAT I NEED...

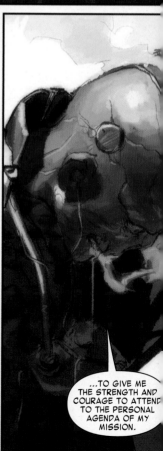

...TO GIVE ME THE STRENGTH AND COURAGE TO ATTEND TO THE PERSONAL AGENDA OF MY MISSION.

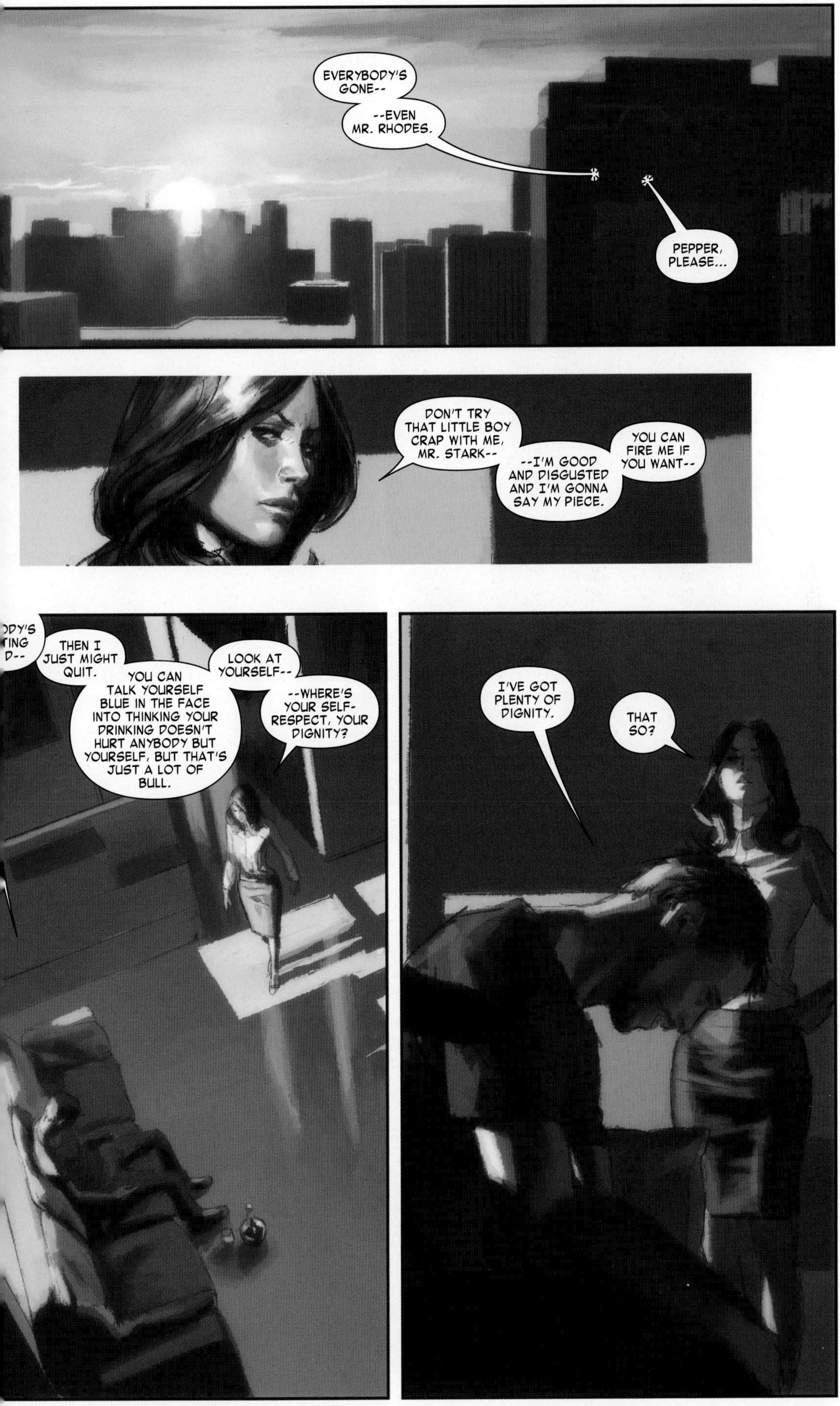
EVERYBODY'S GONE--
--EVEN MR. RHODES.
PEPPER, PLEASE...
DON'T TRY THAT LITTLE BOY CRAP WITH ME, MR. STARK--
--I'M GOOD AND DISGUSTED AND I'M GONNA SAY MY PIECE.
YOU CAN FIRE ME IF YOU WANT--
THEN I JUST MIGHT QUIT.
YOU CAN TALK YOURSELF BLUE IN THE FACE INTO THINKING YOUR DRINKING DOESN'T HURT ANYBODY BUT YOURSELF, BUT THAT'S JUST A LOT OF BULL.
LOOK AT YOURSELF--
--WHERE'S YOUR SELF-RESPECT, YOUR DIGNITY?
I'VE GOT PLENTY OF DIGNITY.
THAT SO?

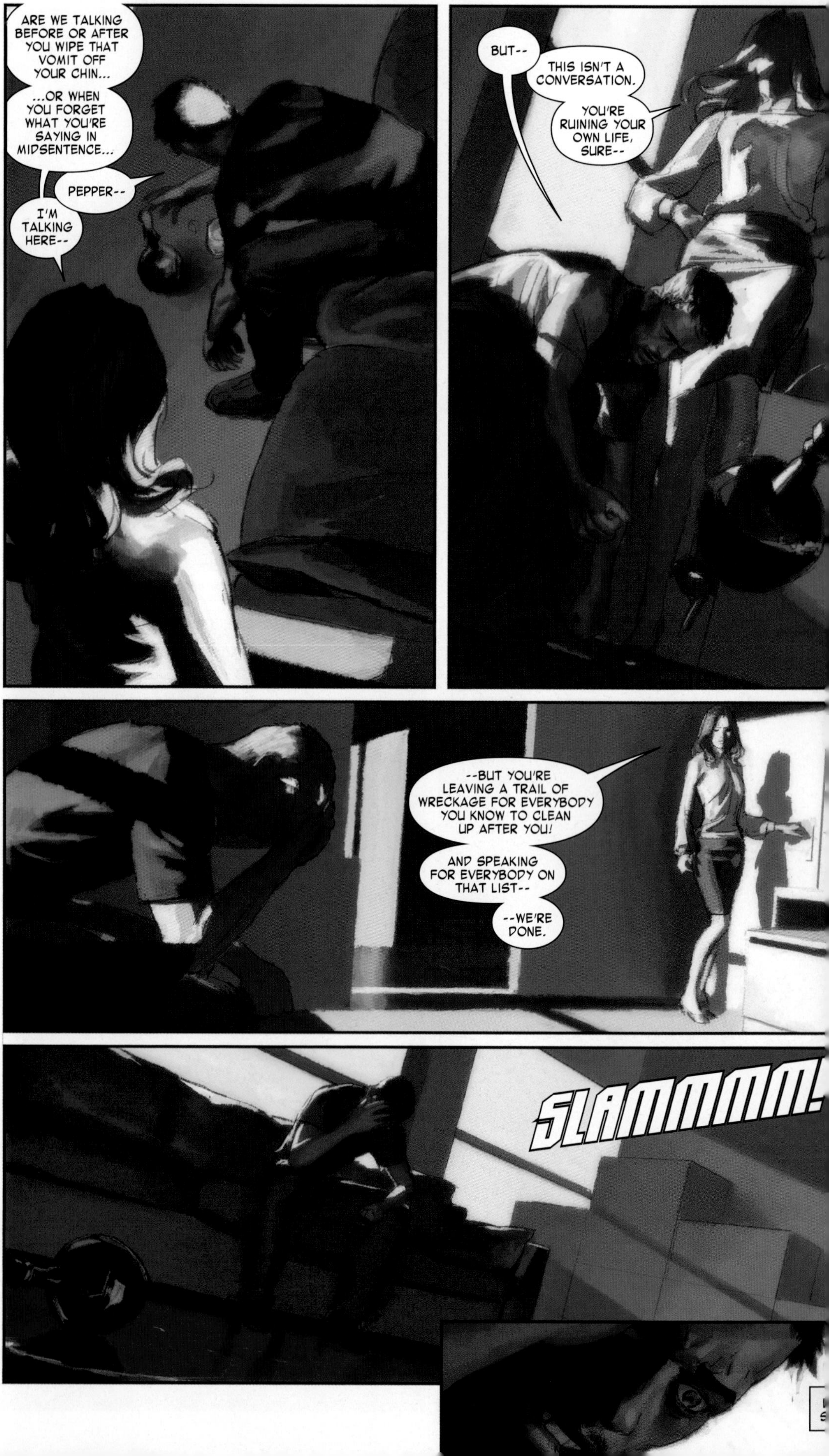
ARE WE TALKING BEFORE OR AFTER YOU WIPE THAT VOMIT OFF YOUR CHIN...
...OR WHEN YOU FORGET WHAT YOU'RE SAYING IN MIDSENTENCE...
PEPPER--
I'M TALKING HERE--
BUT--
THIS ISN'T A CONVERSATION.
YOU'RE RUINING YOUR OWN LIFE, SURE--
--BUT YOU'RE LEAVING A TRAIL OF WRECKAGE FOR EVERYBODY YOU KNOW TO CLEAN UP AFTER YOU!
AND SPEAKING FOR EVERYBODY ON THAT LIST--
--WE'RE DONE.
SLAMMMMM!

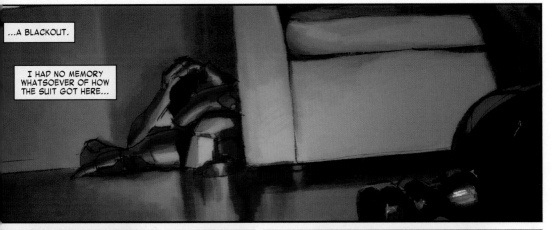

...A BLACKOUT.

I HAD NO MEMORY WHATSOEVER OF HOW THE SUIT GOT HERE...

...LET ALONE HOW IT GOT SO BATTERED, SOAKING WET AND FILTHY.

I LOOKED LIKE I'D BEEN RODE HARD AND PUT AWAY WET MYSELF...

...BUT I STILL WASN'T HIP TO WHAT HAD HAPPENED...

OH GOD...

...WHAT HAVE I DONE?

TO LAY WASTE TO A SMALL CITY.

ARMORED MYSTERY MEN IN AIRBORNE DUEL AFTER U.N. TERRORIST ATTACK.

I WISH I COULD SAY IT ALL CAME BACK TO ME IN A CRUSHING FLOOD...

...THAT SEEING IT UNFOLD BEFORE ME MADE ME RECALL IN VIVID DETAIL WHAT HAD HAPPENED...

...BUT I'D BE LYING.

BUT I'D ALWAYS LIED...

...TO MYSELF, AND EVERYONE AROUND ME...

...AND NOW THAT THE TRUTH HAD HIT ME SMACK IN THE FACE...

...I KNEW JUST WHAT THEY MEANT BY PITIFUL AND INCOMPREHENSIBLE DEMORALIZATION.

THIS ARMORED, SUPER-POWERED TERRORIST WHO CALLS HIMSELF MAOUAD KHOURI...
PITIFUL AND INCOMPREHENSIBLE DEMORALIZATION.
WHAT A MOUTHFUL.
EVEN IN MY DEEPEST DESPAIR...
...I REMAINED GRANDIOSE...
...A WORTHLESS PIECE OF CRAP THE WORLD REVOLVED AROUND.

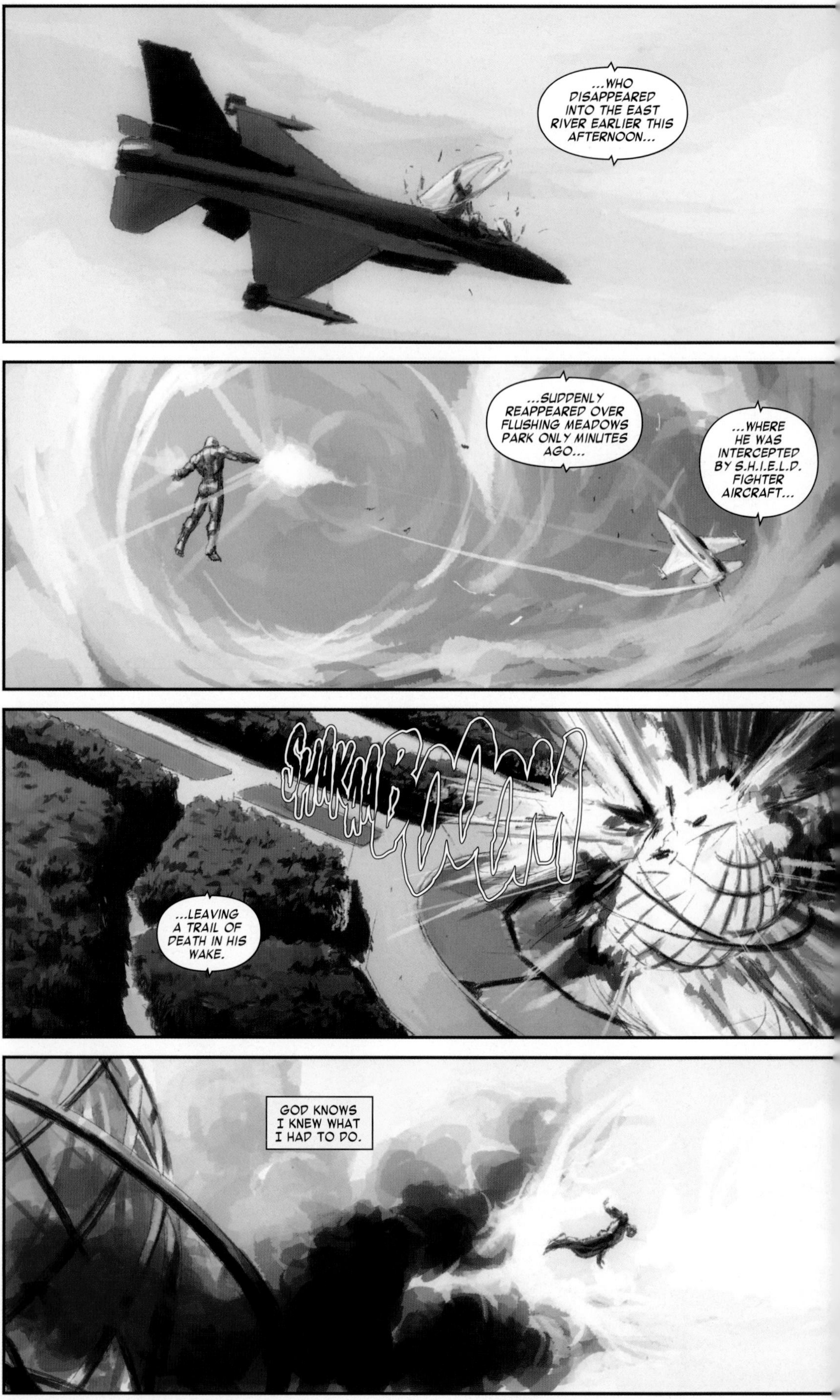
...WHO DISAPPEARED INTO THE EAST RIVER EARLIER THIS AFTERNOON...
...SUDDENLY REAPPEARED OVER FLUSHING MEADOWS PARK ONLY MINUTES AGO...
...WHERE HE WAS INTERCEPTED BY S.H.I.E.L.D. FIGHTER AIRCRAFT...
SHAKAABOOOM
...LEAVING A TRAIL OF DEATH IN HIS WAKE.
GOD KNOWS I KNEW WHAT I HAD TO DO.

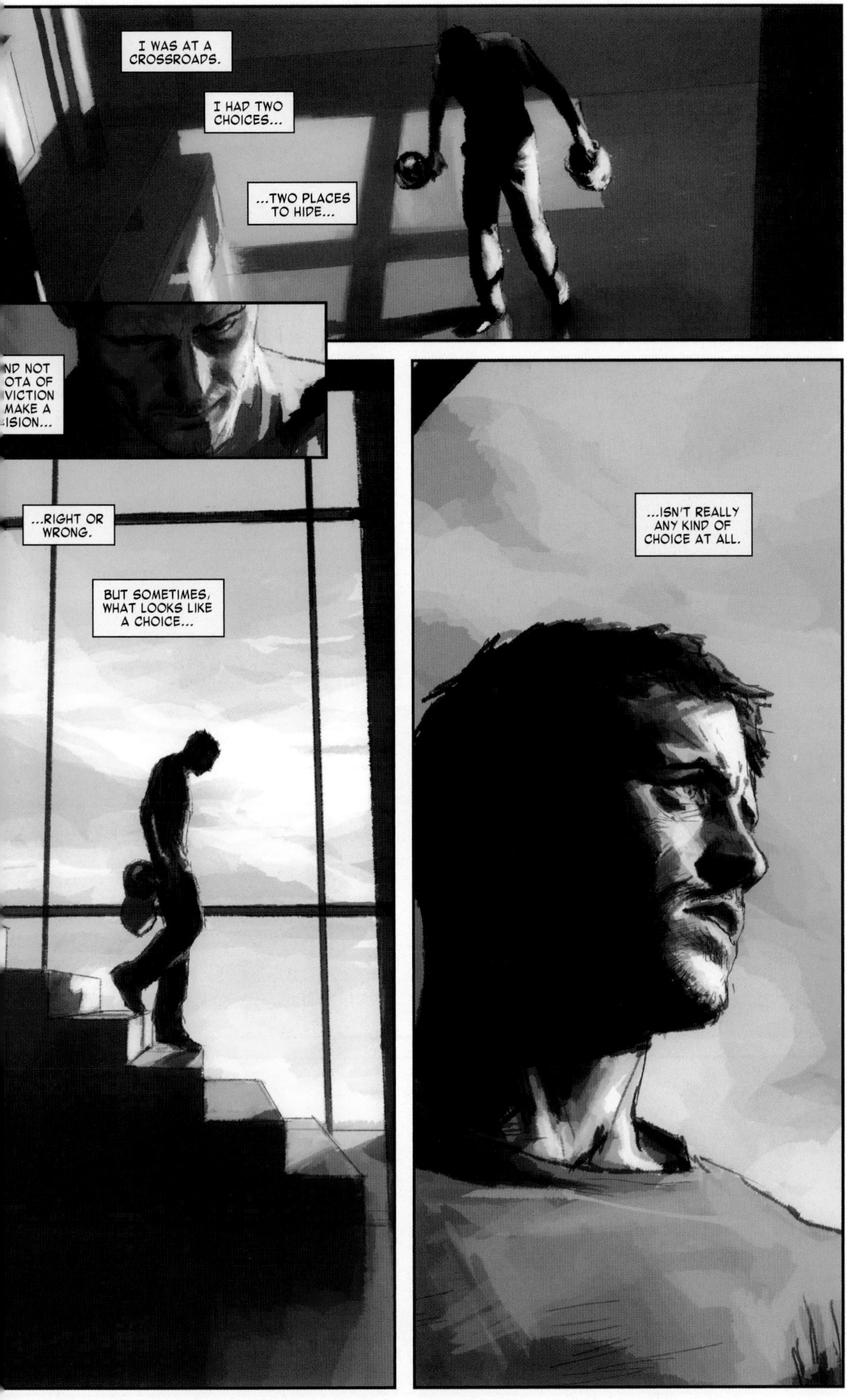
I WAS AT A CROSSROADS.
I HAD TWO CHOICES...
...TWO PLACES TO HIDE...
ND NOT OTA OF VICTION MAKE A ISION...
...RIGHT OR WRONG.
BUT SOMETIMES, WHAT LOOKS LIKE A CHOICE...
...ISN'T REALLY ANY KIND OF CHOICE AT ALL.

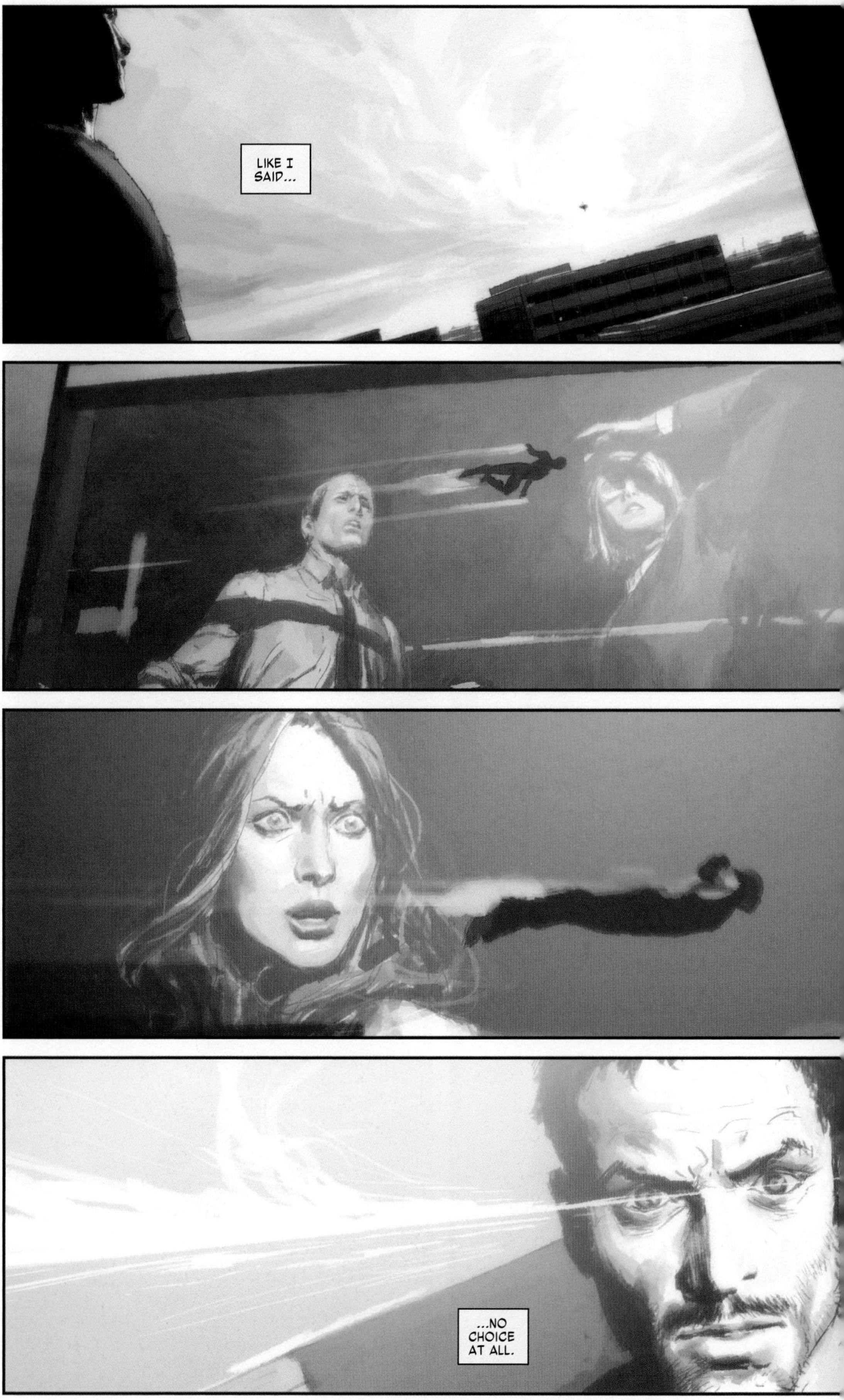
LIKE I SAID...
...NO CHOICE AT ALL.

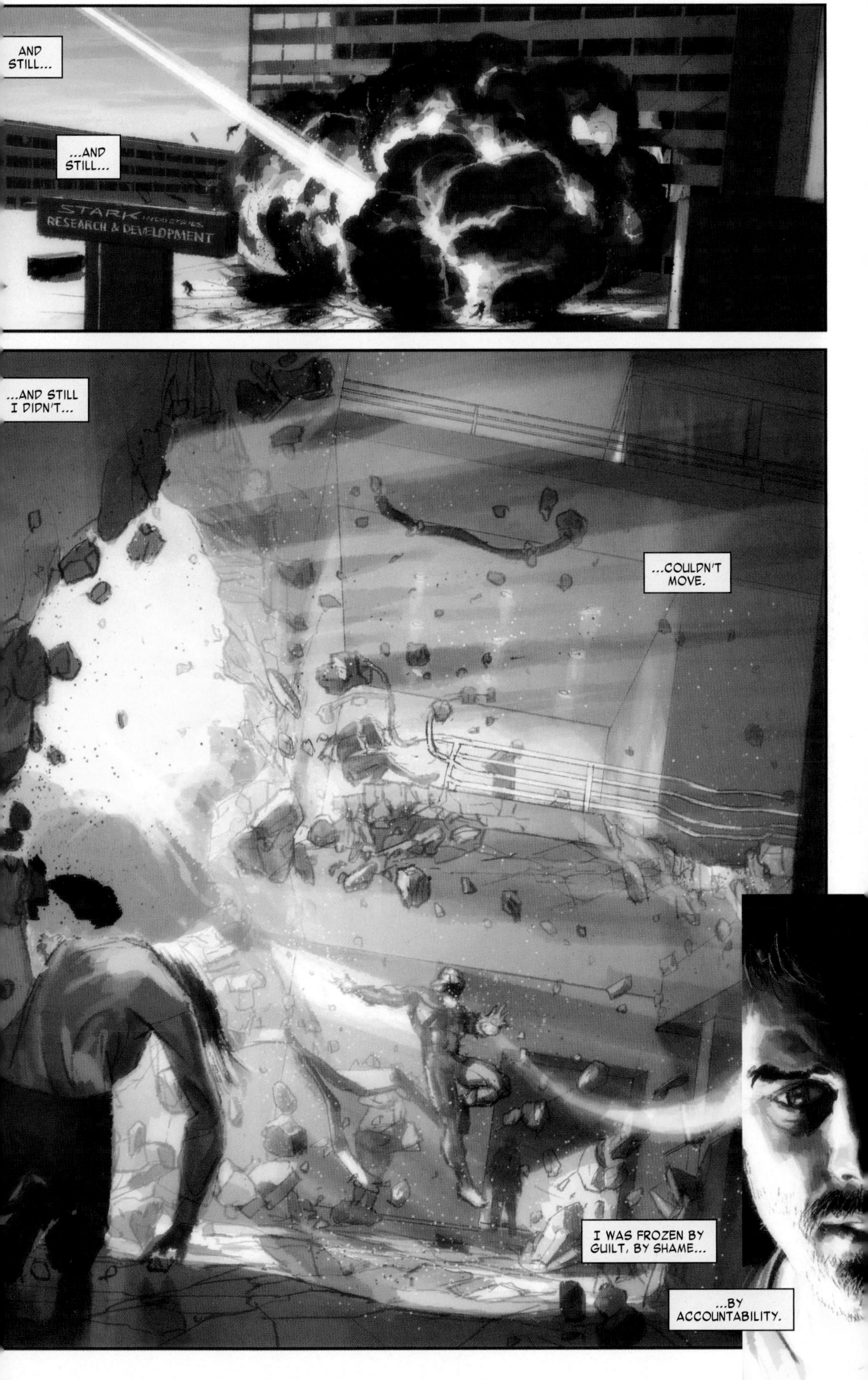
AND STILL...
...AND STILL...
STARK INDUSTRIES
RESEARCH & DEVELOPMENT
...AND STILL I DIDN'T...
...COULDN'T MOVE.
I WAS FROZEN BY GUILT, BY SHAME...
...BY ACCOUNTABILITY.

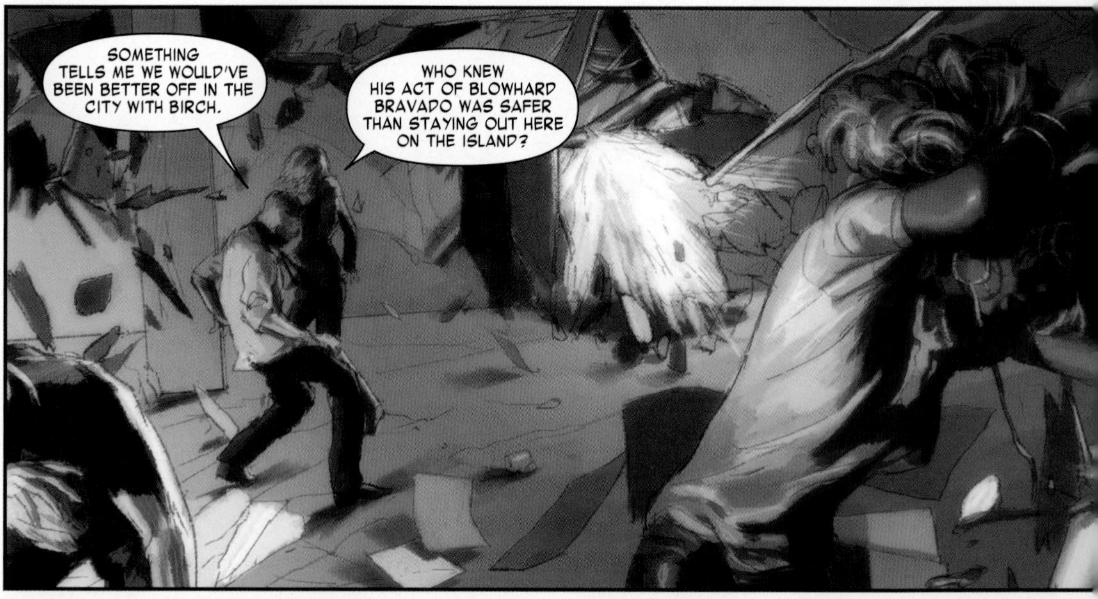
SOMETHING TELLS ME WE WOULD'VE BEEN BETTER OFF IN THE CITY WITH BIRCH.
WHO KNEW HIS ACT OF BLOWHARD BRAVADO WAS SAFER THAN STAYING OUT HERE ON THE ISLAND?

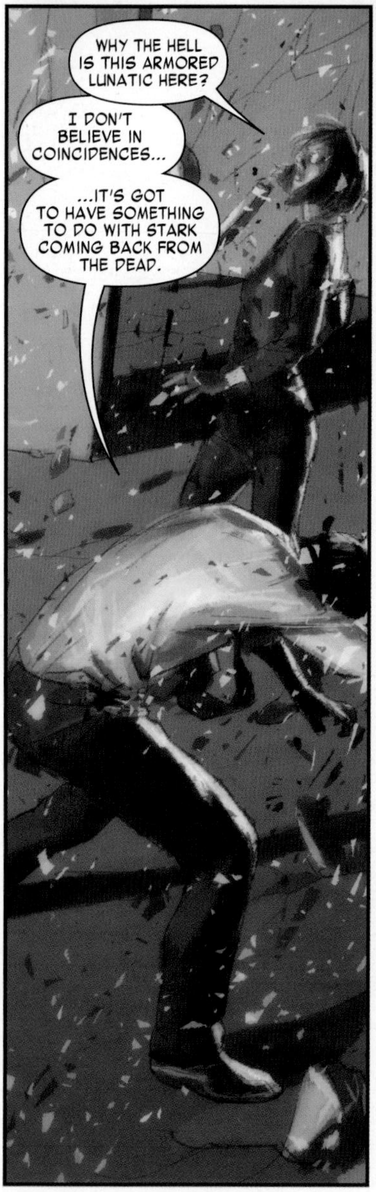
WHY THE HELL IS THIS ARMORED LUNATIC HERE?
I DON'T BELIEVE IN COINCIDENCES...
...IT'S GOT TO HAVE SOMETHING TO DO WITH STARK COMING BACK FROM THE DEAD.

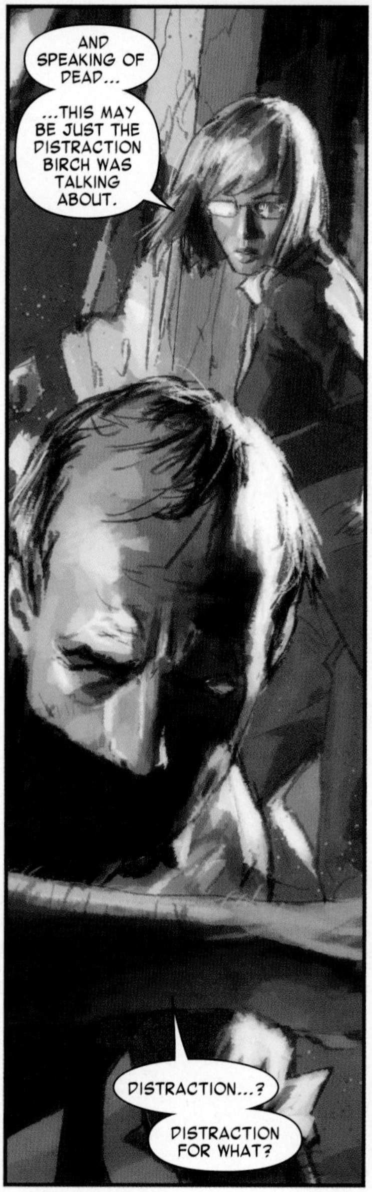
AND SPEAKING OF DEAD...
...THIS MAY BE JUST THE DISTRACTION BIRCH WAS TALKING ABOUT.
DISTRACTION...?
DISTRACTION FOR WHAT?

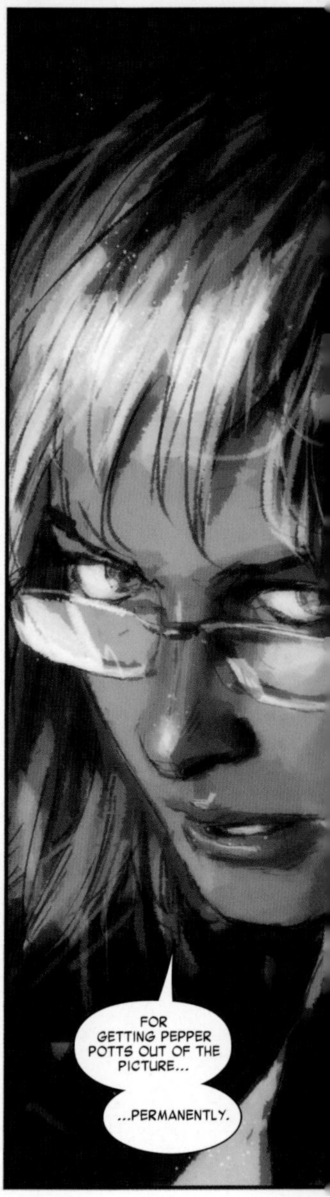
FOR GETTING PEPPER POTTS OUT OF THE PICTURE...
...PERMANENTLY.

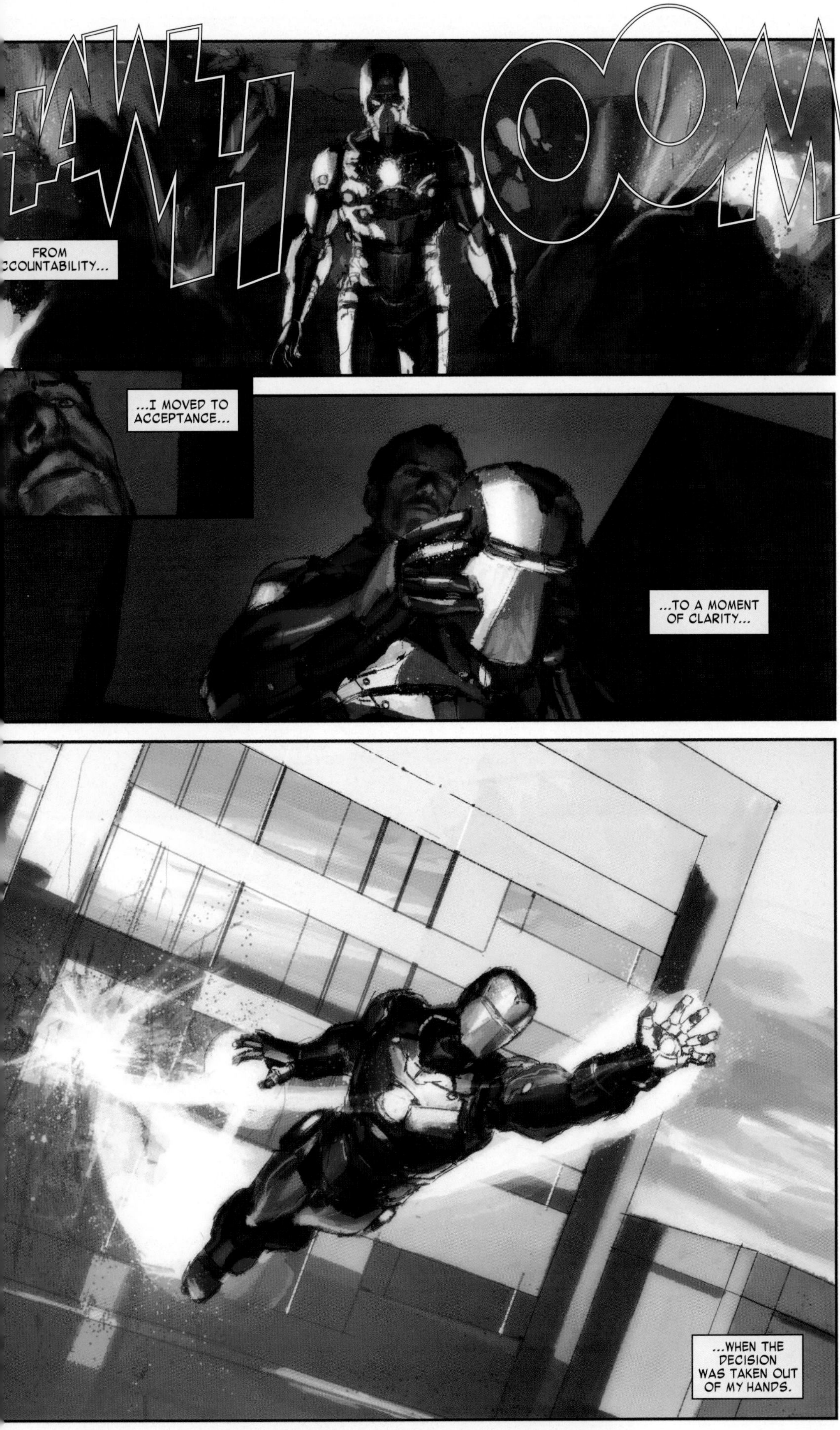

FWAWHOOOM
FROM
ACCOUNTABILITY...
...I MOVED TO
ACCEPTANCE...
...TO A MOMENT
OF CLARITY...
...WHEN THE
DECISION
WAS TAKEN OUT
OF MY HANDS.

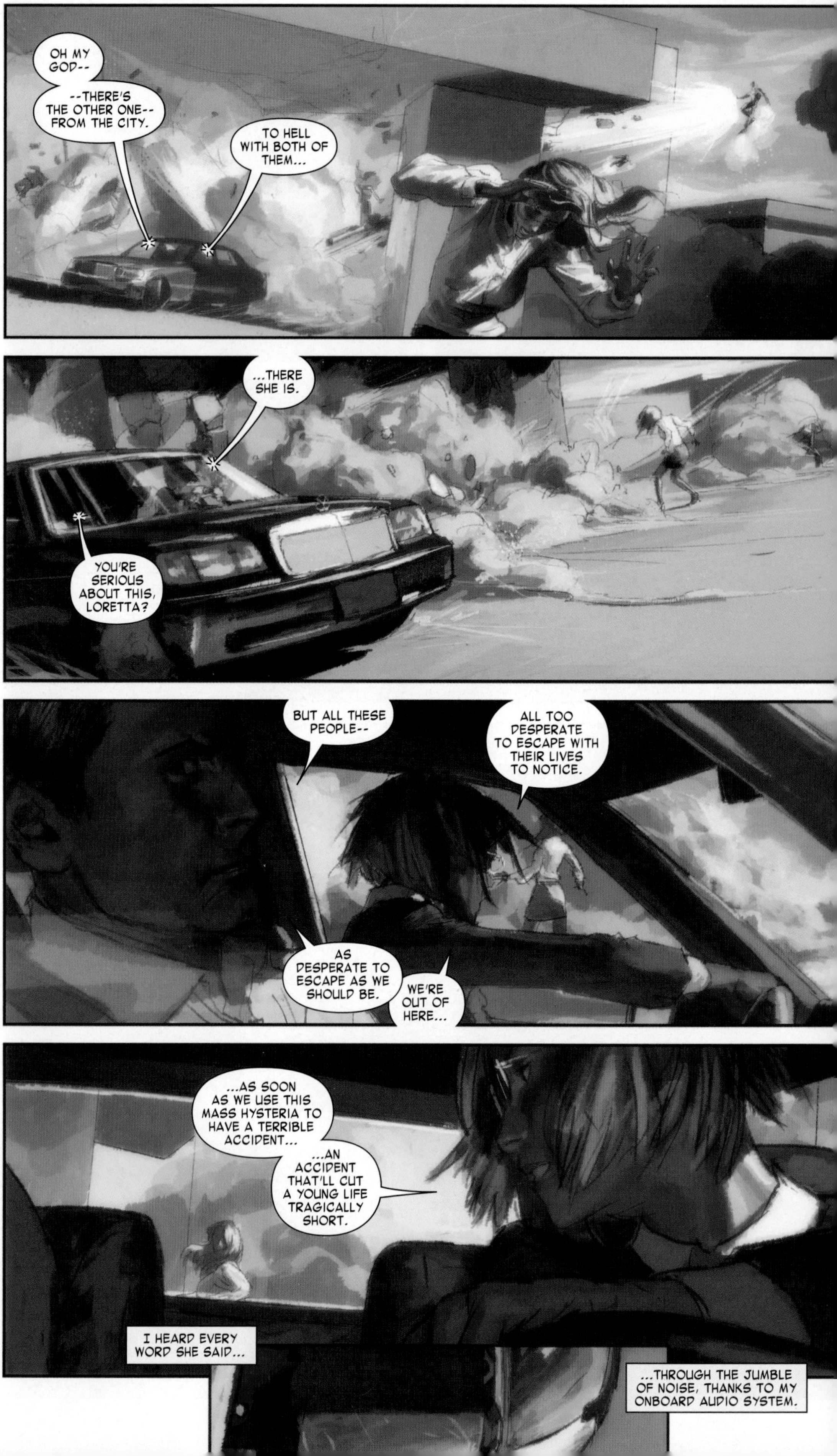

OH MY GOD--
--THERE'S THE OTHER ONE--FROM THE CITY.
TO HELL WITH BOTH OF THEM...
...THERE SHE IS.
YOU'RE SERIOUS ABOUT THIS, LORETTA?
BUT ALL THESE PEOPLE--
ALL TOO DESPERATE TO ESCAPE WITH THEIR LIVES TO NOTICE.
AS DESPERATE TO ESCAPE AS WE SHOULD BE.
WE'RE OUT OF HERE...
...AS SOON AS WE USE THIS MASS HYSTERIA TO HAVE A TERRIBLE ACCIDENT...
...AN ACCIDENT THAT'LL CUT A YOUNG LIFE TRAGICALLY SHORT.
I HEARD EVERY WORD SHE SAID...
...THROUGH THE JUMBLE OF NOISE, THANKS TO MY ONBOARD AUDIO SYSTEM.

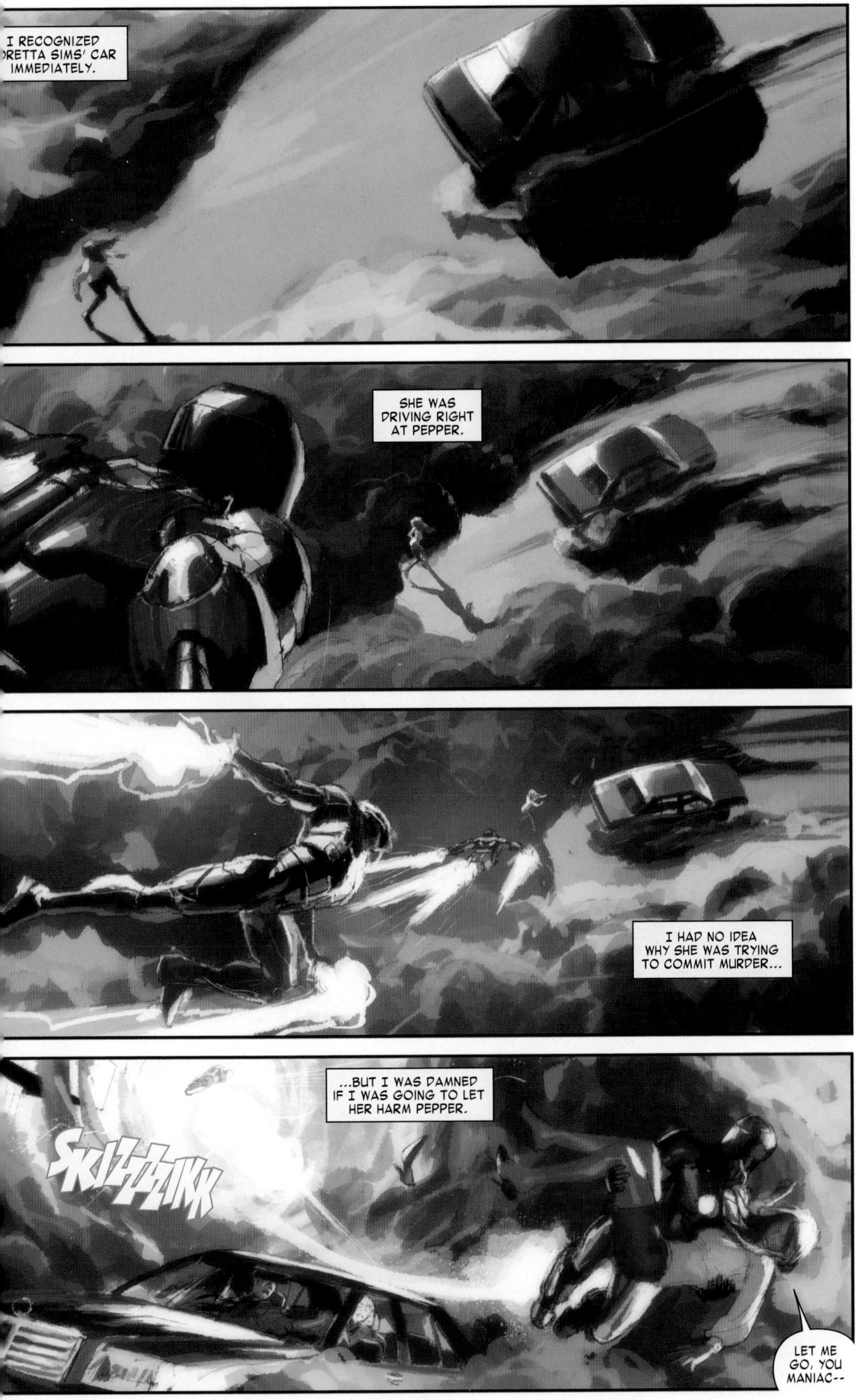
I RECOGNIZED
ORETTA SIMS' CAR
IMMEDIATELY.
SHE WAS
DRIVING RIGHT
AT PEPPER.
I HAD NO IDEA
WHY SHE WAS TRYING
TO COMMIT MURDER...
...BUT I WAS DAMNED
IF I WAS GOING TO LET
HER HARM PEPPER.
SKIZZZZIKK
LET ME
GO, YOU
MANIAC--

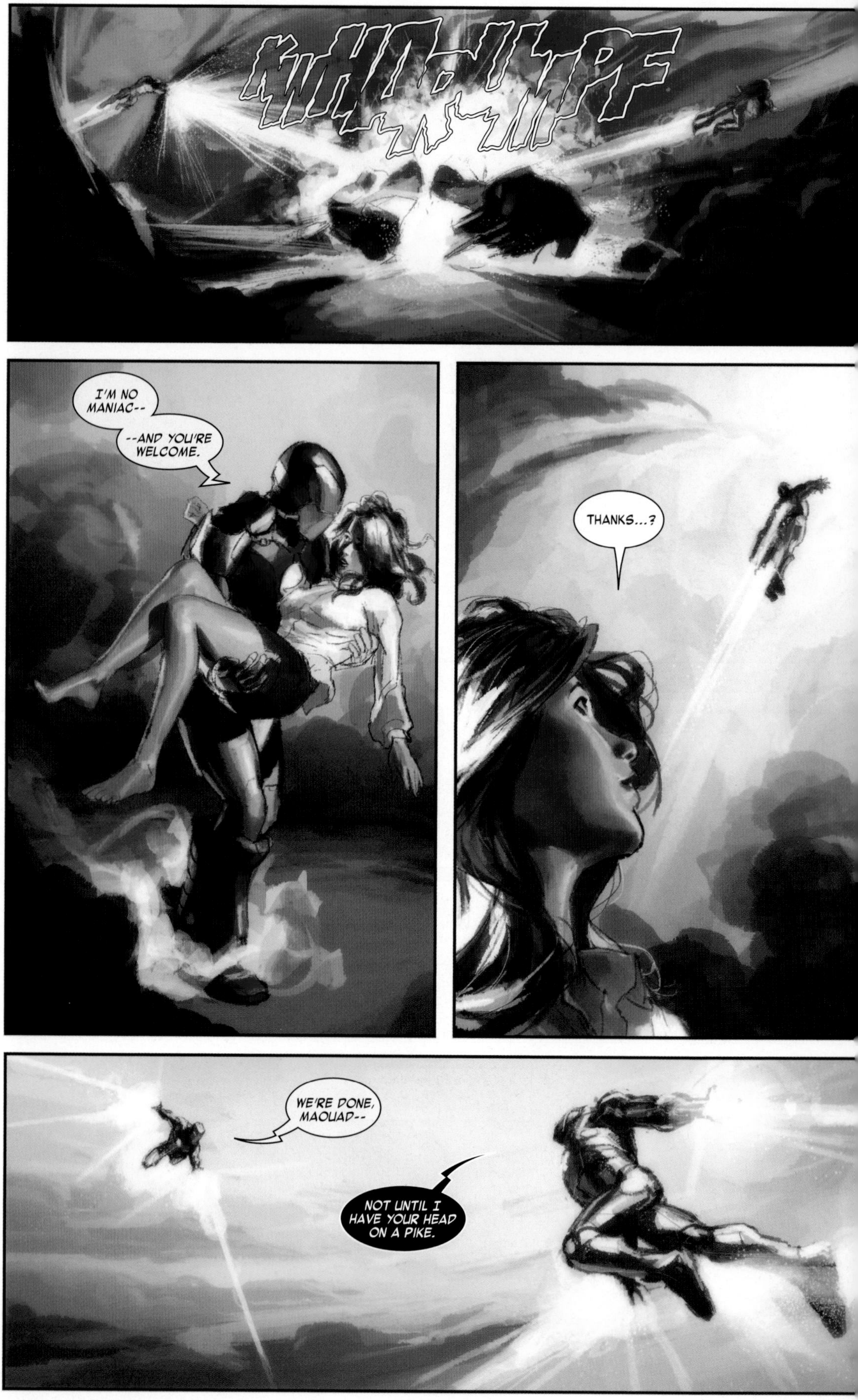
I'M NO MANIAC--
--AND YOU'RE WELCOME.
THANKS...?
WE'RE DONE, MAQUAD--
NOT UNTIL I HAVE YOUR HEAD ON A PIKE.

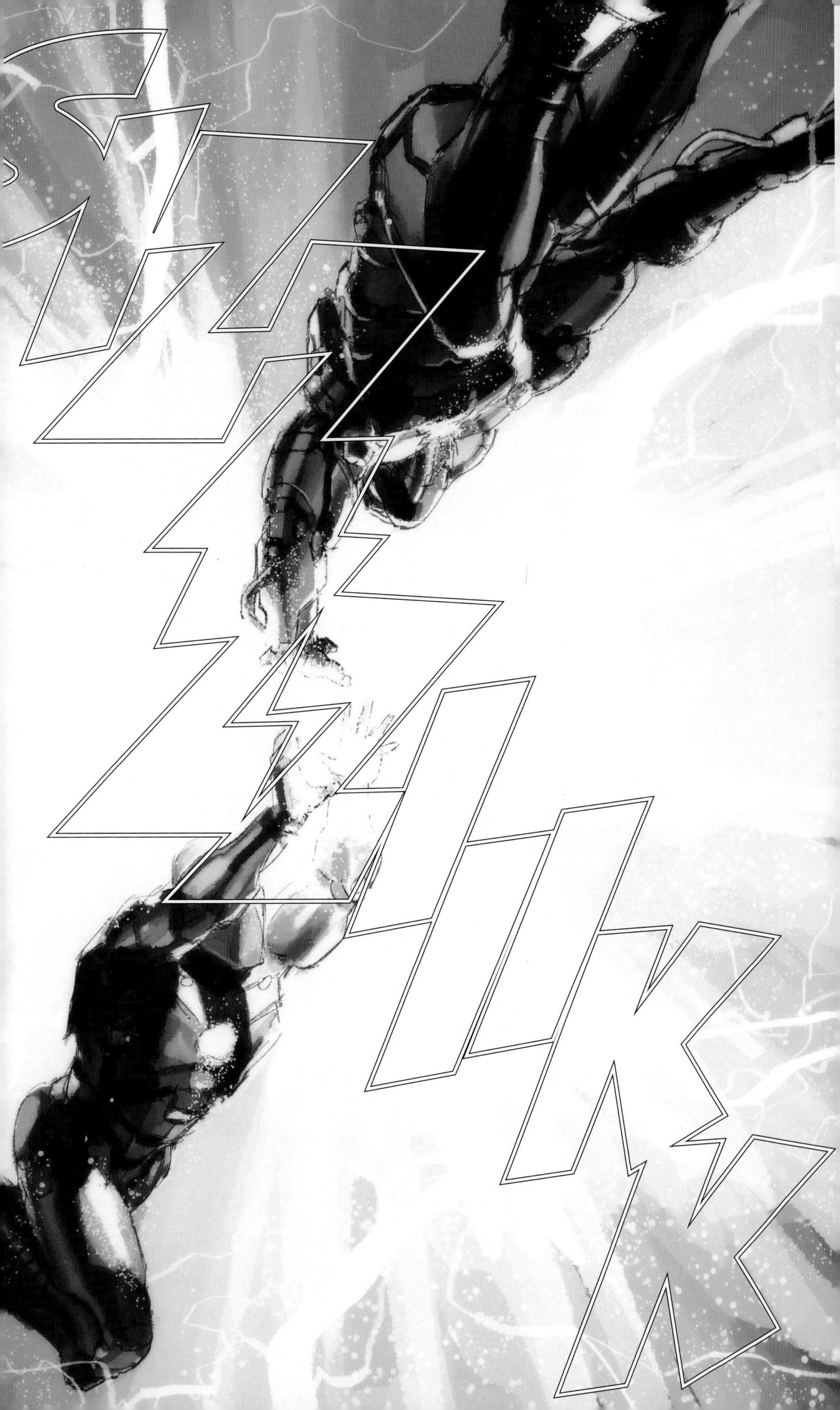

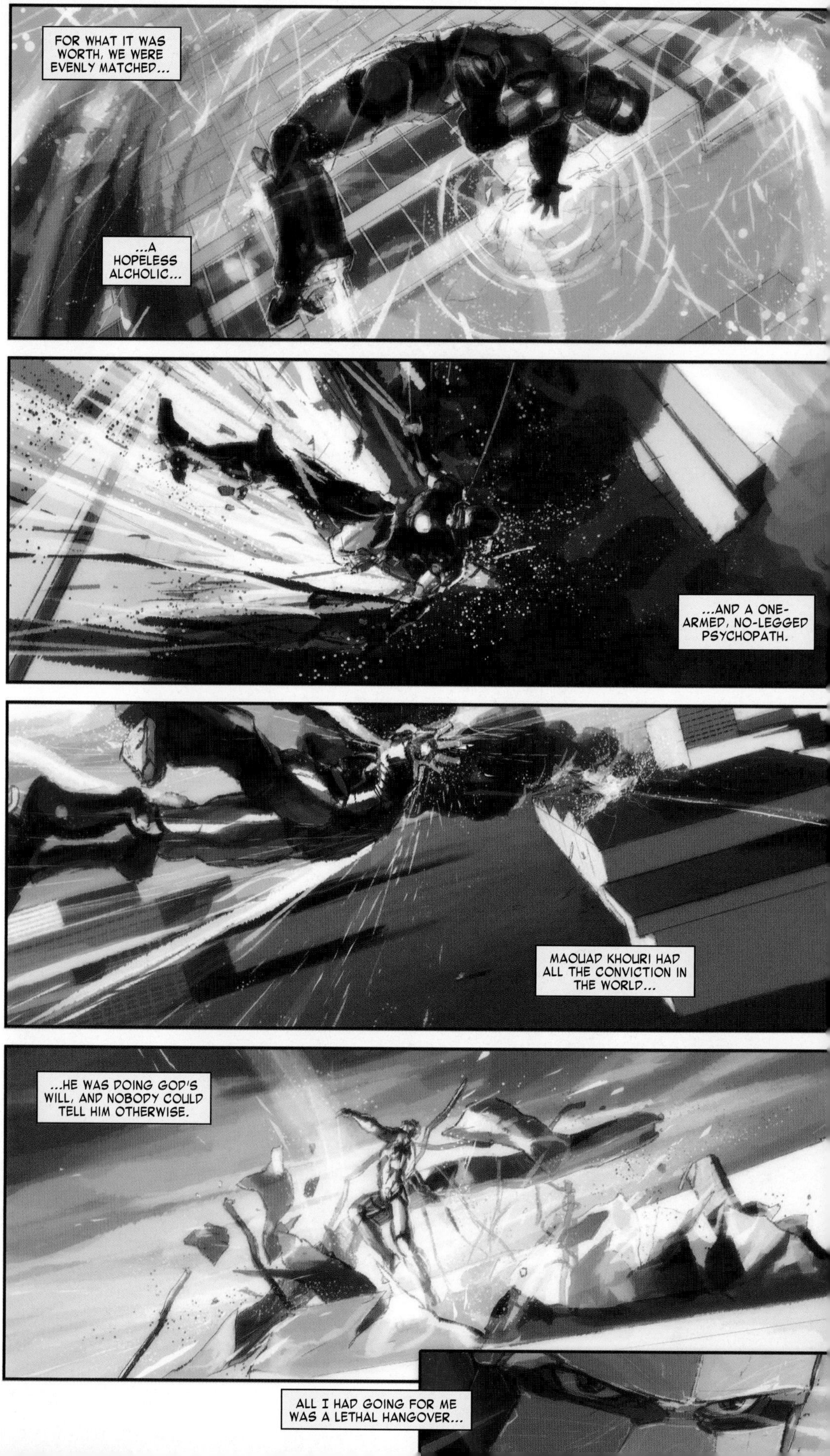
FOR WHAT IT WAS WORTH, WE WERE EVENLY MATCHED...
...A HOPELESS ALCHOLIC...
...AND A ONE-ARMED, NO-LEGGED PSYCHOPATH.
MAOUAD KHOURI HAD ALL THE CONVICTION IN THE WORLD...
...HE WAS DOING GOD'S WILL, AND NOBODY COULD TELL HIM OTHERWISE.
ALL I HAD GOING FOR ME WAS A LETHAL HANGOVER...

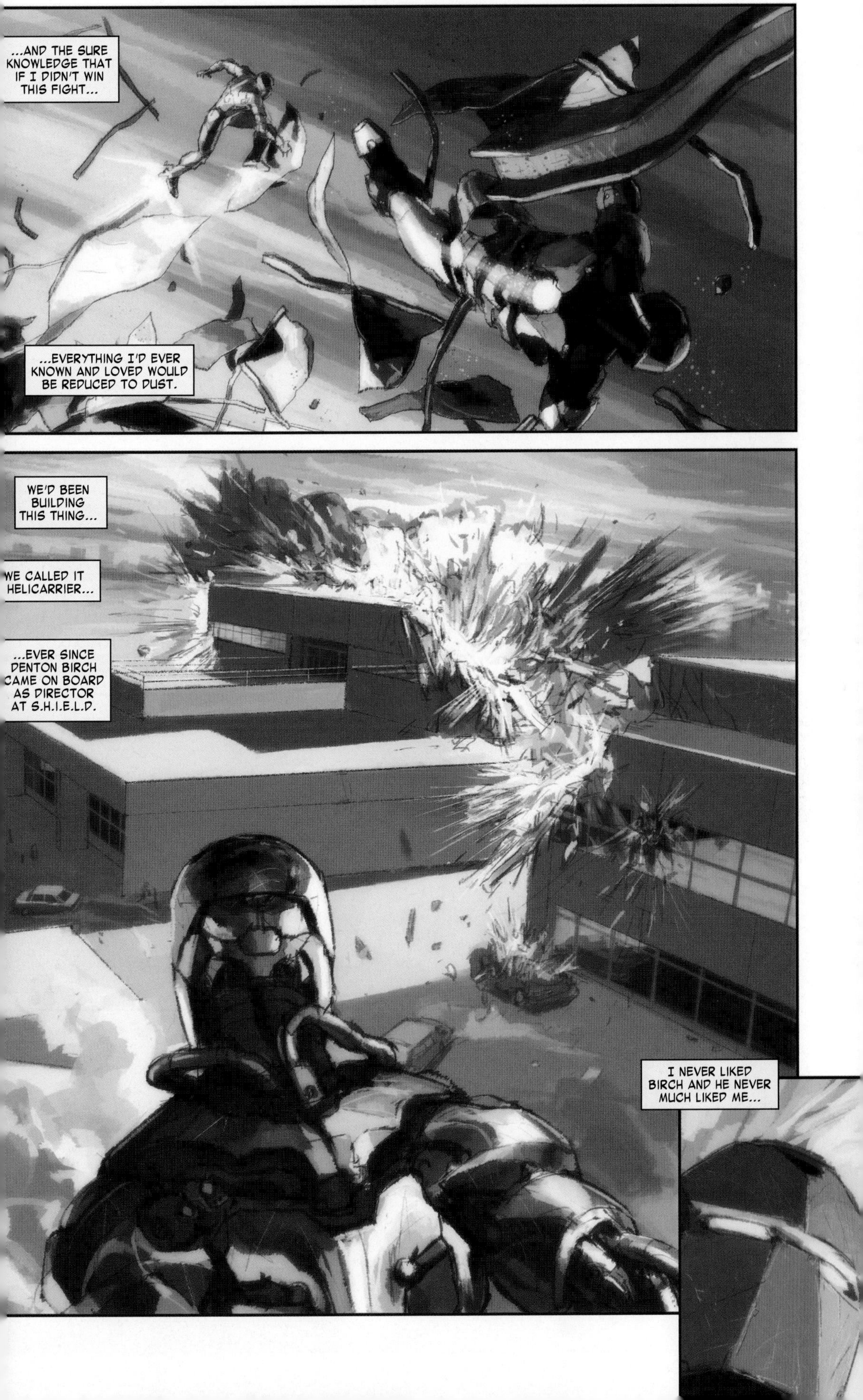
...AND THE SURE KNOWLEDGE THAT IF I DIDN'T WIN THIS FIGHT...
...EVERYTHING I'D EVER KNOWN AND LOVED WOULD BE REDUCED TO DUST.
WE'D BEEN BUILDING THIS THING...
WE CALLED IT HELICARRIER...
...EVER SINCE DENTON BIRCH CAME ON BOARD AS DIRECTOR AT S.H.I.E.L.D.
I NEVER LIKED BIRCH AND HE NEVER MUCH LIKED ME...

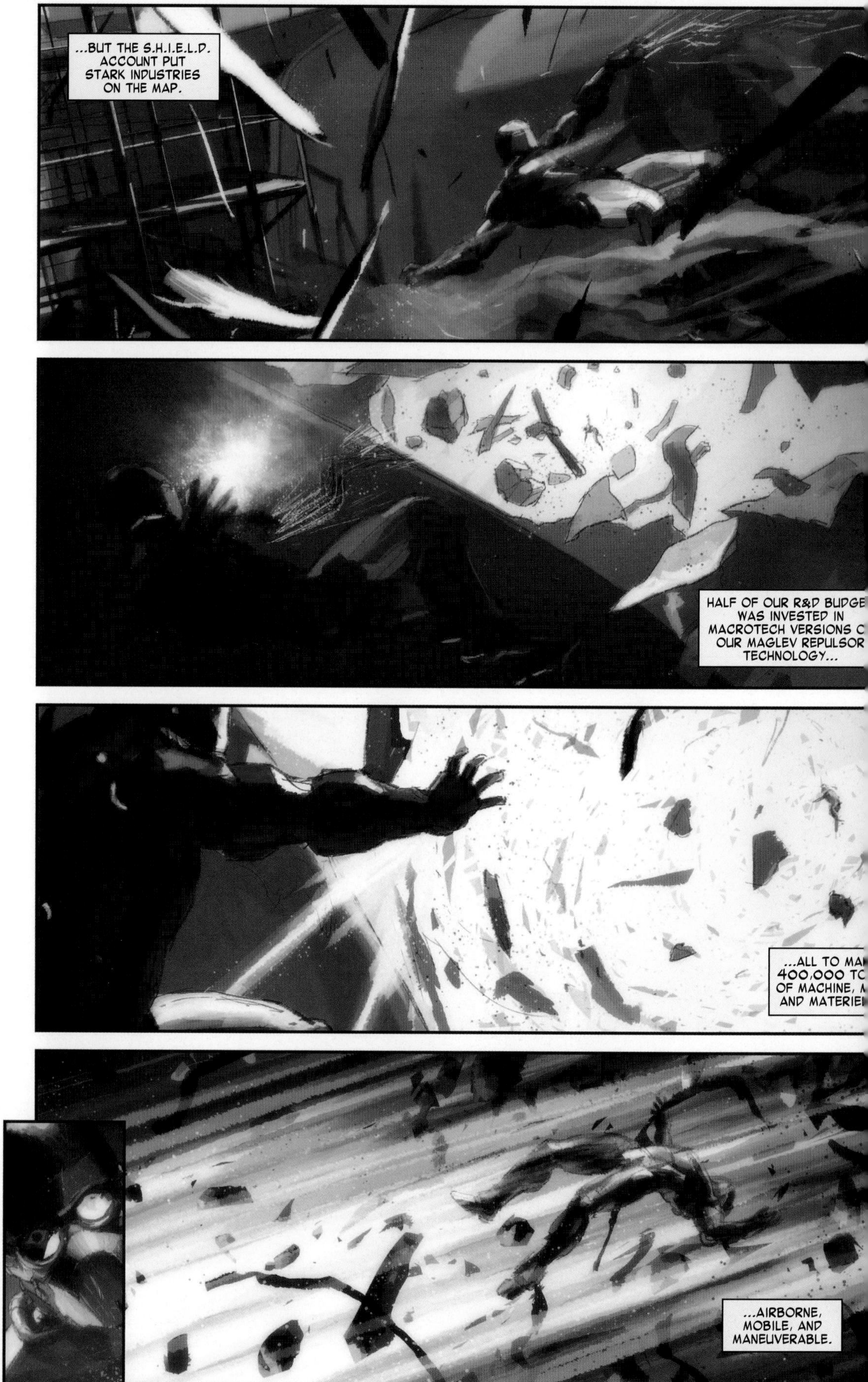
...BUT THE S.H.I.E.L.D. ACCOUNT PUT STARK INDUSTRIES ON THE MAP.
HALF OF OUR R&D BUDGE WAS INVESTED IN MACROTECH VERSIONS O OUR MAGLEV REPULSOR TECHNOLOGY...
...ALL TO MA 400,000 TO OF MACHINE, M AND MATERIE
...AIRBORNE, MOBILE, AND MANEUVERABLE.

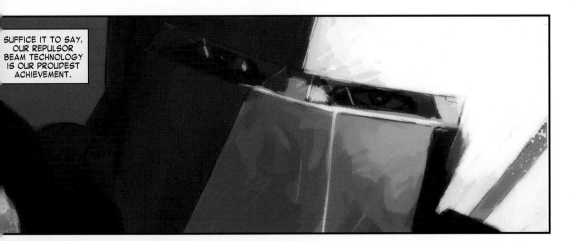

SUFFICE IT TO SAY, OUR REPULSOR BEAM TECHNOLOGY IS OUR PROUDEST ACHIEVEMENT.

SO MUCH FOR PRIDE.

...IT'S NOT LIKE IT HURT, PER SE...

...IT JUST KNOCKED ME AROUND IN MIDAIR A PANTLOAD...

...WHICH GAVE MAOUAD A SHOT AT SHORTING ME OUT...

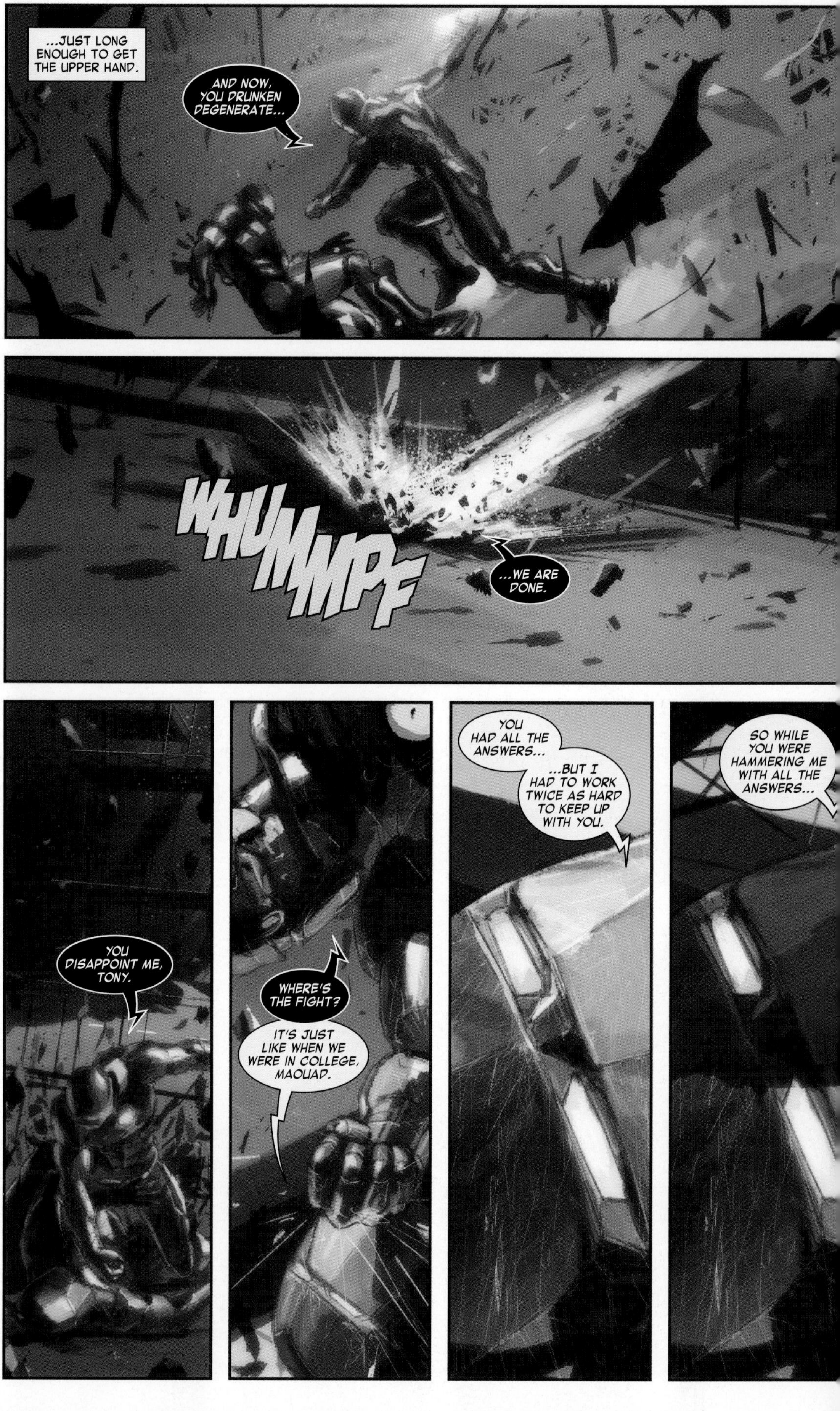
...JUST LONG ENOUGH TO GET THE UPPER HAND.
AND NOW, YOU DRUNKEN DEGENERATE...
WHUMMPF
...WE ARE DONE.
YOU DISAPPOINT ME, TONY.
WHERE'S THE FIGHT?
IT'S JUST LIKE WHEN WE WERE IN COLLEGE, MAOUAD.
YOU HAD ALL THE ANSWERS...
...BUT I HAD TO WORK TWICE AS HARD TO KEEP UP WITH YOU.
SO WHILE YOU WERE HAMMERING ME WITH ALL THE ANSWERS...

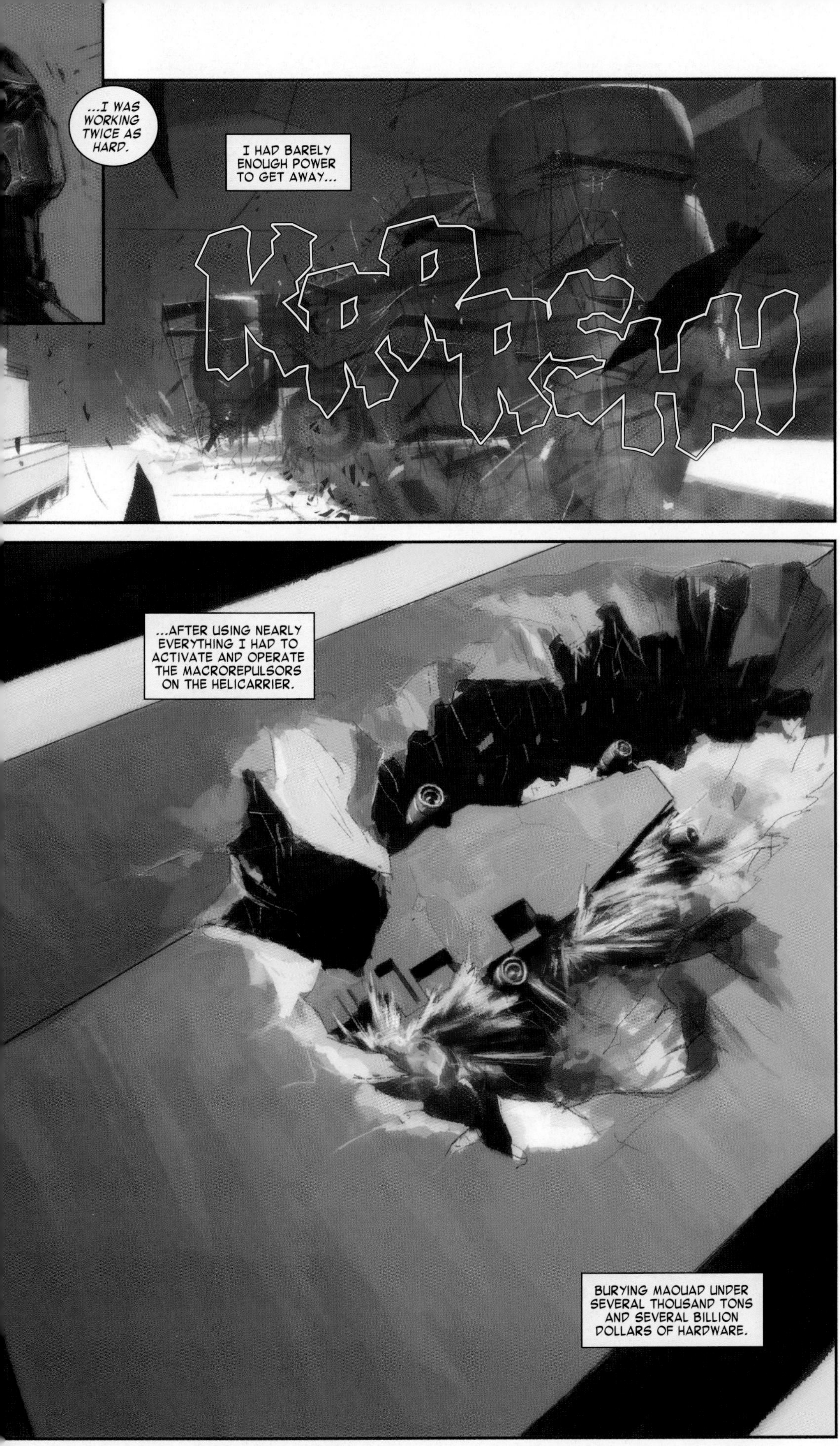
...I WAS WORKING TWICE AS HARD.
I HAD BARELY ENOUGH POWER TO GET AWAY...
...AFTER USING NEARLY EVERYTHING I HAD TO ACTIVATE AND OPERATE THE MACROREPULSORS ON THE HELICARRIER.
BURYING MAQUAD UNDER SEVERAL THOUSAND TONS AND SEVERAL BILLION DOLLARS OF HARDWARE.

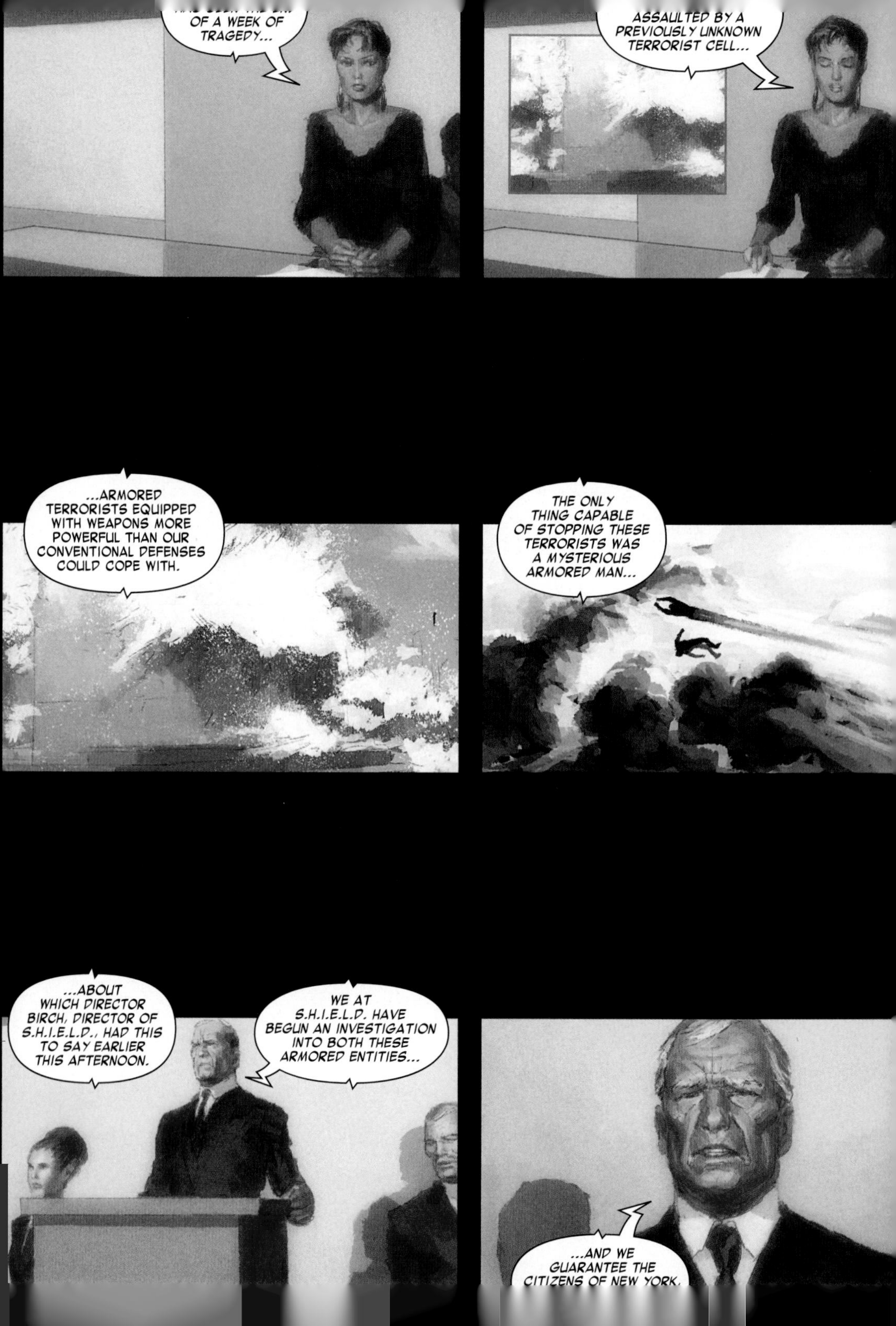

OF A WEEK OF TRAGEDY...
ASSAULTED BY A PREVIOUSLY UNKNOWN TERRORIST CELL...
...ARMORED TERRORISTS EQUIPPED WITH WEAPONS MORE POWERFUL THAN OUR CONVENTIONAL DEFENSES COULD COPE WITH.
THE ONLY THING CAPABLE OF STOPPING THESE TERRORISTS WAS A MYSTERIOUS ARMORED MAN...
...ABOUT WHICH DIRECTOR BIRCH, DIRECTOR OF S.H.I.E.L.D., HAD THIS TO SAY EARLIER THIS AFTERNOON.
WE AT S.H.I.E.L.D. HAVE BEGUN AN INVESTIGATION INTO BOTH THESE ARMORED ENTITIES...
...AND WE GUARANTEE THE CITIZENS OF NEW YORK,

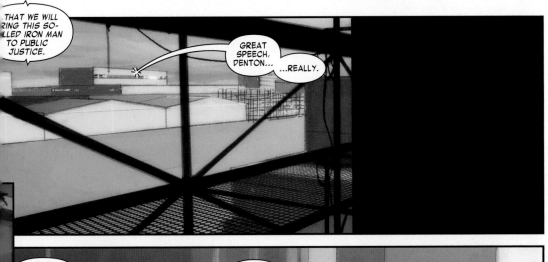

THAT WE WILL BRING THIS SO-CALLED IRON MAN TO PUBLIC JUSTICE.

GREAT SPEECH, DENTON... ...REALLY.

BUT THAT'S WHAT YOU DO BEST, ISN'T IT--

--GIVE SPEECHES.

IS THIS GOING SOMEWHERE, TONY?

I'VE GOT WORK TO DO IN THE CITY, AND I DIDN'T COME OUT HERE TO BE INSULTED.

THEN I GUESS I'D BETTER GET TO THE POINT.

IT WAS A GENUINE TRAGEDY THAT NEAL VAN ZANDT AND LORETTA SIMS DIED THAT DAY.

COULDN'T AGREE MORE. A GENUINE LOSS.

ABSOLUTELY...

...SINCE THEIR DEATHS DENIED THE DEPARTMENT OF JUSTICE THE OPPORTUNITY TO CHARGE THEM WITH EMBEZZLEMENT, FRAUD AND TREASON...

I DON'T--

...SO YOU'LL BE UP THERE ON THE STAND BY YOUR LONESOME, PAL.

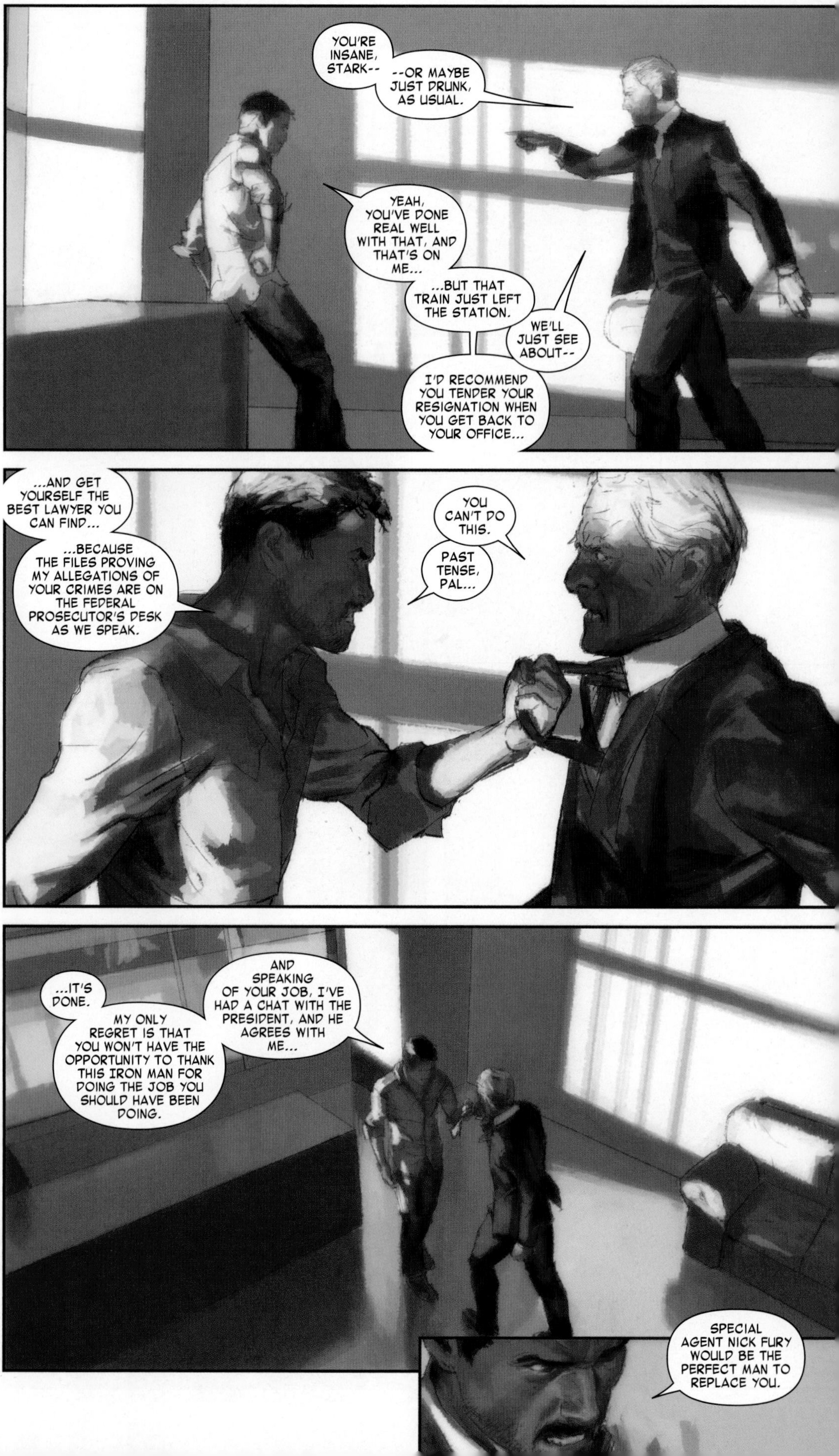
YOU'RE INSANE, STARK--
--OR MAYBE JUST DRUNK, AS USUAL.
YEAH, YOU'VE DONE REAL WELL WITH THAT, AND THAT'S ON ME...
...BUT THAT TRAIN JUST LEFT THE STATION.
WE'LL JUST SEE ABOUT--
I'D RECOMMEND YOU TENDER YOUR RESIGNATION WHEN YOU GET BACK TO YOUR OFFICE...
...AND GET YOURSELF THE BEST LAWYER YOU CAN FIND...
...BECAUSE THE FILES PROVING MY ALLEGATIONS OF YOUR CRIMES ARE ON THE FEDERAL PROSECUTOR'S DESK AS WE SPEAK.
YOU CAN'T DO THIS.
PAST TENSE, PAL...
...IT'S DONE.
MY ONLY REGRET IS THAT YOU WON'T HAVE THE OPPORTUNITY TO THANK THIS IRON MAN FOR DOING THE JOB YOU SHOULD HAVE BEEN DOING.
AND SPEAKING OF YOUR JOB, I'VE HAD A CHAT WITH THE PRESIDENT, AND HE AGREES WITH ME...
SPECIAL AGENT NICK FURY WOULD BE THE PERFECT MAN TO REPLACE YOU.

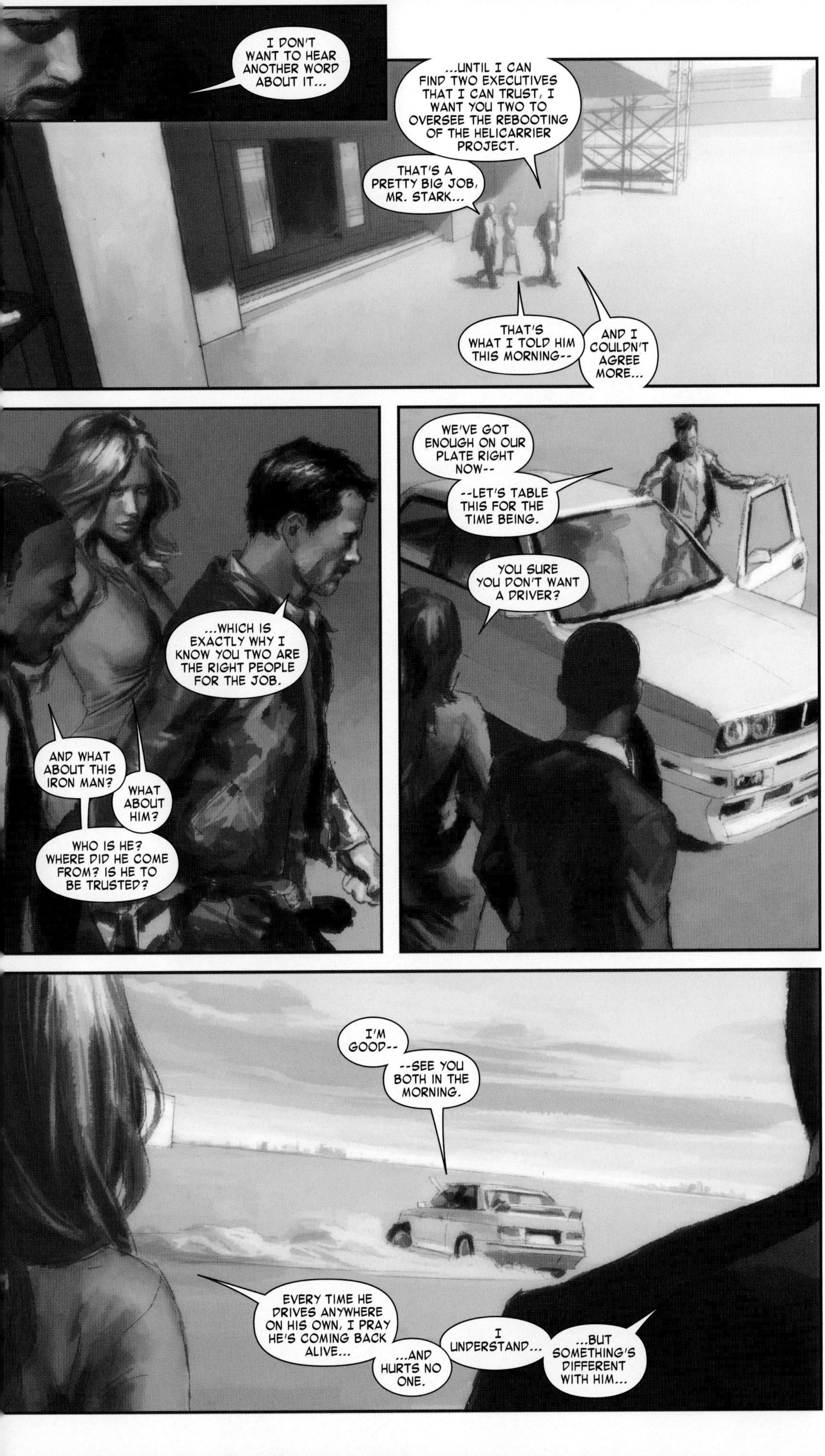
I DON'T WANT TO HEAR ANOTHER WORD ABOUT IT...
...UNTIL I CAN FIND TWO EXECUTIVES THAT I CAN TRUST, I WANT YOU TWO TO OVERSEE THE REBOOTING OF THE HELICARRIER PROJECT.
THAT'S A PRETTY BIG JOB, MR. STARK...
THAT'S WHAT I TOLD HIM THIS MORNING--
AND I COULDN'T AGREE MORE...
...WHICH IS EXACTLY WHY I KNOW YOU TWO ARE THE RIGHT PEOPLE FOR THE JOB.
AND WHAT ABOUT THIS IRON MAN?
WHAT ABOUT HIM?
WHO IS HE? WHERE DID HE COME FROM? IS HE TO BE TRUSTED?
WE'VE GOT ENOUGH ON OUR PLATE RIGHT NOW--
--LET'S TABLE THIS FOR THE TIME BEING.
YOU SURE YOU DON'T WANT A DRIVER?
I'M GOOD--
--SEE YOU BOTH IN THE MORNING.
EVERY TIME HE DRIVES ANYWHERE ON HIS OWN, I PRAY HE'S COMING BACK ALIVE...
...AND HURTS NO ONE.
I UNDERSTAND...
...BUT SOMETHING'S DIFFERENT WITH HIM...

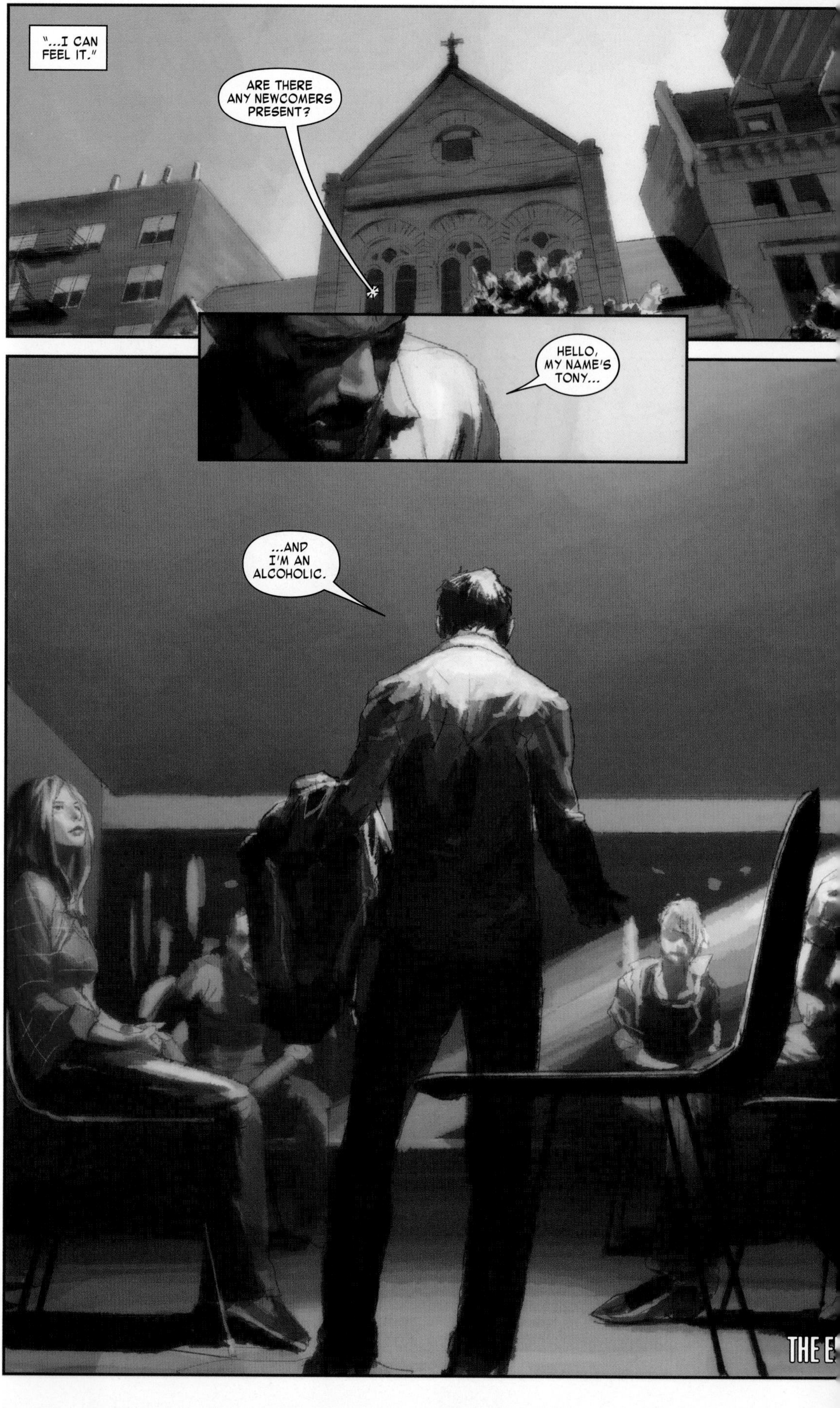

"...I CAN FEEL IT."
ARE THERE ANY NEWCOMERS PRESENT?
HELLO, MY NAME'S TONY...
...AND I'M AN ALCOHOLIC.
THE E

LAYOUTS

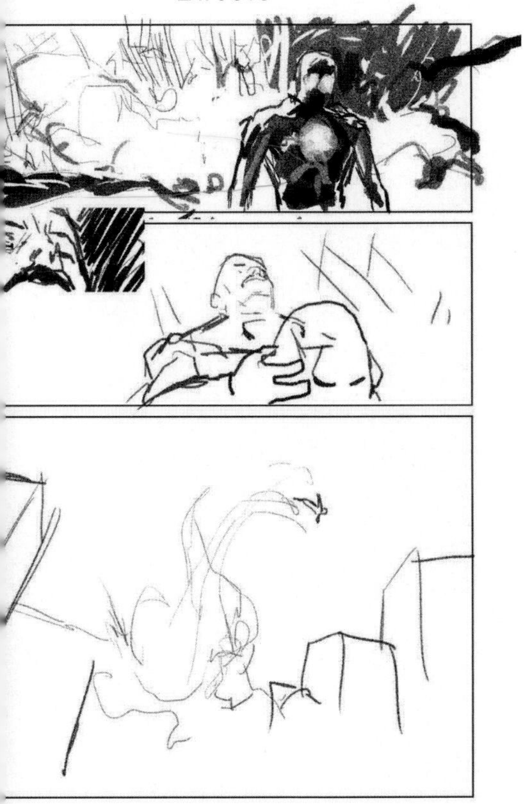

BLACK & WHITE

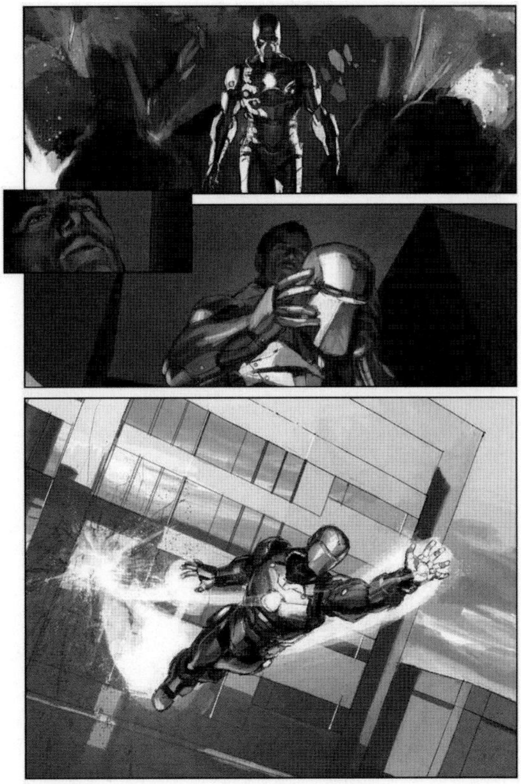

FINAL

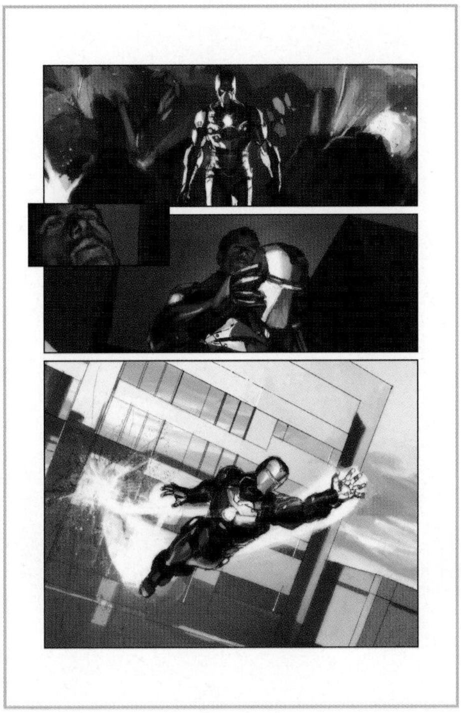

PAGE 117

LAYOUTS

BLACK & WHITE

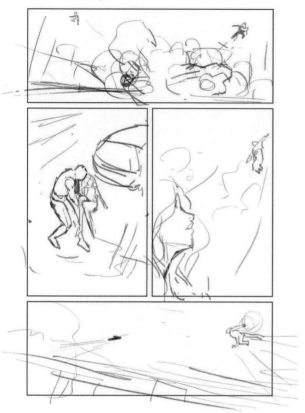

FINAL

LAYOUTS

BLACK & WHITE

FINAL

PAGE 121

LAYOUTS

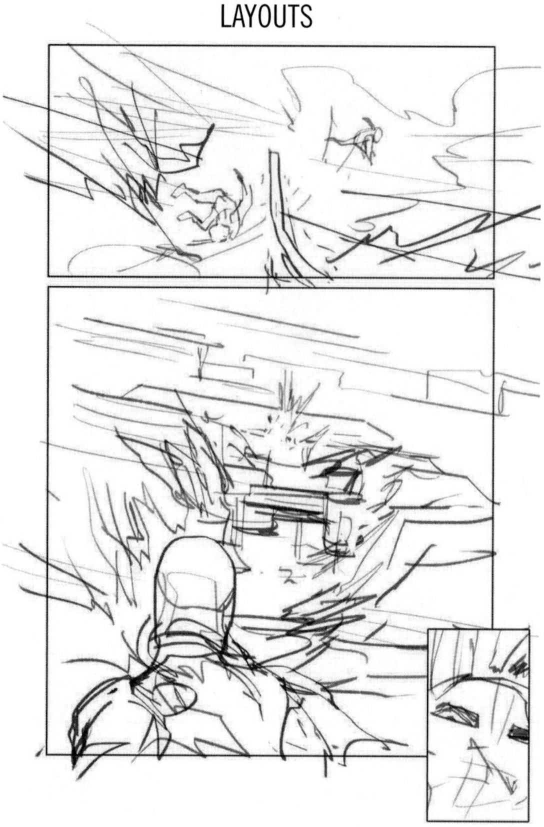

BLACK & WHITE

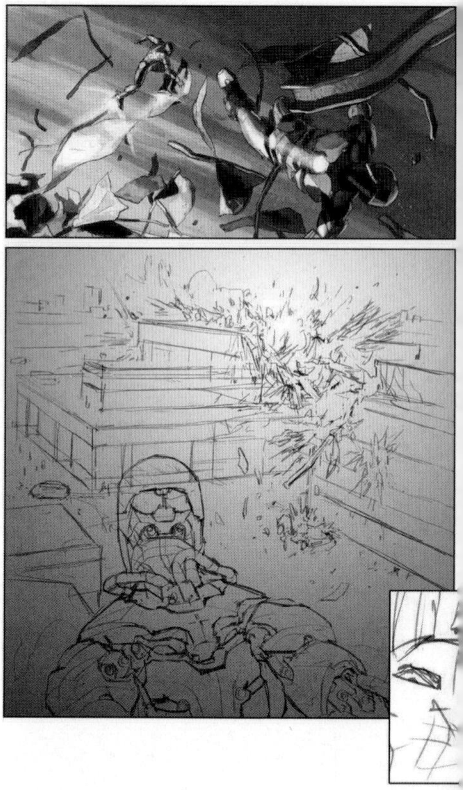

FINAL

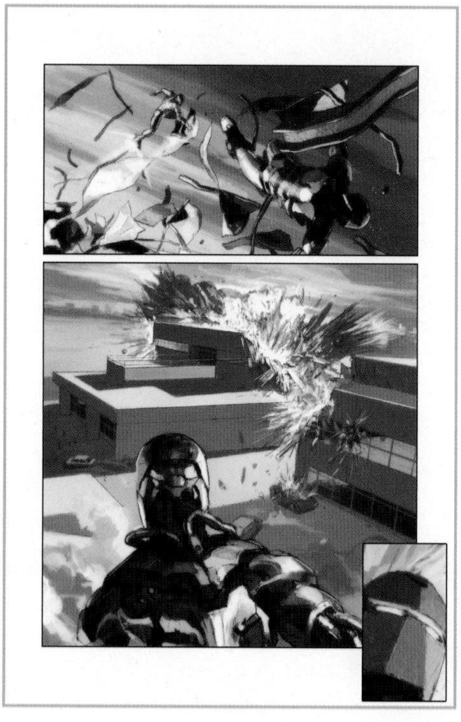

PAGE 123

LAYOUTS

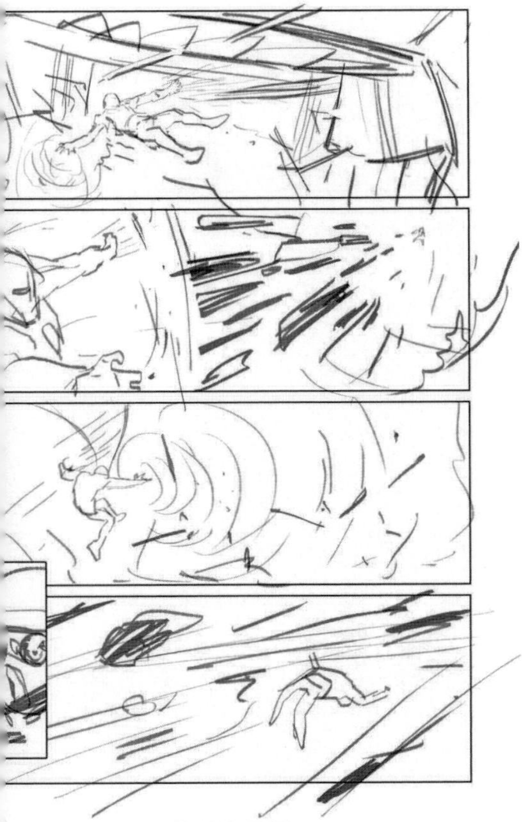

BLACK & WHITE

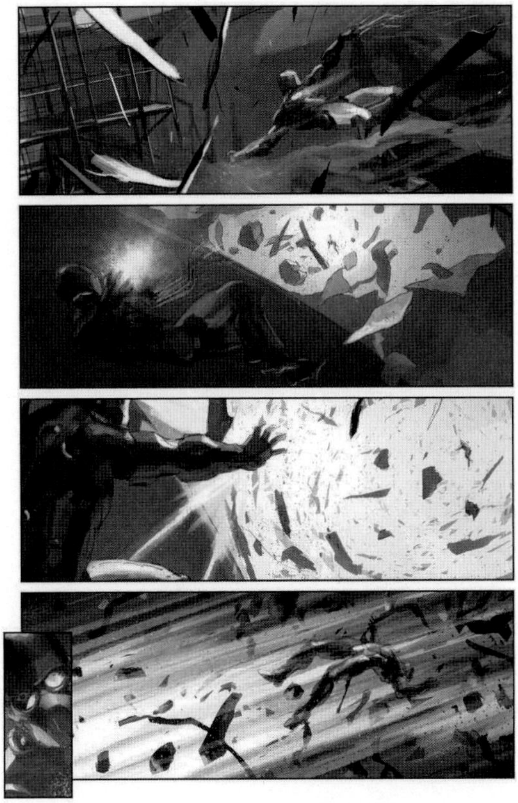

TRANSITION

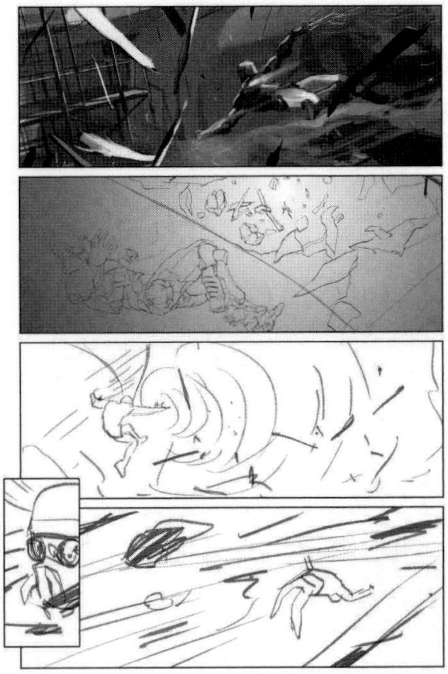

FINAL

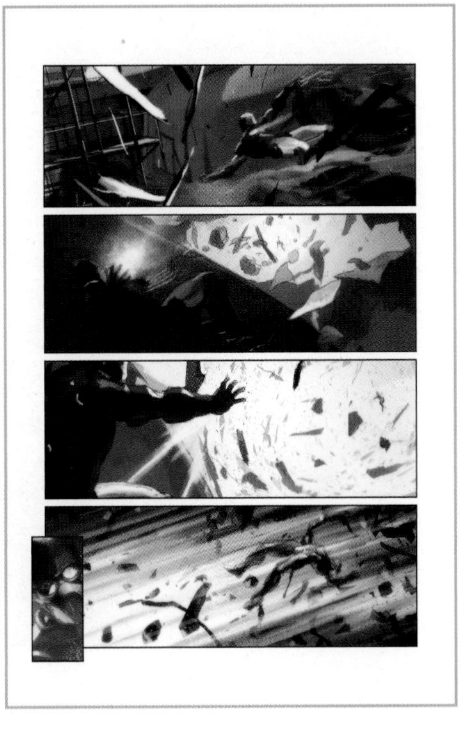

LAYOUTS

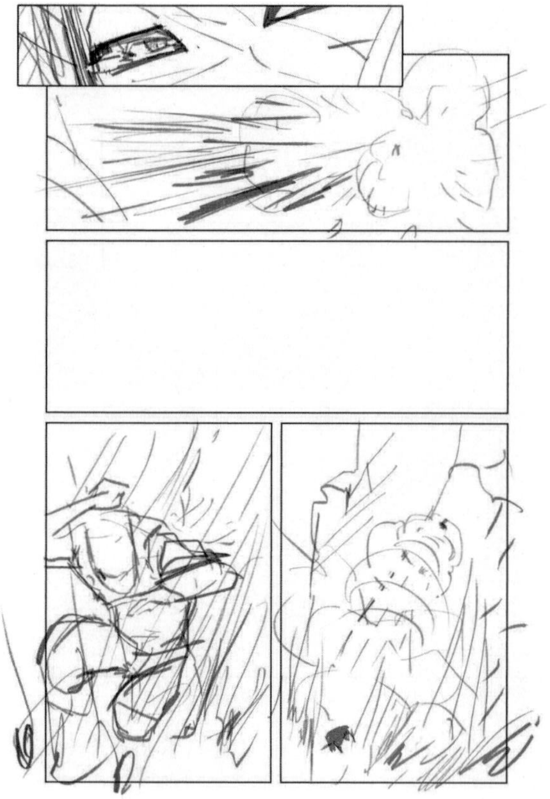

BLACK & WHITE

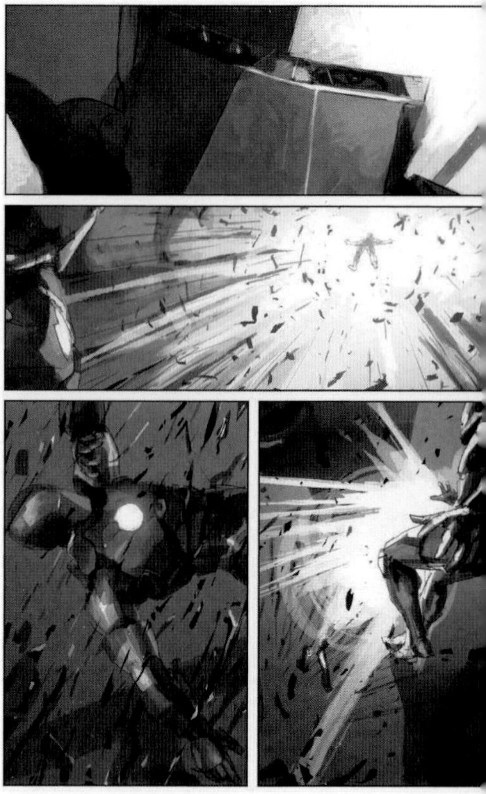

FINAL

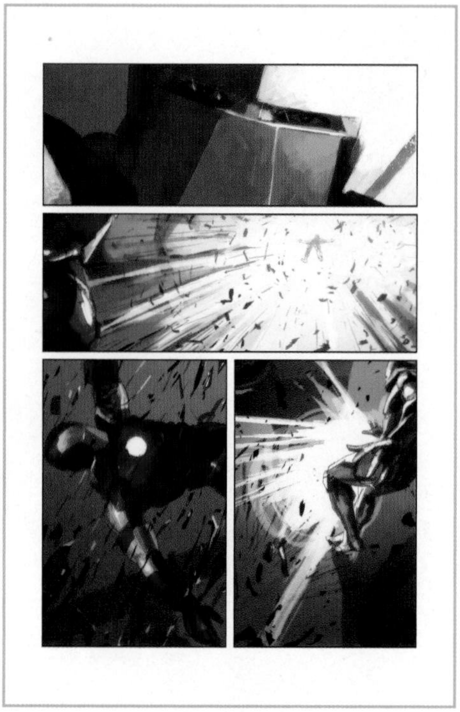

PAGE 125

LAYOUTS

BLACK & WHITE

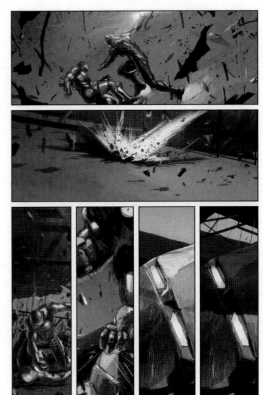

FINAL

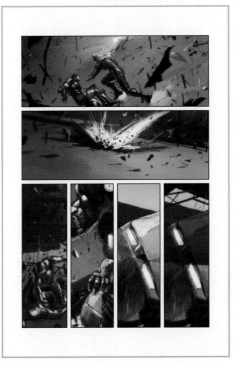

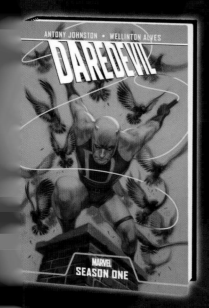

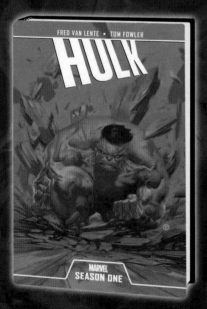

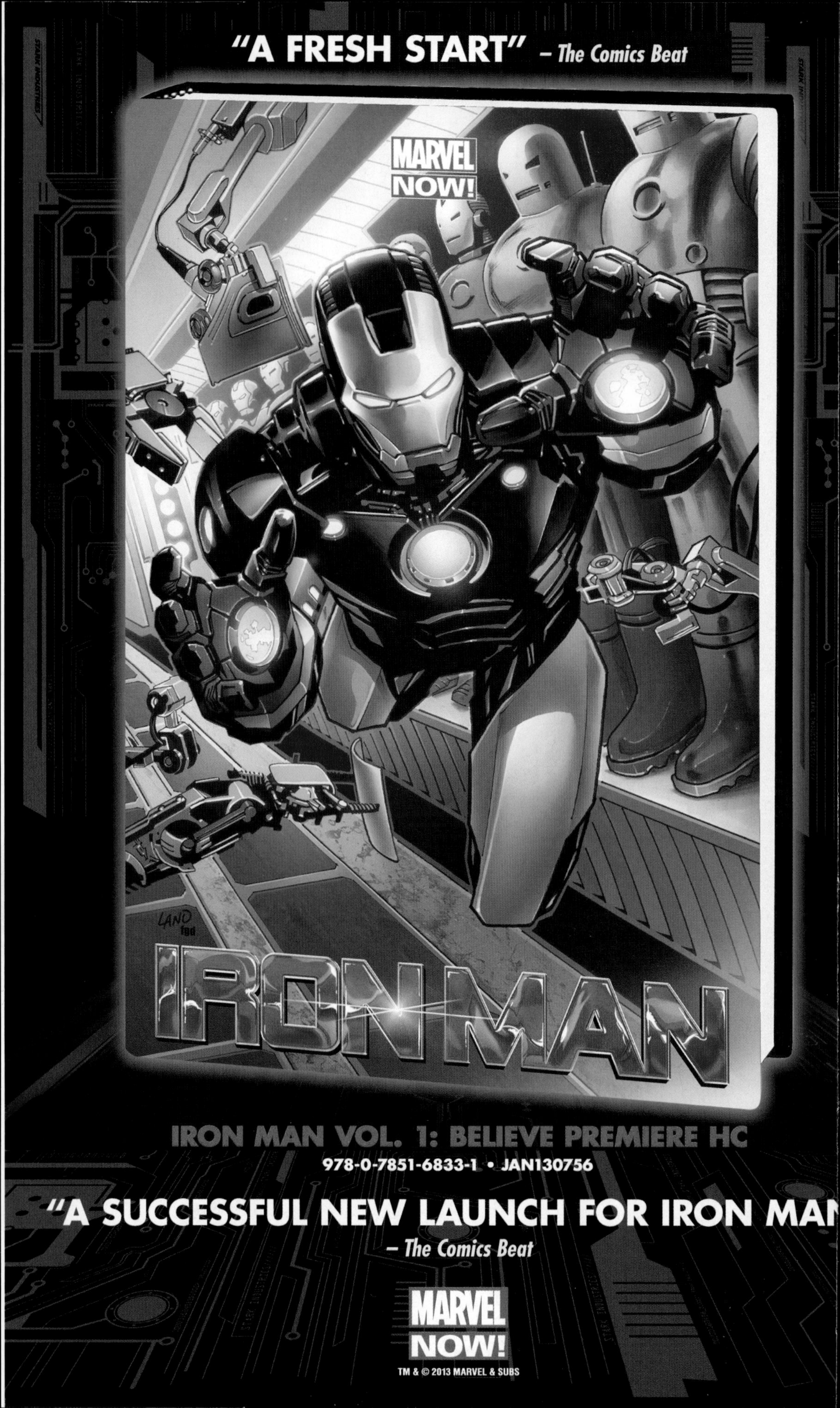
"A FRESH START" – The Comics Beat
MARVEL NOW!
LAND fgd
IRON MAN
IRON MAN VOL. 1: BELIEVE PREMIERE HC
978-0-7851-6833-1 • JAN130756
"A SUCCESSFUL NEW LAUNCH FOR IRON MA
– The Comics Beat
MARVEL NOW!
TM & © 2013 MARVEL & SUBS

DATE DUE
